*Presented to*

_____

*By*

_____

*On the Occasion of*

_____

*Date*

_____

# FILL ME WITH HOPE

## Daily Devotional Insights from Classic Christian Writings

### COMPILED BY PAUL M. MILLER

BARBOUR
PUBLISHING

# FILL ME WITH HOPE,

© 2004 by Barbour Publishing, Inc.

ISBN 1-59310-377-8

Additional editorial assistance from Toni Sortor, Rachel Quillin, Jennifer Hahn, and JoAnne Willett.

Published by Barbour Publishing, Inc., P.O. Box 719, Uhrichsville, Ohio 44683, www.barbourbooks.com

*Our mission is to publish and distribute inspirational products offering exceptional value and biblical encouragement to the masses.*

Member of the
Evangelical Christian
Publishers Association

Printed in the United States of America.
5 4 3 2 1

# Introduction

For the next 365 days (or 366 in a leap year) you are going to discover the many facets of *hope*. Hope is a word that has long been in our vocabularies—we use it to mean expectation, desire, longing, and wishing. While "wish" is the most common connotation, our devotional concerns are focused on the absolute sureties of life. As D. L. Moody might say, "No sense wishing for hope. Claim it in the name of Jesus!"

As you will discover, religious writers of other centuries didn't approach the topic of hope with sentimentality, as do many of today's popular self-help writers. To the Moodys and Sankeys, hope was the bedrock benefit of scripture, of life in Christ, and of His Second Coming. It wasn't something people generated inside themselves.

Today's reader brings to these pages his or her personal discouragement, doubt, disappointment, and perhaps even nagging questions about God. A serious reading of these classic excerpts may be difficult at times—they weren't spoken or penned by contemporary communicators—but they are very much worth the effort. Each one will confront you with God's provision for hope!

Paul M. Miller

"*May the Christ in you
be the hope of glory
to all who read.*"

BROTHER LAWRENCE

# Hope for a New Year

*But as for me, I will always have hope;*
*I will praise you more and more.*
PSALM 71:14 NIV

Take twelve fine, full-grown months; see that they are thoroughly free from old memories of bitterness, rancor, hate, and jealousy; cleanse them completely from every clinging spite; pick off all specks of pettiness; in short, see that these months ahead are free from all the past—have them as fresh and clean as when they came from heaven's great hope chest of time.

Cut these months into thirty or thirty-one equal parts. This batch will keep for one year only. Do not attempt to make up the whole batch at one time, but prepare one day at a time, as follows:

Into each day put twelve parts of faith, eleven of patience, ten of courage, nine of work (some people omit this ingredient and so spoil the flavor of the rest), eight of hope, seven of fidelity, six of liberality, five of kindness, four of rest, three of prayer, two of meditation, and one of well-selected resolution. Next spice this recipe with a teaspoon of good spirits, a dash of fun, a pinch of joviality, a sprinkling of play, and a heaping cupful of good humor.

Serve with a steaming cup of hope for the year ahead, and anticipate a happy new year in our Lord.

HAROLD M. SMYTHE

# Formula for Hope

*The joy of the LORD is your strength.*
NEHEMIAH 8:10 NIV

Hope may be described as the flower of desire. It expects that the object shall be attained. It bars despondence and anticipates good. It shakes the mind from stagnation, animates to encounter danger, and is the balm of life. Though at times it may be associated with doubt and solicitude, yet when hesitance is displaced, it swells into joy and ecstasy.

Hope may be held to be universal and permanent. It is entwined with every other affection and passion. It always originates beneficial effects. It animates desire and is a secret source of pleasure in the transports of joy. Joy triumphs in the success which hope foreshadows. It administers consolation in distress—quickens all our pursuits and communicates to the mind the pleasure of anticipation. This influence, though mild, is nevertheless exhilarating.

There is no happiness which hope cannot surmount, no grief which it cannot mitigate. It is the wealth of the homeless, the health of the sick, the freedom of the captive, the rest of the laborer.

THEODORE LEDYARD CUYLER

# O God Our Help in Ages Past

*Find rest, O my soul, in God alone;*
*my hope comes from him.*
PSALM 62:5 NIV

O God, our help in ages past, our hope for years to come,
Our shelter from the stormy blast, and our eternal home.

Under the shadow of Thy throne still may we dwell secure;
Sufficient in Thine arm alone, and our defense is sure.

Before the hills in order stood, or earth received her frame,
From everlasting Thou art God, to endless years the same.

A thousand ages, in Thy sight, are like an evening gone;
Short as the watch that ends the night,
        before the rising sun.

O God, our help in ages past, our hope for years to come,
Be Thou our Guide while life shall last,
        and our eternal home.

ISAAC WATTS

# *Looking Forward*

*Forgetting what is behind and straining*
*toward what is ahead,*
*I press on toward the goal to win the prize f*
*or which God has called me*
*heavenward in Christ Jesus.*

PHILIPPIANS 3:13 NIV

Failure will hurt but not hinder us. Disillusion will pain but not dishearten us. Sorrows will shake us but not break us. Hope will set the music ringing and quicken our lagging pace.

We need hope for living the year ahead far more than for dying. Dying is easy work compared to living. Dying is a moment's transition; living is a transaction of years. It is the length of the rope that puts the sag in it. Hope tightens the cords and tunes up the heartstrings.

Work well, then; suffer patiently, rejoicing in hope. God knows all, and yet is the God of hope. And when we have hoped to the end here, He will give us something to look forward to for all eternity. For "hope abides."

*Why?*

This is my Father's world, O let me ne'er forget
That though the wrong seems oft so strong,
    God is the Ruler yet.
This is my Father's world: The battle is not done;
Jesus who died shall be satisfied, and earth and
    heav'n be one.

MALTBIE D. BABCOCK

# *For Facing the New Year*

*Do not be anxious about anything,*
*but in everything, by prayer and petition,*
*with thanksgiving, present your requests to God.*
PHILIPPIANS 4:6 NIV

Take not anxious thought as to the result of your work. If you are doing all that you can, the results, immediate or eventual, are not your affair at all. If we do not see the fruit here, we know nevertheless that here or somewhere they do spring up.

It would be great if we could succeed now; it will be greater if we patiently wait for success, even though we never see it ourselves. For it will come. Do not be worried by bigotry. We cannot help it, if we are not responsible for it—we are responsible to ourselves and for ourselves and for no one else. Do not be angry at opposition either; no one can oppose the decrees of God. Our plans may be upset—remember, there are greater plans than ours.

They may not be completed in the time we would wish, but our works and the work of those who follow us will be carried out.

Therefore let us keep the hope of God in our hearts and quiet in our minds, for though in the flesh we may never stand upon the edifice all of us are building, know that it will never be pulled down.

BOLTON HALL

# Hope and Holy Living

*Everyone who has
this hope in him purifies himself,
just as he is pure.*
1 JOHN 3:3 NIV

Many have no idea of the meaning of Christian hope. They talk of hoping that they are Christians, as if this were Christian hope; but obviously they have no conception of what the Christian's hope is. Theirs is not a true Christian hope, for it has not the right object. They hope they will escape punishment; they hope they shall not be doomed to hell; but this is by no means the true end of a Christian hope. And furthermore, they have not the right expectation of ever attaining the true end; they do not expect to become like Christ. Consequently, both elements of Christian hope are missing.

A good hope is of priceless value. It is the very secret of holy living. One never lives holy while in despair of attaining to the image of Christ. No person lives holy unless he has the conception of holiness and heaven. On the other hand a true hope fires the soul with its desire and expectation and mightily sets one's mind to attain the heart's desire. This is the secret of holy living. I am not saying this will produce a holy life without the aid of the Spirit of God, but I do say that the Spirit cannot produce a holy life without this hope.

CHARLES G. FINNEY

# Great Expectations

*There is hope only for the living.*
ECCLESIASTES 9:4 NLT

While modern people of this world make *hope* to include shades of uncertainty associated with a desired outcome (akin to "wishful thinking"), the biblical understanding of hope is a much deeper concept that contributes significantly to the world view of biblical faith. Included are an expectation of the future, trust in attaining that future, patience while awaiting it, the desirability of the associated benefits, and confidence in the divine promises.

In the Old Testament hope is a prominent theme, especially in the poetic and prophetic books. Hope is a fundamental component of the life of the righteous (Proverbs 23:18, 24:14). Without hope, life loses its meaning (Lamentations 3:18; Job 7:6), and in death there is no hope (Isaiah 38:18; Job 17:15).

For hope to be real and genuine and not foolish or presumptuous, it must be grounded in God and God's promises.

ADAPTED FROM A NINETEENTH-
CENTURY BIBLE DICTIONARY

# The Star of Hope

*In him was life, and that life was the light of men.*
*The light shines in the darkness,*
*but the darkness has not understood it.*
JOHN 1:4–5 NIV

There will be times when the child of God, while depending upon the power and guidance of God's Holy Spirit, faces the black night when only the star of hope provides light for the way. Skeptical physician and essayist Holmes provides food for thought.

No man has earned the right to intellectual ambition until he has learned to lay his course by a star that he has never seen—to dig by the divining rod for springs which he may never reach.

To think great thoughts you must be heroes as well as idealists. Only when you have worked alone—when you have felt around you a black gulf of solitude more isolating than that which surrounds the dying man, and in hope and in despair have trusted your own [God-given] unshaken will. Then only will you have achieved.

Thus only can you can gain the secret isolated joy of the thinker, who knows that a hundred years after he is dead and forgotten, men who never heard of him will be moving to the measure of his thought—the subtle rapture of a postponed power, which the world knows not because it has no external trappings, but which to his prophetic vision is more real than that which commands an army.

OLIVER WENDELL HOLMES

# Prayers of Hope

*Give, and it will be given to you.*
LUKE 6:38 NIV

Lord, make me an instrument of your peace;
Where there is hatred let me sow love;
Where there is injury, pardon;
Where there is doubt, faith;
Where there is despair, hope;
Where there is darkness, light;
And where there is sadness, joy.

O divine Master, grant that I may not so much seek
To be consoled as to console,
To be understood as to understand,
To be loved as to love,
For it is in giving that we receive,
It is in pardoning that we are pardoned
And it is in dying that we are reborn
To eternal life.

Almighty God, and You, my Lord Jesus Christ,
I pray You enlighten me
And to dispel the hopelessness of my spirit;
Give me a faith that is without limit,
A hope that is ever unfailing,
And a love that is universal.
Grant, O my God,
That I may really know You
And that I may be guided in all
Things according to your will.
Amen.

FRANCIS OF ASSISI

## Act of Hope

*Everyone who has this hope in him purifies himself,*
*just as he is pure.*

1 JOHN 3:3 NIV

Allow the words of this fifth-century Christian leader to sink into your mind and heart. It is a prayer appropriate for all of us in the twenty-first century. Here is cleansing for the start of a new year.

For your mercies' sake, O Lord my God, tell me what you are to me. Say to my soul: "I am your salvation." Speak that I may hear, O Lord; my heart is listening to you; open it that I may hear you, and say to my soul: "I am your salvation." After hearing this word, may I come in haste to take hold of you.

Hide not your face from me. Let me see your face even if I die, lest I die with longing to see it. The house of my soul is too small to receive you; let it be enlarged by you. It is all in ruins; do repair it. There are things in it—I confess and I know—that must offend your sight. But who shall cleanse it? Or to what others besides you shall I cry out? From my secret sin cleanse me, O Lord, and from those others spare your servant. Amen.

AUGUSTINE

# The Little While

*In just a little while I will be gone,*
*and you won't see me anymore.*
*Then, just a little while after that,*
*you will see me again.*
JOHN 16:16 NLT

Long seem the moments when we are separated from the friend we love. An absent brother—how his return is looked and longed for! The "Elder Brother"—the "Living Kinsman"—sends a message to His waiting church and people—a word of hope, telling that soon ("a little while") He will be back again, never, never to leave them again.

There are indeed blessed moments of communion in which the believer enjoys His his beloved Lord; but how fitful and transient they can be. Today, life is a brief Emmaus journey—the soul happy in the presence and love of an unseen Savior. Tomorrow, He is gone; and the bereft spirit is led to interrogate itself in plaintive sorrow.

But, in just a little while, all mystery of iniquity will be finished. The absent Brother's footfall will soon be heard to receive His people into the permanent mansions He has been preparing and from which they will go no more out. Oh, blessed day! When our Lord will be enthroned amid the hosannas of a rejoicing universe—angels lauding Him—saints crowning Him—sin extinguished forever—death swallowed up in eternal victory.

JOHN MACDUFF

# *Assurance in a Book*

> *All scripture is God-breathed*
> *and is useful for training, rebuking,*
> *correcting and training in righteousness.*
> 2 TIMOTHY 3:16 NIV

Men's ideas differ about the extent that human skill can go; but the reason we believe the Bible is the basis of our assurance and hope is because it is inspired. The reason we believe the Bible is inspired is so simple that the humblest child of God can comprehend it. If the proof of its divine origin lay in its wisdom alone, a simple and uneducated man might not be able to believe it. We believe it is inspired because there is nothing in it that could not have come from God. God is wise, and God is good. There is nothing in the Bible that is not wise, and there is nothing that is not good.

If the Bible had anything in it that is opposed to reason or to our sense of right, then perhaps we might think that it was like all the books in the world than are written by mere men. Books that are just human books, like human lives, have in them a great deal that is foolish and wrong.

Like the other wonderful things of God, this Book bears the sure stamp of its author. It is like Him. Though man plants the seeds, God makes the flowers, and they are perfect and beautiful like He is. Men wrote what's in the Bible, but the work is God's. People with hope love the Bible.

DWIGHT L. MOODY

# *Hope Is...*

*Now faith is being sure of what we hope for
and certain of what we do not see.*
HEBREWS 11:1 NIV

While the matter of hope is at the very heart of God's written Word, it has also been commented on by great human minds. Evangelical preacher Charles Finney's notebooks contained these unidentified "good words."

❧

HOPE is like the sun, which, as we journey toward it, casts the shadow of our burdens behind us. It is like the cork to a net, which keeps the soul from sinking in despair. And fear is like the lead in the net, which keeps it from floating in presumption. Hope is itself a species of happiness and, perhaps, the chief happiness which this world affords. It is one of those things in life you cannot do without.

HOPE! Of all the ills that men endure, is the only cheap and universal cure. It is the last thing ever lost, and it is putting faith to work when doubting would be easier. Hope is the major weapon against the suicide impulse. It is a much stronger stimulant of life than any realized joy could be. Hope is faith holding our hand in the dark, and it is grief's best music.

HOPE is the only bee that makes honey without flowers. Hope is the word God has written on the brow of every man. Hope is a smile on God's face.

SELECTED FROM NINETEENTH-CENTURY SERMONS

# For a Bright Future

*After the earthquake came a fire,*
*but the Lord was not in the fire.*
*And after the fire came a gentle whisper.*
1 KINGS 19:12 NIV

Do not let your faults discourage you. Be patient with yourself as well as with your neighbor. Thinking too much will exhaust you and cause you to make a lot of mistakes. Learn to pray in all your daily situations. Speak, act, and walk as if you were in prayer. This is how you should live anyway.

Do everything without becoming too excited. As soon as you start to feel yourself getting too eager, quiet yourself before God. Listen to Him as He prompts you inwardly, then do only as He directs. If you do this, your words will be fewer but more effective. You will be calm, and good will be accomplished in greater measure.

I'm not talking about continually trying to reason things out. Simply ask your Lord what He wants of you. This simple and short asking is better than your long-winded inner debates.

Turn toward God and it will be much easier to turn away from your strong natural feelings. Depend on the Lord within you. Your life will become a prayer.

FRANÇOIS FENELON

# The Hope in You

*God has chosen to make known among the Gentiles*
*the glorious riches of this mystery,*
*which is Christ in you, the hope of glory.*
COLOSSIANS 1:27 NIV

"Christ in you is the hope of glory." What is hope? I wish we bore in mind the real significance of the good old Anglo-Saxon word "hope." It does not mean foundationless expectations but rather confidence in something yet to be, with an accompanying endeavor to reach it.

Christ in you is the one unanswerable evidence of the ultimate victory. Thank God for the company in whose lives Christ is singing the anthem of His coming victory. We are in the midst of smoke and the din of battle. There are days when we sit and fold our hands and say, "Where is the promise of His coming?" No Christian has ever wailed that out but that presently there came singing back through his soul the answer of Christ.

But "Christ in you, the hope of glory" means a great deal more than that; he sings an anthem of the future. He who gives us a vision of the ultimate is also present to deal with all the forces that oppose.

His victory is assured. The song of it is in our hearts. God help us to answer the call of the song and hasten the triumph.

G. CAMPBELL MORGAN

# *Tyndale's Great Hope*

*We have heard of your faith in Christ Jesus
and of the love you have for all the saints—
the faith and love that spring from the hope
that is stored up for you in heaven.*

COLOSSIANS 1:4–5 NIV

Oxford University don William Tyndale translated the first New Testament published in English (1526). A man of great passion and hope, Tyndale was later persecuted and murdered for making God's Word so accessible. Colossians and its message of hope was Tyndale's favorite.

❧

(1:1) Paul, an apostle Jesus Christ, and brother Timotheus. (1:2) To the saints which are at Colossae, and brethren that believe in Christ. Grace be with you and peace from God our father, and from the Lord Jesus Christ. (1:3) We give thanks to God the father of our Lord Jesus Christ always praying for you in our prayers, (1:4) since we heard of your faith which ye have in Christ Jesus: and of the love which ye bear to all saints. (1:5) For the hope's sake which is laid up in store for you in heaven, of which hope ye have heard [before] by the true word of the gospel.

An Antwerp contemporary of Tyndale's described the final hours: October 6, 1536. Mr. Tyndale was removed from Castle Vilvorde jail, his person wrapped in iron chains. A boatman's rope was tied around his neck, and he was brought to the cross in the town square. Gunpowder was added to the fags and brush. Before his body was burned, the great man was strangled with the rope, then thrown on the pyre.

*This was he who translated Colossians 1:5, "For the hope's sake which is laid up in store for you in heaven."*

WILLIAM TYNDALE

# A Blessed New Year

*But the land. . .is a land. . .*
*which the LORD thy God careth for:*
*the eyes of the LORD thy God are always upon it,*
*from the beginning of the year*
*even unto the end of the year.*
DEUTERONOMY 11:11–12 KJV

[Two weeks ago] we stood upon the verge of the unknown. There still lies before us a new year, and we are going forth to possess it. Who can tell what we shall find? But here is the cheering, comforting, gladdening message from our Heavenly Father: "His eyes are upon it away to the ending of the year."

The land [our life] is a land of hills and valleys. It is not all smooth nor all downhill. If life were all one level, the dull sameness would oppress us; we want the hills and valleys. The hills collect the rain for a hundred fruitful valleys. So it is with us. It is the hill difficulty that drives us to the throne of grace and brings down the showers of blessing; the hills, the bleak hills of life that we wonder at and perhaps grumble at, bring down the showers.

We cannot tell what loss and sorrow and trial are doing. Trust only. The Father comes near to take our hand and lead us on our way today. This shall be a good, a blessed new year!

MRS. CHARLES E. COWMAN

## *Hope Is Life*

*I have come that they might have life,
and have it to the full.*

JOHN 10:10 NIV

The soul that is compact of harmonies has more life, that is, a larger being, than the soul consumed of cares. The contemplative sage is a larger life than the clown. The poet is more alive than the man whose life flows out so that money may come in. The man who loves his fellow is infinitely more alive than he whose endeavor is to exalt himself. The man who strives to be better than he who longs for the praise of many is the person to whom God is all in all, who feels his life-roots hid with Christ in God. He who knows himself the inheritor of all wealth and worlds and ages, yea, of power essential and in itself, that man has begun to be alive and, indeed, is full of hope.

Let us in all the troubles of life remember that our one lack is life, that what we need is more life—more of the life-making presence in us making us more alive. When most oppressed, when most weary of life, let us think that it is in truth the inroads of death that we are weary of. When most incline to sleep, let us rouse ourselves to live! Let us avoid the false refuge of a weary collapse, a hopeless yielding to things just as they are. It is the life in us that is discontented; we need more of what is discontented, not more of the cause of the discontent.

GEORGE MACDONALD

# Catechism of Hope

*To them God has chosen to make known among the Gentiles the glorious riches of this mystery, which is Christ in you, the hope of glory.*

COLOSSIANS 1:27 NIV

Q: What is the definition of the biblical word "hope"?

A: Hope means certain, sure, confident salvation. Hope is called an "anchor, both sure and steadfast" and a "strong consolation" (Hebrews 6:18–19), an "everlasting consolation" (2 Thessalonians 2:16), the "hope of eternal life" (Titus 1:2), "an helmet" (1 Thessalonians 5:8), and "a living hope" (1 Peter 1:3).

Q: Is there certainty? Why is it called a *hope*?

A: The believer can be absolutely certain his sin is forgiven and that he has eternal life. Our salvation in Christ is called a hope not because it is uncertain [as in "I hope so"], but because we do not yet enjoy the fullness of it (Romans 8:24–25).

Q: Why can a Christian have such confidence?

A: (1) God's promise: Hebrews 6:17–19; Titus 1:2; (2) Jesus' blood: Hebrews 9:27–28; (3) Jesus' Resurrection: 1 Peter 1:3; (4) Jesus' priesthood: Hebrews 6:19–20; (5) God's grace: 2 Thessalonians 2:16.

Q: Is a hope a reward?

A: It is the gift of God's grace through the blood of Jesus Christ, not a reward. The believer's security does not depend upon his own goodness and faithfulness but upon that of the Savior. The Christian's hope is not his faithful service but the Lord Jesus himself. He is our hope!

JOHN KNOX, ADAPTED

# The Christian Hope

*Everyone who has*
*this hope in him purifies himself,*
*just as he is pure.*
1 JOHN 3:3 NIV

Our text [above] is a distinct affirmation of Christian commitment. The apostle positively affirms that every instance of this hope will be manifested by the appropriate effort. How can it be otherwise? The object before the mind is being like Christ. You hope to be like Him when you shall see Him as He is. Now you can see at once that this hope must beget a constant endeavor to become like Christ now.

For what is this hope, and what does it imply? Study this point with care. A true hope of heaven implies a realization of what heaven is; for a man deceives himself if he thinks he has a Christian hope and yet does not rightly apprehend what heaven is.

I knew a woman who, for a long time, thought she wanted to go to heaven and had enjoyed, as she supposed, a Christian hope. But in the process of time truth broke in upon her mind, and she began to see the holiness of heaven. At length the subject came fully before her mind as it were a blaze of heaven's own light; and she said to her husband, "You know I have long been hoping for heaven and have supposed myself in a measure prepared for it; but my mind is entirely changed. I'm not sure I want to go to heaven; they are so holy there."

The answer: Our text—be pure as Christ is pure.

CHARLES G. FINNEY

# The Bishop's Candlesticks, Part 1

*So in everything,*
*do to others what you would have them do to you.*
MATTHEW 7:12 NIV

To many Christians, Victor Hugo's novel *Les Miserables* is an impressive parable of redemption. This incident describes how prison fugitive Jean Valjean discovers the glory of forgiveness, God's grace, and hope.

"See here! My name is Jean Valjean. I am a convict; I have been fourteen years in the galleys. Four days ago I was set free. When I reached this place this evening I went to an inn, but they sent me away. I went to the prison, but the turnkey would not let me in. So I came back to the city to get the shelter of some doorway.

"Just then an old woman came out of the church and asked, 'What are you doing here, my friend?' I told her that I had knocked at every door to find shelter and that everybody had driven me away.

"The woman asked, 'Have you knocked at that door?' pointing to this house. I answered 'No.' She smiled. 'Knock there.' "

*Jean Valjean knocked and found refuge in a bishop's home. The old cleric opened his arms to the stranger.*

"Madame Magloire," the old man said to his housekeeper, "put on another plate." Then he added, "Put some sheets on the bed in the alcove," to which Valjean remarked:

"You will keep me? You won't drive me away? A convict! You call me monsieur and don't say 'Get out, dog!' as everybody else does. You are humane, Monsieur Curé; you don't despise me."

*"Hope is the word which God has written on the brow of every man."*

VICTOR HUGO

# The Bishop's Candlesticks, Part 2

*Do not judge, or you too will be judged.*
MATTHEW 7:1 NIV

The bishop touched Jean Valjean's hand gently and said, "You need not tell me who you are. This is not my house; it is the house of Christ. It does not ask any comer whether he has a name, but whether he has an affliction. You are suffering; you are hungry and thirsty; be welcome."

*After dinner. . .*

"Monsieur, I will show you to your room."

*As the cathedral clock struck two, Jean Valjean awoke and began thinking about the beautiful silver service he'd seen on the table. He got out of bed and went straight to the cupboard, reached in, grabbed the silver pieces, and went out the door, across the garden, and over the wall. The next morning. . .*

"Monseigneur, the man has gone! The silver is stolen!"

Just as the bishop finished breakfast there came a knock at the door. "Come in," said the bishop. The door opened and three men stepped in. They held a fourth man by his collar.

The three men were police; the fourth Jean Valjean.

"Ah, there you are!" said the bishop, looking toward Jean Valjean. "I am glad to see you. But I gave you the candlesticks also, which are silver like the rest. Why did you not take them with the plates?"

"Monseigneur," said the brigadier, "then what this man said was true?" The bishop nodded, so the police released Valjean. "My friend," said the old man, ". . .here are your candlesticks."

*"Hope is the word which God has written on the brow of every man."*

VICTOR HUGO

# The Bishop's Candlesticks, Part 3

*Because of his great love for us, God,*
*who is rich in mercy,*
*made us alive in Christ even when*
*we were dead in transgressions.*
EPHESIANS 2:4–5 NIV

Jean Valjean was trembling in every limb. He took the two candlesticks mechanically and with a puzzled appearance.

"Now," said the bishop, "go in peace." Then turning to the police, he said, "Messieurs, you can retire." The police officers retired bewilderedly.

Jean Valjean felt like a man who is just about to faint. The bishop approached him and said in a low voice, "Forget not; never forget that you have promised me to use this silver to become an honest man."

Jean Valjean, who had no recollection of this promise, stood confounded. The bishop had laid much stress upon these words as he uttered them. He continued solemnly, "Jean Valjean, my brother, you belong no longer to evil, but to good. It is your soul that I am buying for you. I withdraw it from dark thoughts and from the spirit of perdition, and I give it to God!"

*"Hope is the word which God has written on the brow of every man."* That hope was possessed by Jean Valjean.

VICTOR HUGO

*No other narrative, save the Bible, has presented such a story of redemption and hope.*

*The novel continues for 491 more pages with Jean Valjean's story of redemption.*

# The Many Mansions

*In my Father's house are many mansions.*
JOHN 14:2 KJV

What a "home aspect" there is in these words of Jesus. He comforts His church by telling those who will soon be done with their wilderness wanderings—the tented tabernacle suited to their present state exchanged for the enduring mansion. It will not be a strange dwelling place; it will be the Father's home—a Father's welcome awaits them. There will be accommodations for all. Thousands have already entered its shining gates—patriarchs, prophets, saints, martyrs, young and old—and still there is room.

The pilgrim's motto on earth is, "Here we have no continuing location—we can't put our roots down." Even "Sabbath tents" must be taken down. Holy seasons of communion will terminate. "Arise, let us go from here!" is a summons which disturbs the sweetest moments of tranquility in the church here on earth. But in heaven, every believer becomes a pillar in the temple of God, and "He shall go no more out." Here on earth, it is but the lodging of a wayfarer turning aside to tarry for the brief night. Here we are but temporary tenants. Our possessions are but movables—ours today, gone tomorrow. But these many "mansions" are an incorruptible and unfading inheritance. Nothing can touch the heavenly inheritance. Once within the Father's house, we are in the house forever.

JOHN MACDUFF

# Poetic Hope

*Be strong and take heart,*
*all you who hope in the LORD.*
PSALM 31:24 NIV

Hope! Who is insensible to the music of that word? What bosom has not kindled under its utterance? Poetry has sung of it; music has warbled it; oratory has lavished on it its bewitching strains.

Hope! Well may we personify you, lighting up your altar fires in this dark world and dropping a live coal into many desolate hearts; gladdening the sick chamber with visions of returning health; illuminating with rays, brighter than the sunbeam, the captive's cell; crowding the broken slumber of the soldier by his bivouac fire with pictures of his sunny home and his own joyous return.

When all others flee, Hope, with her elastic dreams, elastic step, radiant countenance, and lustrous attire, lingered behind. Hope! Drying the tear on the cheek of woe as the black clouds of sorrow break and fall to earth, arching the descending drops with thine own beautiful rainbow.

Yes, there is more—standing with your lamp in your hand by the gloomy realms of Hades, kindling your torch at Nature's funeral pile, and opening vistas through the gates of glory.

If hope, even with reference to presence and infinite things, be an emotion so joyous—if uninspired poetry can sing so sweetly of its delights, what must be the believer's hope, the hope which has God for its object and heaven its consummation.

JOHN MACDUFF

# Jesus Dwelling

*I pray that out of his glorious riches*
*he may strengthen you with*
*power through his Spirit in your inner being,*
*so that Christ may dwell in your hearts through faith.*

EPHESIANS 3:16–17 NIV

The child of God's hope: If Christ Jesus dwells in a man as his friend and noble leader, that person can endure all things, for Christ helps and strengthens us and will never abandon us. He is a true friend. I clearly see that as a hope-filled one, I must receive an abundance of these graces, which come to you from the hands of Christ. In all of this, God takes delight.

All blessings come to us through our Lord. He will teach us, for in beholding His life, we discover that He is our best example.

What more do we desire from such a good friend, who walks beside us? Unlike our friends in the world, He will never abandon us when we are troubled or distressed. Blessed is the one who truly loves Him and always keeps Him near.

When we think of Christ, we should recall the love that led Him to shower us with so many graces and favors. Our hope is established in God's love—God who gave us Christ as a pledge of His love. This calls for us to return that love. Let us strive to keep this always before our eyes and to rouse us to love Him. As He impresses His love on us, He shares it with others, starting with Him.

TERESA OF AVILA

# Obedience: A Mark of Hope

*Seek first his kingdom and his righteousness,*
*and all these things will be given to you as well.*
MATTHEW 6:33 NIV

When a man goes up in a balloon, he takes along sand as ballast, which he uses to control how fast and high he rises; when he throws out a little sand ballast, he mounts higher; then more sand, and still higher. The higher the balloonist wants to go, the more sand he throws out. The closer we get to God, the more things of the world we have to throw out of our lives. The more we throw out the things of the world, the nearer we get to God.

I must say, let go of those things of the world. Do not let us set our hearts and affections on them. Do what the Master tells us to do: "Lay up for yourselves treasures in heaven."

In England I was told of a lady who had been bedridden for years. She was one of those saints who God polishes up for the kingdom. I believe that there are a good many saints in this world that we never hear about; we never see their names; they live very near the Master; they live very near heaven.

I think it takes a great deal more grace to suffer God's will than it does to do God's will. If a person lies in a bed of sickness and suffers cheerfully and is putting hope to practice, that person is as acceptable to God as if they were out working in His vineyard. Amen!

DWIGHT L. MOODY

# Hoping and Praying

*Ask what ye will, and it shall be done unto you.*
JOHN 15:7 KJV

Let us realize that we can only fulfill our calling to bear much fruit by praying much. In Christ are all the treasures any person needs; in Him all God's children are blessed with all spiritual blessings; He is full of grace and truth. But it needs prayer, much prayer, strong believing prayer, to bring these blessings down.

And let us equally remember that we cannot appropriate the promise (John 15:7) without a deep, life-giving concern for the spiritually lost. Many try to take the promise and then look around for something to ask for. This is not the way but the very opposite. Get the heart burdened with the need of souls and the command to help save them, and the power to claim the promise will come.

Let us claim it as one of the revelations of our wonderful life in Christ: He tells us that if we ask in His name, in virtue of our union with Him, whatsoever it be, it will be given to us. Souls are perishing because there is so little prayer. God's children are feeble because there is so little prayer. The faith of this promise would make us strong to pray; let us not rest till it has entered into our very heart and drawn us in the power of Christ to continue and labor and strive in prayer until the blessing comes in power.

ANDREW MURRAY

# Jesus' Pledge

*Because I live, you will live also.*
JOHN 14:19 NKJV

Sometimes God selects the most stable and enduring objects in the material world to illustrate His unchanging faithfulness and love for the church. But here, the Redeemer uses an argument from His own everlasting nature. He stakes, so to speak, His own existence on that of His saints—"Because I live, you will live also."

Believer, read in these words of Jesus your glorious title-deed. Your Savior lives—and His life is the guarantee for your own life. But with Christ for our life, how inviolable is our security. The great Fountain of being must first be dried up before the streamlet can. The great Sun must first be quenched, before one of His light-filled disciples can. Satan must first pluck the crown from that glorified Head before he can touch one jewel in His people's crown. "If we perish," says Martin Luther, "Christ perishes with us."

Reader, is your life now "hidden with Christ in God?" Do you know the blessedness of a vital and living union with a living, life-giving Savior? Can you say with humble and joyous confidence, amid the confidence, amid the fitfulness of your own ever-changing frames and feelings, "Nevertheless I live, yet not I, but Christ lives in me" (Galatians 2:20)?

*Those are the happiest words a lost soul and a lost world can hear, the sublime utterance with which He was addressed by that same "Kinsman," when He appeared arrayed in the luster of His glorified humanity.*

JOHN MACDUFF

# Commissioning Souls

*The fruit of the righteous is a tree of life,*
*and he who is wise wins souls.*

PROVERBS 11:30 NASB

Every born-again Christian possesses a measure of the Spirit of Christ, enough of the Holy Spirit to lead us to true consecration and inspire us with the faith that is essential to our prevalence in prayer. Let us, then, not grieve or resist Him, but accept the commission, fully consecrate ourselves with all we have, to the saving of our great and only life work.

Let us get onto the altar, with all we have and are, and lie there and persist in prayer until we receive the provision.

Now, observe, conversion to Christ is not to be confounded with the acceptance of this commission to convert the world. The first is a personal transaction between the soul and Christ relating to its own salvation. The second is the soul's acceptance of the service in which Christ proposes to employ it. Christ does not require us to make brick without straw. To whom He gives the commission He also gives the admonition and the promise. If the commission is heartily accepted, if the promise is believed, if the admonition to wait upon the Lord until our strength is renewed be complied with, we shall receive the provision.

CHARLES G. FINNEY

# Finding Our Life in Him

*We do not want you to become lazy,*
*but to imitate those who through faith*
*and patience inherit what has been promised.*
HEBREWS 6:12 NIV

It is the highest stage of manhood to have no wish, no thought, no desire, but Christ—to feel that to die were bliss, if it were for Christ—that to live in poverty and woe and scorn and contempt and misery were sweet for Christ—to feel that it matters nothing what becomes of one's self, so that our Master is but exalted—to feel that though, like a mere leaf, we are blown in the blast, we are quite careless where we are going, so long as we feel the that the Master's hand is guiding us according to His will. Or, rather, to feel that though, like a diamond, we must be exercised with sharp tools, yet we care not how sharply we may be cut, so that we may be made fit brilliants to adorn His crown.

I do think that one of the worst sins a person can be guilty of in this world is to be idle. I can almost forgive a drunkard, but a lazy man I do think there is very little pardon. I think a person who is idle has a good reason to be a penitent before God. God never sent an individual into the world to be idle. And there are some who make a tolerably fair profession but who do nothing from one new year to the next.

CHARLES H. SPURGEON

# Always Reason to Hope

*Why art thou cast down, O my soul?*
PSALM 43:5 KJV

Is there ever any ground to be cast down? There are two reasons, but only two. If we are as yet unconverted, we have ground to be cast down; or if we have been converted and live in sin, then we are rightly cast down.

But except for these two things there is no ground to be cast down, for all else may be brought before God in prayer with supplication and thanksgiving. And regarding all our necessities, all our difficulties, all our trials, we may exercise faith in the power of God, and in the love of God.

*"Hope thou in God."* Oh, remember this: there is never a time when we may not hope in God. Whatever our necessities, however great our difficulties, and though to all appearance help is impossible, yet our business is to hope in God, and it will be found that it is not in vain. In the Lord's own time help will come.

Oh, the hundreds, yes, the thousands of times that I have found it so within the past seventy years and four months!

When it seemed impossible that help would come, help did come; for God has His own resources. He is not confined. In ten thousand different ways, and at ten thousand different times, God may help us.

GEORGE MÜLLER

# Hope in Him

*I know whom I have believed,*
*and am persuaded that he is able to keep that which*
*I have committed unto him against that day.*
2 TIMOTHY 1:12 KJV

I well recall an old Christian woman who lived down the lane from me. In her younger days she had fallen in love with Jesus Christ, when He had given her Hope for her future. At one time she knew much of the Bible by heart. Her favorite verse was "I know whom I have believed and am persuaded that he is able to keep that which I have committed to him against that day."

As age came on and began to take its toll, her memory began to fail. Eventually her deteriorating memory caused only one precious bit of that verse to stay with her, "To keep that which I have committed unto him against that day." By and by only a phrase of the verse kept its focus, and she would quietly repeat, "That which I have committed unto him."

When at last, as she hovered on the borderland between this and the world to come, her loved ones noticed her lips moving. They bent down to see if she needed anything. She was repeating over and over to herself the one word of the text, "Him—Him—Him." She had lost the whole Bible but held on to her hope in one word.

S. D. GORDON

# No Despair for Pilgrim

*Those who hope in the LORD will renew their strength.*
*They will soar on wings like eagles;*
*they will run and not grow weary,*
*they will walk and not be faint.*

ISAIAH 40:31 NIV

You who have read *Pilgrim's Progress,* do you recall where John Bunyan pictures Christian as getting right under the old dragon's foot? He is very heavy and presses the very breath out of a fellow when he makes him his footstool.

Poor Christian lay there with the dragon's foot on his breast, but he was just able to stretch out his hand and lay hold on his sword, which by good providence, lay within his reach. Then he gave Apollyon a deadly thrust which made him spread his dragon wings and fly away. The poor crushed and broken pilgrim [Christian], as he gave the stab to his foe, cried, "Rejoice not over me, O mine enemy; though I fall, yet shall I rise again."

Brother, do you do the same? You who are near despair, let this be the strength that strengthens your arm and steels your heart. Jesus Christ of the seed of David was raised from the dead according to Paul's gospel.

This is the genuine hope for the believer. Just like Jesus, we to are able to "mount up with wings as eagles" (Isaiah 40:31 KJV). God grant that we all mount to higher plains of living in Jesus Christ our Lord.

CHARLES H. SPURGEON

# The Solid Rock

*No one can lay any foundation other than the one already laid,
which is Jesus Christ.*
1 CORINTHIANS 3:11 NIV

My hope is built on nothing else than Jesus' blood
    and righteousness.
I dare not trust the sweetest frame,
    but wholly lean on Jesus' name.

When darkness seems to hide His face,
    I rest on His unchanging grace.
In ev'ry high and stormy gale,
    my anchor holds within the veil.

His oath, His covenant, His blood,
    support me in the whelming flood.
When all around my soul gives way,
    He then is all my hope and stay.

When He shall come with trumpet sound,
    O may I then in Him be found!
Dressed in His righteousness alone,
    faultless to stand before the throne.

On Christ the solid Rock I stand;
    all other ground is sinking sand,
All other ground is sinking sand.

EDWARD MOTE

# Enough for the Present

*May the God of hope fill you with
all joy and peace as you trust in him,
so that you may overflow with hope
by the power of the Holy Spirit.*

ROMANS 15:13 NIV

Professor Dr. James McCosh addressed his students at Princeton University in a day when the learned could practice and describe the hope within him, and class members would listen with respect and open hearts.

Religion is full of questions that we cannot answer, because we only know in part—*but we know!*

There are things of which we may be positively certain though we cannot comprehend all their connections and relations. We know that our souls exist as truly as our bodies. We know that there is a God who is not a blind force, but a Spirit who answers the souls who seek peace and joy. Evil brings discord and death to the soul. We know that Jesus Christ is absolutely good, the perfect union of the Divine and the human spirits. We know through Him that love continues after death.

Beyond our ken lie the mysteries unexplored. But we have light enough to steer by. We know as much as we need. If we live with hope, by it we shall know more someday.

JAMES McCOSH

# He's Here!

*The Master is come, and calleth for thee.*
JOHN 11:28 KJV

It must have been a remarkable family that lived in the Bethany home—Martha, Mary, and Lazarus. Jesus loved to tarry there with them. Their home was hospitable and filled with high expectation. What did He experience in their company? Perhaps it can be best summed up in the death of Lazarus. The sisters' hope was unbounded when they called for the Master.

When Jesus stood by Lazarus's grave, I can hear Him saying: "Take away the stone." He could have done it Himself, but the Master will not do what you must do yourself. [He has great hope in us.] When the sisters took away the stone at the grave of their brother Lazarus, can you see their Lord? Hallelujah! What a Savior! I can shut my eyes and see Him as He stoops down and looks into the tomb. I can hear Him say, "Lazarus, come forth!" Mr. Moody once said that Jesus called Lazarus by name because if He had said, "Come forth," everyone who was dead would have heard him and gotten up ahead of time.

Let me say the text over again: "The Master is come, and calleth for thee." There can be no doubt about it. Maybe you are a Christian, and maybe you are not. "Screw your hope to the sticking point" and trust Jesus Christ to make you right with God.

J. WILBUR CHAPMAN

# The Hope of Glory

*He called you to this through our gospel,*
*that you might share in the glory*
*of our Lord Jesus Christ.*

2 THESSALONIANS 2:14 NIV

The hope of glory refers to the great consummation in which God's purposes are to be perfectly fulfilled; in which the church, with one voice, shall say, "You, O Christ, are all I want"; and in which the whole creation will find its groaning cease and join the chorus of praise to Him who sits upon the throne. God's glory consists in the realization of the purpose of His love.

Christ in you is the hope of this glory.

Without hope none can attain the glory of holiness. You cannot attain sanctification without first having the hope of attaining it, and then being stimulated by this hope to make appropriate efforts. Hence, you must expect to attain as a condition of attaining.

No hope can be kept secret. Some people talk of having a secret hope and speak of others as having a secret hope. The fact is, a hope that can be kept secret, shows itself to be poor and vain—the antithesis of holy living. If it were a good hope, it would lead its possessor to purify himself. No man can throw the energies of his being into the struggle for Christian purity and still keep his religion a secret. The world will know him; Christian brethren will feel the warmth of his heart.

CHARLES G. FINNEY

# Our Great Savior

*Looking for that blessed hope, and the glorious appearing of the great God and our Saviour Jesus Christ; who gave himself for us, that he might redeem us from all iniquity, and purify unto himself a peculiar people, zealous of good works.*
TITUS 2:13–14 KJV

Through the centuries, artists and poets who have been impressed with Christ have tried valiantly to present His portrait both with brush and pen. Yet even the most noble efforts of these dedicated artisans seem feeble and inadequate.

Evangelist J. Wilbur Chapman has provided a worthy text extolling various attributes of Christ as they relate to our personal lives—the world's only hope.

> Jesus! What a Friend for sinners! Jesus! Lover of my soul;
> Friends may fail me, foes assail me, He, my Savior,
>     makes me whole.
>
> Jesus! What a Strength in weakness! Let me hide myself
>     in Him.
> Tempted, tried, and sometimes failing, He, my Strength,
>     my victory wins.
>
> Jesus! What a Help in sorrow! While the billows over
>     me roll,
> Even when my heart is breaking, He, my comfort,
>     helps my soul.
>
> Jesus! I do now receive Him, More than all in Him I find,
> He hath granted me forgiveness, I am His, and He is mine.

J. WILBUR CHAPMAN

# Give to the Winds Thy Fears

*Cast all your anxiety on him because he cares for you.*

1 PETER 5:7 NIV

Give to the winds thy fears, Hope, and be undismay'd;
God hears thy sighs and counts thy tears;
    God shall lift up thy head.

Through waves and clouds and storms He gently clears
        thy way;
Wait thou His time, so shall this night soon end in
        joyous day.

Still heavy is thy heart? Still sink thy spirits down?
Cast off the weight, let fear depart, and every care be gone.

Thou seest our weakness, Lord, our hearts are known
        to Thee;
Oh, lift thou up the sinking hand, confirm the feeble knee.

Let us in life, in death, Thy steadfast truth declare,
And publish with our latest breath Thy love and
        guardian care!

PAULUS GERHARDT
JOHN WESLEY, TRANSLATED

# Hope at Rest

*If any man be in Christ, he is a new creature:*
*old things are passed away;*
*behold, all things are become new.*
2 CORINTHIANS 5:17 KJV

This scripture [above] speaks of the great change that came to Billy Sunday when he heard the gospel at the Pacific Garden Mission in this city [Chicago] and received the Lord Jesus Christ as his own personal Savior. This is what the Bible calls "conversion" or "regeneration." This great change came to Billy Sunday, as it comes to every truly saved soul, as a great miracle. One moment he was without Christ, the next, to his joy and amazement, he was in Christ. Doubtless he did not fully understand the meaning of this at the time, but his life all through the years since has proven the reality of it.

Now the man who is in Christ is the man who has been born again, has become a partaker of the Divine nature, and is indwelt by the Holy Spirit. The person who is in Christ is justified before God and freed from condemnation.

And now, Billy Sunday has finished his course, he has kept the faith, and he is at home. To this hope-filled man of God, what did death mean? It is to be with Christ. It is "absent from the body, present with the Lord." And we may be sure of this, as we are here to pay our respects to the memory of our departed brother: We are not burying the real Billy Sunday. He is with Christ. We are simply laying away the tabernacle in which he dwelt for a season.

HARRY IRONSIDE

# Moody on Hope

*The LORD is my rock,
my fortress and my deliverer;
my God is my rock,
in whom I take refuge.*

PSALM 18:2 NIV

Take your stand on the Rock of Ages. Let death, let the judgment come: The victory is Christ's and yours through Him.

No matter how low down you are, no matter what your disposition has been, you may be low in your thoughts, words, and actions; you may be selfish; your heart may be overflowing with corruption and wickedness; yet Jesus will have compassion upon you. He will speak comforting words to you—words of love and affection and kindness. He is a faithful friend—a friend that sticks closer than a brother.

No person in the world should be so happy as a man or woman of God. It is one continual source of gladness. He can look up and say, "God is my Father, Christ is my Savior, and the church is my mother."

Keep your eyes on Christ. He is the Savior of the world. He came from the throne to this earth: He came from the very bosom of the Father. God gave Him up freely for us, and all we have to do is to accept Him as Savior. Look at Him on the cross, crucified between two thieves; hear that piercing cry, "Father, Father, forgive them; they know not what they do." And as you look into that face, as you look into those wounds on His feet or His hands, will you say He has not the power to save you? Will you say He has not the power to redeem you?

DWIGHT L. MOODY

# *Hope Is Trust*

*All things work together for good to those who love God,*
*to those who are the called according to His purpose.*
ROMANS 8:28 NKJV

My soul! Be still! You are in the hands of your God. Were all the strange circumstances in your history the result of accident or chance, you might well be overwhelmed. But "all things," and this thing (be what it may) which may be now disquieting you, is one of these "all things" that are so working mysteriously for your good. Trust your God! He will not deceive you—your interests are with Him in safe custody. When sight says, "All these things are against me," let faith rebuke the hasty conclusion and say, "Shall not the Judge of all the earth do right?" How often does God hedge up your way with thorns to elicit simple trust! How seldom can we see all things so working for our good! But it is better discipline to believe it. Oh for faith amid frowning providences to say, "I know that your judgments are good"; and, relying in the dark to exclaim, "Though He slay me, yet will I trust Him!" (Job 13:15 NKJV).

Blessed Jesus, to You are committed the reins of this universal empire. The same hand that was once nailed to the cross is now wielding the scepter on the throne—all power in heaven and in earth is given unto You. How can I doubt the wisdom and the faithfulness and the love of our Father in Heaven who gave His Son for me?

JOHN MACDUFF

# A Many-Splendored Savior

*Jesus answered,
"I am the way and the truth and the life."*
JOHN 14:6 NIV

Our hope is based on nothing less than a Savior who knows us, and is "all things to all people."

I tell you that Jesus challenges the attention of this world by his many-sidedness. He meets the needs of all classes and conditions of all men. He responds to the movings of each man's soul. Call the roll of the world's workers and ask, "What think ye of Christ?"

To the artist, He is the one Altogether Lovely. To the architect, He is the Chief Cornerstone. To the astronomer, He is the Sun of Righteousness. To the baker, He is the Living Bread. To the biologist, He is the Life. To the builder, He is the Sure Foundation. To the carpenter, He is the Door.

To the doctor, He is the Great Physician. To the Educator, He is the Great Teacher. To the farmer, He is the Sower. To the florist, He is the Rose of Sharon. To the geologist He is the Rock of Ages. To the philanthropist, He is the Unspeakable Gift. To the servant, He is the Good Master.

To the cartographer, He is the Way. To the lawyer, He is the Truth. To the biologist, He is Life. To the sinner, He is Salvation. What is He to you?

R. A. TORREY

# An Eternal Love Story

*For God so loved the world*
*that he gave his one and only Son,*
*that whoever believes in him should not perish*
*but have eternal life.*

JOHN 3:16 NIV

While it's debatable if there ever was a historical character by the name of St. Valentine, it cannot be debated that his influence has been with us for centuries. Undebatable is the influence of God's love for us and the gift of His Son.

❧

(1) God—the greatest lover, (2) So loved—the greatest degree, (3) The world—the greatest company, (4) That He gave—the greatest act, (5) His one and only Son—the greatest gift, (6) That whoever—the greatest opportunity, (7) Believes—the greatest simplicity, (8) In Him—the greatest attraction, (9) Should not perish—the greatest promise, (10) But—the greatest difference, (11) Have—the greatest certainty, (12) Everlasting life—the greatest possession.

JOHN L. DAVIES

# Spirituality for Two

> [Jesus] entered a certain village,
> where a woman named Martha
> welcomed him into her home.
>
> LUKE 10:38 NRSV

Mystic writer Meister Eckhart (1260–1328) does not fault Martha for her busyness but holds both sisters as women who loved their Lord. Each demonstrated her love for and hope in Jesus.

There were three reasons that made Mary sit at her Lord's feet. First, it was because God's goodness had reached out and embraced her soul. The second cause was a great, unspeakable longing; she yearned without knowing what it was she was yearning for. The third was the sweet consolation and happiness that she derived from the words of life that she heard from Jesus' mouth.

Then there were three things that inspired Martha to busy herself in serving her dear Lord. The first thing was her maturity and depth of age, which she thoroughly trained to be responsive to physical needs. Because of this, Martha believed no one else was as well suited to do this as she. The second reason was a wise prudence that knew how to accomplish acts to the highest degree that love demands. The third was the dignity of her honored guest.

Those who are experts on the topic of spiritual life say that God is ready for every person's spiritual and physical satisfaction to the degree that a person desires. There is certainly a spirituality that is tailored to everyone's personality and readiness.

MEISTER ECKHART

# *Holy Affection*

*[God has given his people the spirit] of power,*
*and of love, and of a sound mind.*
2 TIMOTHY 1:7 KJV

If we are not earnest in our religion, and if our wills and inclinations are not strongly exercised, we are nothing. The importance of religion is so great that no halfhearted exercise will do. In nothing is the state of our heart so crucial as in religion, and in nothing is lukewarmness so odious.

True religion is a powerful thing. It is the basis of hope in the Christian life. Its power appears in the inward exercises of the heart (which is the seat of all religion). Therefore, true religion is called "the power of godliness," in contrast to the external appearances of it, i.e., the mere "form": "Having the form of godliness but denying the power of it" (2 Timothy 3:5). The Spirit of God is a spirit of powerful holy affection in the lives of those who have a sound and solid religion.

When we receive the Spirit of God, we receive the baptism of the Holy Ghost who is like "fire," and along with it the sanctifying and saving influences of God. When this happens, when grace is at work within us, it sometimes "burns" within us, as it was for Jesus' disciples (Luke 24:32).

JONATHAN EDWARDS

# Genuine Religion

*Happy is [one]. . .*
*whose hope is in the LORD.*
PSALM 146:5 KJV

Jonathan Edwards has carried the stigma of a firebrand preacher because of his renowned sermon, "Sinners in the Hands of an Angry God." Yet in this, the man's tender heart and note of hope shines through.

❧

The holy scriptures clearly see religion as a result of the affections, namely the affections of fear, hope, love, hatred, joy, desire, sorrow, gratitude, compassion, and zeal.

The scriptures see religion as the result of *holy fear*. Truly religious persons tremble at the Word of God. It is His holiness that makes them fear. The fear of God is a great part of godliness.

So also *hope* in God and in the promises of God, according to the scriptures, is a very important part of true religion. It is recorded as one of the three great things of which religion consists: "And now faith, hope, and love abide" (1 Corinthians 13:13 NRSV). Hope is spoken of as the helmet of the Christian soldier, "the hope of salvation" (1 Thessalonians 5:8). It is a sure and steadfast anchor of the soul (Hebrews 6:19).

"Hope does not disappoint us, because God's love has been poured into our hearts through the Holy Spirit" (Romans 5:5 NRSV).

JONATHAN EDWARDS

# Believer's Conversation

*Let your conversation be always full of grace,*
*seasoned with salt,*
*so that you may know how to answer everyone.*
COLOSSIANS 4:6 NIV

Ever-practical Charles Spurgeon provides guidance for spirit-filled conversationalists.

≈

It has become very popular to join the church in our day. But are there fewer cheats than there used to be? Are there less frauds committed? The lives and conversations of too many men and women of the church give the world cause to wonder if there really is godliness in any of them.

Let us take a look at the conversation of many professing Christians. You might spend from the first of January to the end of December and never hear them speak about their faith. They will scarcely even mention the name of their Lord Jesus Christ at all. On Sunday afternoon, what will they talk about at the dinner table? It will not be about the minister's sermon, unless they want to point out some faults.

Do they ever talk about what Jesus said and did? What He suffered for us? When we go to each other's houses what will we talk about? I have concluded this: You will not know how to get to heaven simply by eavesdropping on the members of the church.

We talk too little about our Lord. Is this not the truth? Many of us need pray, "O Lord, revive your work in my soul, that my conversation might be more Christlike, seasoned with salt, and kept by the Holy Spirit."

CHARLES H. SPURGEON

# Teach Us to Pray

*Lord, teach us to pray.*
LUKE 11:1 KJV

One day the disciples said to Jesus Christ: "Lord, teach us to pray." It was the Holy Spirit who inspired them to make this request. The Holy Spirit convinced them of their inability to pray in their own strength, and He moved their hearts to draw near to Jesus as their only Master who could teach them how they ought to pray. It was then that Jesus taught them the Lord's Prayer.

There is no Christian who is not in the same case as the disciples. Every Christian ought to say to the Savior as humbly as the disciples, "Lord, teach us to pray." Ah, if we were only convinced of our ignorance and of our need of a teacher like Jesus Christ! If we would only approach Him with confidence, asking Him to teach us Himself and desiring to be taught by His grace how to converse with God!

How soon we should be skilled in it and how many of its secrets we should discover. Do not let us say that we know how to pray the prayer they learned from Him. We may know the words, but without the grace we cannot understand the meaning—and we cannot ask or receive what it expresses.

JEAN-NICHOLAS GROU

# There's Hope in Silence

*Be still, and know that I am God.*
PSALM 46:10 KJV

Imagine a soul so closely united to God that it has no need of outward acts to remain attentive to the inward prayer. In these moments of silence and peace when it pays no heed to what is happening within itself, it prays and prays excellently, with a simple and direct prayer that God will understand perfectly by the action of grace.

The heart will be full of aspirations toward God without any clear expression. If it is the heart that prays, it is evident that sometimes and even continuously, it can pray by itself without any help from words, spoken or not. Here is something that few people understand. Though prayers may elude our own consciousness, they will not escape the consciousness of God.

This prayer, so empty of all images and perceptions, apparently so passive and yet so active, is—so far as the limitations of this life allow—pure adoration in spirit and in truth. It is adoration fully worthy of God in which the soul is united to Him as its ground, the created intelligence to the uncreated, without anything but a very simple attention of the mind and an equally simple application of the will. This is what is called the prayer of silent or of quiet or of bare faith.

JEAN-NICHOLAS GROU

# Praying the Scripture

*Jesus told his disciples. . .*
*that they should always pray and not give up.*

LUKE 18:1 NIV

"Praying the scripture" is a unique way of dealing with the scripture; it involves both reading and prayer. Turn to the scripture; choose some passage that is simple and fairly practical. Next, come to the Lord. Come quietly and humbly. There, before Him, read a small portion of the passage of scripture you have opened to.

Be careful as you read. Take in fully, gently, and carefully what you are reading. Taste it and digest it as you read. In the past it may have been your habit, while reading, to move very quickly from one verse of scripture to another until you have read the whole passage.

Coming to the Lord by means of "praying the scripture," you do not read quickly; you read very slowly. You do not move on to the next thought until you have sensed the very heart of what you have read. You may then want to take that portion of scripture that has touched you and turn it into a prayer.

After you have sensed something of the passage and after you know that the essence of that portion has been extracted and all the deeper sense of it is gone, then, very slowly, gently, and in a calm manner begin to read the next portion. You will be surprised to find that when your time with the Lord has ended, you will have been drawn closely to Him.

MADAME GUYON

# The Grace of Humility, Part 1

*"All who exalt themselves will be humbled,
and those who humble themselves will be exalted."*
LUKE 14:11 NRSV

*Holy Living,* the book for which author Jeremy Taylor is best known, discusses humility—an important mark of Christlikeness. The following are excerpts of his instructions.

❧

The grace of humility is exercised in the following rules.

First, do not think better of yourself because of any outward circumstance that happens to you. Although you may—because of the gifts that have been bestowed upon you—be better at something than someone else (as one horse runs faster than another), know that it is for the benefit of others, not for yourself.

Second, humility does not consist in criticizing yourself or wearing ragged clothes or walking around submissively wherever you go. Humility is a realistic opinion of yourself.

Third, when you hold this opinion of yourself, be content that others think the same of you. If you realize that you are not wise, do not be surprised if someone else should agree.

Fourth, nurture a love to do good things in secret, concealed from the eyes of others and therefore not highly esteemed because of them. Be content to go without praise, never being troubled when someone has slighted or undervalued you.

Fifth, never be ashamed of your birth, of your parents, your occupation, or your present employment, or the lowly status of any them. When there is an occasion to speak about them to others, do not be shy but speak readily.

JEREMY TAYLOR

# The Grace of Humility, Part 2

*I say to everyone among you not to think of yourself
more highly than you ought to think.*

ROMANS 12:3 NRSV

More from Jeremy Taylor's *Holy Living:*

Sixth, never say anything, directly or indirectly, that will provoke praise or elicit compliments from others. Do not let your praise be the intended end of what you say. If it so happens that someone speaks well of you, you are not to stop the conversation.

Seventh, when you do receive praise for something you have done, take it indifferently and return it to God. Reflect it back to God, the giver of the gift, the blesser of the action, the aid of the project. Always give God thanks.

Eighth, make a good name for yourself by being a person of virtue and humility. It is a benefit for others who hear of you to hear good things about you. As an example, they can use your humility to their advantage.

Ninth, do not take pride in any praise given to you. Rejoice in God who gives gifts others can see in you, but let it be mixed with a holy respect so that good does not turn into evil. If praise comes, put it to work by letting it serve others.

Tenth, when you are slighted by someone or feel undervalued, do not harbor any secret anger, supposing that you actually deserve praise and that they overlooked your value or that they neglected to praise you because of their own envy.

JEREMY TAYLOR

# *Only Source of Hope*

*The tax collector stood at a distance.*
*He would not even look up to heaven,*
*but beat his breast and said,*
*"God, have mercy on me, a sinner."*
LUKE 18:13 NIV

And now, being brought to this distress, to his utter loss, his despair drives him to the only source of hope that is left open.

Christ will be acceptable, when he sees none but Christ can help him: The apostle tells us (Galatians 3:23 KJV), "We were kept under the law, shut up unto the faith which should afterwards be revealed": All other doors were shut; there was no hope of escaping but by that one door that was left open—the faith that was afterwards to be revealed. As the besieged in a city that have every gate blocked up and but one difficult passage left open, by which there is any possibility of escaping, thither throng for the saving of their lives; they are shut up unto that door, to which (if there had been any other way open) they would never have come.

And as Christ will never be accepted, so can the sinner never be received of Him until he lets go all other props and trusts on Christ alone. Jesus Christ will have no sharer with Him in the work of saving souls. "If you seek me, let these go their way," as He said in another case: Let not only your sins go, but let your righteousness go.

*Sinners, come to Me. Find true hope in Me. I am come to this end, to seek and to save them that are lost.*

JOHN WESLEY

# The Hope of Eternity

*The High and Lofty One*
*who inhabits eternity,*
*whose name is Holy. . .*
ISAIAH 57:15 NKJV

I was preaching in Lincoln, Nebraska, when a professor of mathematics stepped up behind me and said, "Eternity begins where computation ends."

I said, "Professor, what does that mean?"

"It means this," he said. "When the man with the greatest mind that world has known thinks his way out into the future and his mind fails because it can go no farther, that is the beginning of eternity."

There is no end. Sometimes men try to measure the depth of dark caverns, but the plummet is not long enough. So they measure the depth like this: They take a stopwatch in one hand and a piece of rock in the other, note when the rock drops from their fingers, and listen as it strikes the bottom, noting the time it has taken to fall. If you know the weight of the rock and the time of the falling, you can measure with some degree of accuracy the depth of the darkness.

They tell me that sometimes they let the stone fall and there comes back no answer from below. That is closer to what I believe about eternity. I stand on the edge of the precipice of time and I cry up into the light and into the darkness: "How long art thou, Eternity?" I get the answer from the Book: "The peace of the righteous is everlasting. The doom of the wicked is without end."

J. WILBER CHAPMAN

# A Better Hope

*A better hope.*
HEBREWS 7:19 KJV

The theme of Hebrews is found in the word better. The writer of this letter introduces the better theme in his discussion of the law, which "made nothing perfect," which introduces the subject of a "better hope."

Who or what is this "better hope"? It is our blessed Savior, the Lord Jesus Christ, who is able to give the believer a sense of hope that includes a deep peace, a vision of the future, a satisfaction, a desire to share it with those whose hope is really more like, "I hope so." The hope that the Son of God offers does not come to fruition as the result of a resolution. Neither can it be realized through laboring for good causes, like the church.

Spiritual hope springs eternally from a forgiven heart, a dedicated will, a stewardship of time, talent, and treasure, a love for Christ and His people. This is what the Hebrews author includes when he declares that there is "better hope." Since that hope is found in Jesus, what does He expect in return?

When you accept Him as Lord and Savior, you begin by getting better acquainted with Him. That demands a personal quiet time for prayer and devotional reading, including the Bible.

You begin to share your hope with those around you, beginning with family and then friends and business acquaintances.

Finally, you take what you discover about Jesus and begin adapting it to your own life and lifestyle.

BROTHER UGOLINO, ADAPTED

# The Hope of Assurance

> *Your heavenly Father knows that*
> *you need all these things.*
> MATTHEW 6:32 NASB

Though spoken originally by Jesus regarding temporal things, this may be taken as a motto for the child of God amid all the changing vicissitudes of his changing history. How it should lull all misgivings, silence all murmuring, lead to a lowly, unquestioning submissiveness—"My heavenly Father knows that I have need of these things."

Where can a child be safer or better off than in a father's hands? Where can the believer be better off than in the hands of his God? We are usually poor judges of what is best. We are under safe guidance with infallible wisdom. If we are tempted in a moment of rash presumption to say "All these things are against me," let this "word" rebuke that hasty and unworthy surmise. Unerring wisdom and Fatherly love have pronounced all to be needful.

Seek to cherish a spirit of more childlike confidence in your heavenly Father's will. You are not left friendless and alone to buffet the storms out in the wilderness. Absolutely not! A gracious pillar-cloud is before you. Follow it through sunshine and storm. He will lead you about, but He will not lead you wrong. Tenderness is the characteristic of all His dealings.

JOHN MACDUFF

# Asking with Hope

*I will do whatever you ask in my name,*
*so that the Son may bring glory to the Father.*
JOHN 14:13 NIV

Blessed Jesus! It is You who has unlocked to Your people the gates of prayer. Without You they must have been shut up forever. It was Your atoning merit on earth that first opened them; it is Your intercessory work in heaven that keeps them open still.

How unlimited the promise—"Whatever you ask!" It is the pledge that all believers and unbelievers require. To us His faithful servants, He seems to say, "Bring your requests and under my superscription, write what you please." And then He further endorses each petition with the words, "I *will* do it!"

He further encourages us to ask "in His name." Because of our humanity, there are some pleas that seem more influential in obtaining a benefit than others. Jesus speaks of this as forming the key to the heart of God. As David loved the helpless cripple of Saul's house "for Jonathan's sake" (2 Samuel 9:7), so will the Father, by virtue of our covenant relationship, take delight in giving us even "exceeding abundantly above all that we can ask or think" (Ephesians 3:20).

Reader, do you know the blessedness of confiding your every need and every care—your every sorrow and every cross—into the ear of the Savior? He is the Wonderful Counselor. With tender sympathy, He can enter into the innermost depths of your need. That need may be great, but the everlasting arms are underneath it all.

JOHN MACDUFF

# He Absolutely Knows Me

*The very hairs of your head are all numbered.*
MATTHEW 10:30 KJV

Those are Jesus' own words. All that befalls you, to the very numbering of your hairs, is known to God. Nothing can happen by accident or chance. Nothing can elude His inspection. The fall of the forest leaf, the fluttering of the insect, the waving of the angel's wing, the annihilation of a world—all are equally noted by Him. Man speaks of great things and small things—God knows no such distinction.

How especially comforting to think of this tender solicitude with reference to His own covenant people—that He metes out joys and their sorrows! Every sweet and every bitter is known by Him—even a wearisome night. He puts my tears into His bottle. Every moment the everlasting arms are underneath and around me. He keeps me "as the apple of His eye." He bears me as a man bears his own son.

Do I look to the future and see much uncertainty and mystery hanging over it? It may be a foreboding of evil. But trust Him! All is marked out for me. Dangers will be averted; bewildering mazes will show themselves to be interlaced and interwoven with mercy. He keeps you the apple of His eye.

JOHN MACDUFF

# Be Still My Soul

*Rest, and be still.*
JEREMIAH 47:6 KJV

Be still, my soul: the Lord is on thy side.
Bear patiently the cross of grief or pain;
Leave to thy God to order and provide;
In every change He faithful will remain.
Be still, my soul: thy best, thy heav'nly Friend
Through thorny ways leads to a joyful end.

Be still, my soul: thy God doth undertake
To guide the future as He has the past.
Thy hope, thy confidence let nothing shake;
All now mysterious shall be bright at last.
Be still, my soul: the waves and wind still know
His voice who ruled them while He dwelt below.

Be still, my soul: the hour is hast'ning on
When we shall be forever with the Lord,
When disappointment, grief, and fear are gone,
Sorrow forgot, love's purest joys restored.
Be still, my soul: when change and fear are past,
All safe and blessed we shall meet at last.

KATHARINA VON SCHLEGEL,
TRANSLATED BY JANE BORTHWICK

# *Heaven—Its Hope*

*They were longing for a better country—
a heavenly one.*

HEBREWS 11:16 NIV

It seems perfectly reasonable that God should encourage us by giving us a glimpse of the future. When a loved one is taken away from us, how often we ask, "Where have they gone?" followed by, "Will I ever see them again?" It is then that we turn to the blessed Book, for there is no other book in all the world that can give us the slightest hope and comfort; no other book can tell us where the loved ones have gone.

Not long ago I met an old friend, and as I took his hand and asked about his family, the tears came trickling down his cheeks as he said, "Haven't any now."

"What?" I said. "Is your wife dead?"

"Yes, sir."

"And all your children, too?"

"Yes, all gone," he responded, "and I am left here desolate *and alone.*"

Would anyone take from this man the hope that he will meet his dear ones again? Would anyone persuade him that there is not a future where the lost will be found? No, we need not forget our dear loved ones; but we fly and cling forever to the enduring hope that there will be a time when we can meet unfettered and be blest in that land of everlasting suns, where the soul drinks from the living streams of love that roll by God's high throne.

DWIGHT L. MOODY

# Abba, Father

*[In] a spirit of adoption. . .we cry, "Abba, Father."*
ROMANS 8:15 NRSV

There may be among my readers—alas for such!—to whom the word father brings no cheer, no dawn, in whose heart it rouses no tremble of even a vanished emotion. It is hardly likely to be their fault. For though as children we seldom love up to the mark of reason, though we often offend—and although the conduct of some children is inexplicable to the parent who loves them—yet if the parent has been but ordinarily kind, even the son who has grown up a worthless man will now and then feel, in his better moments, some dim reflex of childhood, some faintly pleasant, some slightly sorrowful remembrance of the father around whose neck his arms had sometimes clung. In my own childhood my father was the refuge from all the ills of life, even pain.

Therefore I say to the son or daughter who has no pleasure in the name *father*, "You must interpret the word by all that you have missed in life, even sharp pain itself. Take hope."

Our Father would make to himself sons and daughters indeed—that is, such sons and daughters as shall be his sons and daughters not merely by having come from his heart, but He will have them share in His being and nature.

GEORGE MACDONALD

# *Hope Sees a Star*

*He will wipe every tear from their eyes.*
*There will be no more death or*
*mourning or crying or pain.*
REVELATION 21:4 NIV

The following reading was spoken by a grieving skeptic, Robert G. Ingersoll, at his brother's grave, June 2, 1879.

Life is a narrow vale between the cold and barren peaks of two eternities. We strive in the vale to look beyond the heights. We cry aloud—and the only answer is the echo of our wailing cry. From the voiceless lips of the unreplying dead there comes no word.

But in the night of death, Hope sees a star, and, listening, Love can hear the rustling of a wing.

He who sleeps here when dying, mistaking the approach of death for the return of health, whispered with his latest breath, "I am better now."

Let us believe, in spite of doubts and fears, that these dear words are true of all the countless dead.

Hope lights a candle instead of cursing the darkness.

ROBERT G. INGERSOLL

# A Father's Hope

*Whatever was to my profit*
*I now consider loss for the sake of Christ.*
PHILIPPIANS 3:7 NIV

When I was in Dublin, they were telling me about a father who had lost his little boy. Adding to his great pain was the fact that he had not thought much about the future because he was so taken up with this world and its affairs. When that little boy, his only son, died, that father's heart was broken, and every night when he got home from work, he could be found with his yellowed tallow candle and his family Bible in his room. He was hunting up all that he could find there about heaven. When someone asked him what he was doing, the father replied, "I am trying to find out where my boy has gone. I need to know."

This story reflects man's interest in the afterlife. Some call it an undiscovered country from where no traveler returns. But the hope of every Christian is the place called heaven—a better country. While men constantly seek to find some better place, some lovelier place than we have now, Christians have this hope. They don't look down to this earth, but they lift their eyes

My friends, let us believe this good old Book, that our hope is based on the fact that heaven is not a myth. Let us be prepared to follow dear ones who have gone before.

There, and there alone, can we find the peace we seek for.

DWIGHT L. MOODY

# Lincoln's "Last Best Hope"

> *"I have raised you up for this very purpose,*
> *that I might show you my power*
> *and that my name might be*
> *proclaimed in all the earth."*
>
> EXODUS 9:16 NIV

From the president's second Inaugural Address, delivered a bit more than a month before his death.

❧

The Almighty has His own purposes. He now wills to remove, and that gives to both North and South this terrible war as the woe due to those by whom the offense came; shall we discern there in any departure from those divine attributes which the believers in a living God always ascribes to Him?

Fondly do we hope—fervently do we pray—that this mighty scourge of war may speedily pass away. Yet, if God wills that it continue until all the wealth piled up by the bondsman's 250 years of unrequited toil shall be sunk and until every drop of blood drawn with the lash shall be paid by another drawn with the sword as was said three thousand years ago, so still it must be said, "The judgments of the Lord are true and righteous altogether."

With malice toward none, with charity for all, with firmness in the right as God gives us to see the right, let us strive on to finish the work we are in, to bind up the nation's wounds, to care for him who shall have borne the battle and for his widow and his orphan, to do all which may achieve and cherish a just and a lasting peace among ourselves and with all nations.

ABRAHAM LINCOLN

# Re: The Reverend John Fletcher

*Mark the blameless man,*
*and behold the upright.*
PSALM 37:37 NASB

John Wesley's choice for his replacement to lead Methodism was the Reverend John Fletcher, "a man of great hope and industry." Problem: Wesley outlived him by six years. The following is from the address Wesley delivered at Fletcher's funeral.

He would often say, "It is my business in all events to hang upon the Lord, with a sure trust and confidence, that He will order all things in the best time and manner. Indeed, it would be nothing to be a believer; nay, in truth, there would be no room for faith if everything were seen here. But against hope to believe in hope, to have a full confidence in that unseen power which so mightily supports us in all our dangers and difficulties—this is the believing which is acceptable to God."

Sometimes when I have expressed some apprehension of an approaching trial, he would answer, "I do not doubt but the Lord orders all; therefore I leave everything to Him." In outward dangers, if they were ever so great, he seemed to know no shadow of fear. When I was speaking once, concerning a danger to which we were then particularly exposed, he answered, "I know God always gives His angels charge concerning us; therefore we are equally safe everywhere."

JOHN WESLEY

# St. Benedict Hopes

*Make every effort to keep the unity of
the Spirit through the bond of peace.*

EPHESIANS 4:3 NIV

Two of Benedict's gifts were organization and belief in his fellow man.
The monastery reflected Benedict's positive personality and his strong
belief in God's guidance. He tried to express this in his "Rules."

❧

If any pilgrim monk come from distant parts as a guest to dwell
in the monastery and will be content with the customs which he
finds in the place and does not perchance by his lavishness dis-
turb the monastery but is simply content with what he finds, he
shall be received for as long a time as he desires.

If, indeed, he find fault with anything, the Abbot shall discuss it prudently, lest perchance God has sent this very thing. But,
if he is found to be gossipy and contumacious in the time of his
sojourn as guest, not only ought he not to be joined to the body
of the monastery, but also it shall be said to him, honestly, that he
must depart. If he does not go, let two stout monks, in the name
of God, explain the matter to him.

Make an effort to find God in all. Disciplines made part of
the Christian life provide hope in a believer's heart.

BENEDICT OF NURSIA

# A Mother's Hope

*Train children in the right way,*
*and when old, they will not stray.*
PROVERBS 22:6 NRSV

Epworth, October, 1709

My dear Sammy:

I hope that you retain the impressions of your education, nor have forgot that the vows of God are upon you. You know that the first fruits are heaven's by an unalienable right, and that, as your parents devoted you to the service of the altar, so you yourself made it your choice when your father [John Wesley] was offered another way of life for you. But have you duly considered what such a choice [ministry] and such a dedication imports? Consider well what separation from the world, what purity, what devotion, what exemplary virtue are required in those who are to guide others to glory.

Begin and end the day with Him who is the Alpha and Omega, and if you really experience what it is to love God, you will redeem all the time you can for His more immediate service.

I beg, I beseech you to be very strict in observing the Lord's Day. In all things endeavor to act on principle, and do not live like the rest of mankind. Often put this question to yourself: Why do I do this or that? Why do I pray, read, study, or use devotions, etc.? By which means you will come to such a steadiness and consistency in your words and actions as becomes a reasonable creature and a good Christian. Your affectionate mother,

SUSANNA WESLEY

# A Sermon Outline

*Every man that hath this hope in him purifieth himself,*
*even as he is pure.*

1 JOHN 3:3 KJV

The Christian is a person whose main possessions lie in reversion. Most people have a hope, but it is a peculiar one; and its effect is special, for it causes the need to purify one's self.

The Believer's Hope. "Every man that hath this hope in him."

It is the hope of being like Jesus.
It is based on divine love.
It arises out of sonship.
It rests upon our union to Jesus.
It is the hope of the second Advent.

The Operation of that Hope
The believer purifies himself from:
his grosser sins like evil company;
his secret sins of neglects, imaginings, desires;
his besetting sins of heart, temper, body, relationships;
his relative sins in the family, the shop, the church;
his sins of word, thought, omission.
He does this in a perfectly natural way:
by understanding what purity is;
by keeping a tender conscience;
by having an eye to God and continual presence;
by asking the Lord to search him.
He sets Jesus as his model.

CHARLES H. SPURGEON

# Mr. Sankey's Prayer

*Why are you downcast, O my soul?*
*Why so disturbed within me?*
*Put your hope in God, for I will yet praise him.*
PSALM 42:5 NIV

A broken street man sat across from the great hymn writer and song leader for Dwight L. Moody. His body language announced he had lost all hope. His will to live was shattered. The three children of his family had been lost to a terrible fire, causing him to lose the will to live and to walk away from his wife. For him, Mr. Sankey prayed. . .

O God, we ask Thy blessing upon all who need prayer but especially bless this—our dear brother, who is now passing through the deep waters of affliction. Grant, O Lord, that when he is away from those who love him and is tempted by the evil one, that he may see that to yield he must give up something of the hope of seeing his little ones, who are in their heavenly home. O God, may he receive grace from Thee. There is none of us who doesn't need Christ, and we come to Thee today. O our Father, take away doubt and give hope. Take away longing and give peace. Remove any discord and bring harmony. May this man's heart begin to sing again. May new life be planted here, O God.

Light a lamp in his heart and reunite him with your Son and with his wife. May both experience forgiveness and hope for tomorrow. Amen.

IRA SANKEY

# A Seeker of Hope

*"You will seek me and find me
when you seek me with all your heart."*

JEREMIAH 29:13 NIV

Reformer and preacher John Wesley searched for his own spiritual hope. He sailed to America to preach to the Indians of Georgia but returned to England still dissatisfied. In his journal of 1738, he wrote what follows. This struggle is reconciled in the reading for December 1.

I went to America to convert the Indians but, oh, who shall convert me? Who, what is he that will deliver me from this evil heart of unbelief? I have a fair summer religion. I can talk well, nay, and believe myself while no danger is near. My spirit is troubled. Nor can I say, *to die is gain.*

I think if the gospel be true, I am safe, for I not only have given and do give all my goods to feed the poor; I not only give my body to be burned, drowned, or whatever God shall appoint for me, but I also follow after charity if haply I may attain it. I now believe the gospel is true. *I show my faith by my works* by staking my all upon it. I would do so again and again a thousand times, if the choices were still to make.

JOHN WESLEY

# The Assurance of Christian Hope

*Now the God of hope fill you with*
*all joy and peace in believing,*
*that ye may abound in hope,*
*through the power of the Holy Spirit.*

ROMANS 15:13 KJV

There is nothing in life that heals the soul from grieving pain and from the gaping wounds of loss. . .and that comforts, heals, and restores one from a state of hopelessness and discouragement more than biblical hope.

Biblical hope is not wishing, and it is not aching for something better; it is anticipating in earnest expectation *with joy* something—better and true and sure—yet to happen in the future. It is desire with expectation of fulfillment.

People do not anticipate with joy something in the future that is negative and destructive. They earnestly anticipate future events with joy when something is positive and better and fulfilling.

Therefore, if the return of Christ is to be a negative experience yet to come in the future, then how could we have joyful, earnest expectation in anticipation regarding its fulfillment? Biblical "hope" cannot be a negative to dread, but it is a joy to be anticipated.

God gives and fills believers with hope in all joy. We do not dread the second coming of Christ but have abounding hope in joy and peace in believing. We believe God's Word, and God's Word fills us with all joy and peace. We abound in hope via the power of God.

W. M. RAMSEY

## A Quaker Psalm

*Since the creation of the world*
*God's invisible qualities—*
*his eternal powers and divine nature—*
*have been clearly seen. . .*
*so that men are without excuse.*

ROMANS 1:20 NIV

One morning as I sat, a great cloud came over me—but I sat still.

"All things came by nature," it was said, and the elements and the stars came over me, so I was quite clouded.

Yet, people perceived nothing inasmuch as I sat still and silent under it.

And let it alone. Then a living hope rose in me and a true voice said, "There is a living God who made all things."

Cloud and temptation vanished. Life arose over all and my heart danced with gladness. And I praised my living God!

"To eat bread without hope is still slowly to starve to death."

GEORGE FOX

# How to Go to God

*The Spirit of the LORD God is upon me.*
ISAIAH 61:1 KJV

Brother Lawrence (1611–1691) practiced what he called "the presence of God" while washing pots and pans in the monastery scullery. What follows is a conversation reported by a visitor, with all its overlong sentences and seventeenth-century vocabulary.

❧

He [Brother Lawrence] discussed with me frequently, with great openness of heart, concerning his manner of going to God, to coming into His presence. To do so, there must be a hearty renunciation of everything that does not lead us to God and a continual conversation with Him, with freedom and in simplicity. We will recognize that God is intimately present with us, importuning us to address ourselves to Him, that we may beg His assistance for knowing His will in things doubtful, and for rightfully performing those which we plainly see He requires of us.

In this conversation with God, we are also employed in praising, adoring, and loving him incessantly for His infinite goodness and perfection.

That, without being discouraged on account of our sins, we should take His Spirit upon us and pray for His grace with a perfect confidence. Our sanctification does not depend upon changing our works but in doing that for God's sake, which we commonly do for our own.

It is a great delusion to think that the times of prayer ought differ from other times. It is also a great delusion to believe that we are as strictly obliged to adhere to God by action in the time of action, as by prayer in its season.

BROTHER LAWRENCE

# Reinforcing Your Hope

*You are receiving the outcome of your faith,*
*the salvation of your souls.*

1 PETER 1:9 NRSV

I do not know anything that would wake up Chicago better than for every man and woman here who loves Him to begin to talk about Him to their friends and just tell them what He has done for you.

I can't help thinking about the old woman who started out when the war commenced with a poker in her hand. When asked what she was going to do with it, she replied, "I can't do much with it, but I can show which side I'm on." My friends, even if you can't do a whole lot, you can surely show which side you're on.

Thanks be to God, there is hope today—great swelling hope! This very hour you can know His presence in your life, His love in your soul, His mind in your mind, His concern for those without hope in your heart.

When Christ was on earth, there was a woman in the temple who was bowed almost to the ground. Satan had her bound for eighteen years; but after all these years of bondage, Christ delivered her. He spoke one word and she was free. She got up and walked home. Imagined how astonished those at home must have been to see her walking into her home.

If you believe on the Lord Jesus Christ, you are free! Take heart, man and woman of God—He is in control. He gives you hope.

D. L. MOODY

# St. Patrick on Hope

*They will come and bind themselves to the LORD
in an everlasting covenant.*
JEREMIAH 50:5 NIV

I bind unto myself today
The power of God to hold and lead,
His eye to watch, His might to stay,
His ear to hearken to my need,
The wisdom of my God to teach,
His hand to guide, His shield to ward;
The word of God to give me speech,
His heavenly host to be my guard.

I bind unto myself the name,
The strong name of the Trinity;
By invocation of the same
The Three in One and One in Three,
Of whom all nature hath creation;
Eternal Father, Spirit, Word;
Praise to the Lord of my salvation,
Salvation is of CHRIST the LORD.

PATRICK, APOSTLE OF IRELAND

# Hope and Grace, Part 1

*Come now, and let us reason together, saith the LORD:*
*though your sins be as scarlet, they shall be as white as snow;*
*though they be red like crimson, they shall be as wool.*

ISAIAH 1:18 KJV

The following is God's provision for my hope.

Pardoning Grace. My soul! Your God summons you to his audience chamber! Infinite purity seeks to reason with infinite vileness. Deity swoops to speak to dust. Dread not the meeting. It is most gracious, as well as most wondrous of all conferences. Jehovah Himself breaks silence. He utters the best tidings a lost soul or a lost world can hear—"God [is] in Christ, reconciling the world unto himself, not imputing [unto men] their trespasses" (2 Corinthians 5:19 KJV).

What! Scarlet sins and crimson sins—and these all to be forgiven and forgotten. The just God "justifying" the unjust—the mightiest of all beings, the kindest of all.

Oh! What is there in you to merit such love as this? You might have known your God only as the "consuming fire" and had nothing before you except "a fearful looking full of vengeance." This gracious conference bids you dispel your fears. It tells you it is no longer a "fearful," but a blessed thing to fall into His hands.

Until you are at peace with Him, happiness must be a stranger to your bosom. Though you have all else beside, bereft of God you must be "bereft indeed." Lord! I come. As Your pardoning grace is freely tendered, so shall I freely accept it. May it be mine, even now, to listen to the gladdening accents: "Son! Daughter! Be of good cheer! Your sins, which are many are all forgiven."

JOHN MACDUFF

# Hope and Grace, Part 2

*As your days, so shall your strength be.*
DEUTERONOMY 33:25 NKJV

Needful Grace. God does not give grace until the hour the trial comes. But when it does come, the amount of grace and the nature of the special grace required are granted. My soul! Do not dwell with painful apprehension on the future. Do not anticipate coming sorrows, perplexing yourself with the grace needed for future emergencies; tomorrow will bring its promised grace along with tomorrow's trials.

God, wishing to keep His people humble and dependent on Himself, does not give a stock of grace; He metes it out for every day's exigencies, that they may be constantly "traveling between their own emptiness and Christ's fullness"—their own weakness and Christ's strength. But when the exigency comes, you may safely trust an Almighty arm to bear you through!

Is there now some "thorn in the flesh" sent to lacerate you? You may have been entreating the Lord for its removal. Your prayer has doubtless been heard and answered, but not in the way, perhaps, expected or desired by you. The "thorn" may still be left to prick, the trial may still be left to buffet; but "more grace" has been given to endure them. Oh, how often have His people thus been led to glory in their infirmities and triumph in their afflictions, seeing the power of Christ rests more abundantly upon them! The strength which the hour of trial brings often makes the Christian a wonder to himself.

JOHN MACDUFF

# Hope and Grace, Part 3

*God is able to make all grace abound toward you;*
*that you, always having all sufficiency in all things,*
*may abound to every good word and work.*

2 CORINTHIANS 9:8 KJV

All-Sufficient Grace. All sufficiency in all things! Believer, surely you are "thoroughly furnished." Grace is no scanty thing doled out in pittance. It is a glorious treasury which the key of prayer can always unlock, but it is never empty. A fountain, "full, flowing, overflowing." Mark these three "alls" in this precious promise. It is a threefold link in a golden chain, let down from a throne of grace. All grace—"all sufficiency" in "all things" and these to "abound."

Oh, precious thought! My need cannot impoverish that inexhaustible treasury of grace. Myriads are hourly hanging on it and drawing from it, and yet there is no diminution—"out of that fullness all we, too, may receive, and grace for grace."

My soul, do you not love to dwell on that all-abounding grace? Your own insufficiency in everything met with an "all-sufficiency in all things." Grace in all circumstances and situations, in all problems and changes, in all the various phases of Christian being.

Grace in sunshine and storm, in health and in sickness, in life and in death. Grace for the old believer and the young believer, the tired believer and the weak believer, and the tempted believer. Grace for duty and grace in duty, grace to carry the joyous cup with a steady hand, grace to drink the bitter cup with a hopeful spirit, and grace to have prosperity sanctified. And finally, grace to say, through tears, "Your will be done."

JOHN MACDUFF

# Hope and Grace, Part 4

*I am sure that God, who began the good work within you,
will continue his work until it is finally finished
on that day when Christ Jesus comes back again.*

PHILIPPIANS 1:6 NLT

Sanctifying Grace. Hope-filled reader, is the good work begun in you? Are you holy? Is sin being crucified? Are your heart's idols one by one abolished? Does the world mean less to you and eternity more? Is more of your Savior's image impressed on your character and your Savior's love more enthroned in your heart?

There is no standing still in the life of faith. "The man," says Augustine, "who says 'enough,' that man's soul is lost!" Let this be the superscription in all your ways and doings. "Holiness to the Lord." Let that word *holiness* sweep over you with its power. "Without holiness, no man shall see the Lord."

Moreover, remember that to be holy is to be happy. The two terms are equivalent. Holiness! It is the secret and the spring of the joy of angels; and the more of holiness attained on earth, the nearer and closer my walk is with God—the more of a sweet earnest shall I have of the bliss that awaits me in a holy heaven.

Oh, my soul, let it be your sacred ambition to be holy.

*Has grace begun in you? Do not delay the momentous question. Your
hope is dependant upon offered grace. The day of offered grace is on
the wing; its hours are fast numbering—and, "no grace, no glory."*

JOHN MACDUFF

# A Scotsman Finds Hope

*For God so loved the world,*
*that he gave his only begotten Son,*
*that whosoever believeth in him should not perish,*
*but have everlasting life.*

JOHN 3:16 KJV

You may have heard the story of the old Scot who had been brought up with the idea that God had predetermined just so many people to be saved and all the rest were created to be damned. He felt he ought to be willing to say, "O God, if it is Thy will to damn me, I do not want to be saved"; but he did want to be saved. But they all said, *"If* you are not one of the elect, you cannot be saved."

One day he was out in the field plowing when he found a piece of paper with a text on it. He tried to spell it out, but he wasn't very good at reading. "For—God—so—loved—the—world —that—he—gave—his—only—be-got-ten—Son—that— who–so–ever. . ." He wondered what that long word meant. He passed on to the next part; "That—who-so-ever—believeth— in—him—should—not—perish—but—have—ever-last-ing— life." He scratched his head, "I wonder what this means?" Then he saw a boy going by. "Here, laddie, can you read this to me?"

The boy read the verse aloud to the old man. "Does it really say someone can be saved by just believing?" the old man asked. "What does that long word mean?"

*"Whosoever* means you or me or anybody."

The old man stood there and reread it, "Man!" he shouted. "That's hope for a sinner like me. Praise the Lord!"

HARRY IRONSIDE

# A Habitual Sense of God, Part 1

*Let this mind be in you, which was also in Christ Jesus.*
PHILIPPIANS 2:5 KJV

A letter instructing how the seeker of hope can develop a habitual sense of God's presence:

. . .Since you desire so earnestly that I should communicate to you the method by which I arrived at that habitual sense of God's presence, which our Lord has been pleased to vouchsafe to me.

Having found in many books different methods of going to God, various practices of the spiritual life, I reckoned that so much instruction only puzzled me. Simply put, all I was looking for was how to become wholly God's.

This made me resolve to give my all for His all. So, after giving myself wholly to God—that is, making satisfaction for sins by renouncing them—I renounced them for the love of Him, and I began to live as if there were none but Him and I in the world.

Sometimes I considered myself before Him as a poor criminal at the feet of his judge; at other times I beheld Him in my heart as my Father, as my God. I worshiped Him the oftenest I could, keeping my mind in His holy presence and recalling it as often as I found it wandered from Him. I found no small pain in this exercise, and yet I continued it. I made this my business, as much as all the daylong as at the appointed times of prayer. I drove away from my mind everything that was capable of interrupting my thoughts of God.

BROTHER LAWRENCE

# A Habitual Sense of God, Part 2

*Worship the LORD with gladness;*
*come into his presence with singing.*

PSALM 100:2 NRSV

At my entrance into religion I took a resolution to give myself up to God the best I could—and for the love of Him, to renounce all besides Him.

Such has been my common practice ever since I entered into religion; and though I have done it imperfectly, still I have found great advantages by it. These, I well know, are to be given over to God's goodness and mercy, because we can do nothing without Him.

When we are faithful to keep ourselves in His holy presence, we are hindered from offending Him and doing anything that may displease Him, at least willfully. But it also begets within us a holy freedom, and if I may so speak, a familiarity with God. Therefore we ask, He will give aid in making this practice habitual, and be awarded the graces I need.

In time, by often repeating these acts, they become habitual, and the presence of God is rendered as it were natural to us. Give Him thanks, if you please, with me, for His great goodness toward me, which I can never sufficiently admire, for the many favors He has done to me—so miserable a sinner as I am. May all things praise Him. Amen.

BROTHER LAWRENCE

# *Take Hope!*

*I will set out and go back to my father.*
LUKE 15:18 NIV

Welshman Christmas Evans was a nineteenth-century, self-taught religionist who, in his spiritual search, became enamored with various unorthodox theological thoughts. Learning English, he was finally made aware of his need for a personal relationship with Jesus Christ.

I was weary of a cold heart toward Christ and His sacrifice and the work of His spirit, of a cold heart in the pulpit, in secret, and in the study. I realized that I had no hope for heaven. For fifteen years previously I felt my heart burning within as if going to Emmaus with Jesus.

On a day ever to be remembered, as I was going from Dolgellau to Machynlleth [Welsh towns], I considered it to be incumbent upon me to pray, regardless of how hard I felt in my heart and worldly in my spirit. Having begun praying in the name of Jesus, I soon felt as it were fetters loosening and the old hardness of my heart softening. It was as if mountains of frost and snow were dissolving and melting within me. This engendered confidence in my soul in the promise of the Holy Ghost.

I felt my whole mind relieved from some great bondage. Tears flowed copiously, and I was constrained out for the gracious visits of God. I resigned myself to Christ, body and soul, gifts and labors, every hour of every day that remained for me and all my cares I committed to Christ. The road ahead was mountainous and lonely, and I was wholly alone with God.

CHRISTMAS EVANS

# A Good Hope

*We have this hope as
an anchor for the soul,
firm and secure.*
HEBREWS 6:19 NIV

A good hope must reveal itself in holy living. What can an unsanctifying hope be good for? It can only deceive and curse its possessor. A hope that makes a man careless and prayerless—what good is it for? Just nothing at all—save to ruin his soul. Such a hope is sheer presumption. So far from being any title to heaven, it is certainly a lure to hell. It is a nuisance to him and to everybody else.

If his hope leads him into sin, it is the greatest curse he can have upon him. It is a nuisance to all his acquaintances. The existence of false hopes in the church is one of the greatest evils in the world. False hopes beget a vast amount of spurious religion. They lead men naturally to misconceptions of what true religion is.

By false hopes, as I now use the phrase, I mean those who do not purify. That is the certain make of the spurious nature. Many are too proud to confess their hope to be false, when they inwardly know it to be so. They can see that they are surely deceived—but alas, the pride of their heart rebels against any confession of the truth.

To the contrary, no good hope can be kept secret. A good hope will lead its professor to purify himself. The world will know him; Christian brethren will feel the warmth of his heart.

CHARLES G. FINNEY

# Hope for Success

*You shall make your way prosperous, and. . .be successful.*
JOSHUA 1:8 NRSV

I leave these words with you. It is only a Christian's message to the young. There's nothing impossible about it to any young person (or any person) so long as you bear in mind these salient points:

First, spiritual success means being successful at being, as well as doing, your best at whatsoever He directs you to undertake. Second, the price of success is hard work, patience, prayer, and a few sacrifices.

Then, the keys of godly success—in your spiritual life, a firm, unwavering belief in God, in prayer, in holy living, and a life consistent with "God first, others second, and myself last." In your social life: moderation and abstinence in activity that does not reflect your Christian standards. In your marriage: love. In business: thoroughness—not thoroughness only in large things or for whatever is obvious to the eye, but thoroughness in all things. Never slight small things. Remember? "What is worth doing at all is worth doing well."

Finally, the hope for success: "Strive first for the kingdom of God and his righteousness, and all these [good] things will be given to you" (Matthew 6:33 NRSV). Without a doubt, God is waiting to help us succeed, but you who are young (and old) must seek the things of God first.

EDWARD BLOK

# *Possibilities of Hope*

> *Grow in the grace and knowledge*
> *of our Lord and Savior Jesus Christ.*
>
> 2 PETER 3:18 NIV

A young lady of my acquaintance received a proposal of marriage. She frankly confessed her interest in the proposal; she felt the highest esteem for the gentleman who made it. It was this very esteem, coupled with her own deficiencies, which led her to reply, "I am not prepared now to become your wife, because I cannot be to you all that a wife ought to be. I can accept your proposal on the condition that it shall not be consummated for some time to come."

Her condition was accepted, and the engagement made. Then the young lady entered upon an era of hope. She thenceforth expected to become a wife and earnestly desired to become all that the wife of such a man ought to be. What must be the effect of this hope on her mind? Obviously, it put her upon most earnest efforts to make all those improvements in her habits and character which it is conscious of needing.

The Christian says, "I must be prepared to dwell with Christ. I must be in readiness for those divine joys and employments which constitute heaven." The heart is set upon it, and the assured hope of it inspires intense efforts. Such a hope will make a Christian avoid everything that can displease Christ.

CHARLES G. FINNEY

# It Is Done

*He is able also to save them to the uttermost.*
HEBREWS 7:25 KJV

Believe that God has promised to save you from all sin and to fill you with all holiness. Believe that He is able to save you to the uttermost, to purify you from all sin and fill up all your heart with love. Believe that He is not only able but also willing to do it now. Not when you die, not tomorrow, but today. He will then enable you to believe it is done, according to His word.

You shall be delivered from every evil work; from every evil word; from every sinful thought; yes, from every evil desire, passion, temper; from all inbred corruption, from all remains of the carnal mind, from the body of sin; and you shall be renewed in the spirit of your mind, in every right temper, after the image of Him that created you, in righteousness and true holiness.

You shall be entire [Greek: *holokleroi*]. This seems to refer not so much to the *kind* as to the *degree* of holiness; the Lord, being your Shepherd, your Father, your Redeemer, your Sanctifier, your God, and your all, will feed you with the bread of heaven. He will lead you beside the waters of comfort and keep you every moment, so that loving Him with all your heart (which is the sum of all perfection), you will "rejoice evermore, pray without ceasing, and in everything give thanks."

JOHN WESLEY

# Hands of the Father

*"No one can snatch them out of my Father's hand."*

JOHN 10:29 NIV

Think, brothers, think, sisters; we walk in the air of an eternal fatherhood. Every uplifting of the heart is a looking up to the Father. Graciousness and truth are around, above, beneath us, yea, in us. When we are least worthy, then most tempted, hardest, unkindest, let us yet commend our spirits into His hands.

Whither else dare we send them? How the earthly father would love a child who would creep into his room with an angry, troubled face and sit down at his feet, saying, when we asked what he wanted: "I feel so naughty, Papa, and I want to get good!" Would he say to his child: "How dare you! Go away and be good, and then come to me!" And shall we dare to think God would send us away? Would we not let all the tenderness of our nature flow forth upon such a child? And shall we dare think that if we being evil know how to give good gifts to our children, God will not give us His Spirit when we come to ask Him?

Nor is there anything we can ask for ourselves that we may not ask for another. We may commend any brother, any sister, to the common fatherhood. He that loves not his brother whom he has seen, how can he love God whom he has not seen? To rest, I say, at last, even in those hands into which the Lord commended His spirit, we must have learned already to love our neighbor as ourselves.

GEORGE MACDONALD

# *Inheriting Glory*

*The wise shall inherit glory.*
PROVERBS 3:35 KJV

Glory is the concentrated essence of all that is holy, excellent, and beautiful. For a being has its more and its less perfect parts. And its glory is that which is most perfect about it, to which of course that which is less perfect has, according to its measure contributed. Light is the glory of the sun. Transparency is the glory of the stream. The flower is the glory of the plant. The soul is the glory of the man. The face is the glory of the body. And this glory is strangely manifold: "There is one glory of the sun, and another of the moon, and another glory of the stars; stars differ from the sun glory."

What is really glorious is so hidden that scripture always speaks as if the whole glory were yet in reserve. When He came to earth, who was "the brightness of Jehovah's glory," He was not recognized as the possessor of such glory; it was hidden. Few eyes saw any glory at all in Him; none saw the greatness of it. Even in His case it did not appear what He was and what He shall be when He comes "to be glorified in his saints."

The hope of this glory cheers us. The warfare is ending, and the tear shall be shall be dried up. In that day we shall be presented faultless before the presence of His glory with exceeding great joy!

HORATIUS BONAR

# How Salvation Brings Hope

*At that time you were separate from Christ. . .*
*without hope and without God in the world.*
*But now in Christ Jesus you who once were far away*
*have been brought near through the blood of Christ.*

EPHESIANS 2:12–13 NIV

On a Sabbath evening in the autumn of 1821, I made up my mind that I would settle the question of my soul's salvation at once. While I was very busy in the affairs of my office, I knew that without firmness of purpose I should never effectively attend to give myself to the work of securing the salvation of my soul. When I was truthful to myself, I knew that I was without hope of glory.

I must confess, I was very proud without knowing it. I had in fact been most neglectful in attending prayer meetings and in the degree of attention that I had paid to religion. In this respect I had been so deceitful as to lead the church at times into thinking that I must be an anxious seeker. But I found, when I came to face the truth of my seeking, that I was very unwilling to have anyone know that I needed to seek the salvation of my soul.

When I prayed, I would only whisper my prayer, after having stopped the keyhole to the door. Before that I had my Bible lying on the desk with my law books; it never occurred to me to be ashamed to be found reading it, any more than I should be ashamed of being found reading any of my other books.

During Monday and Tuesday my convictions increased; I knew I had no hope for heaven. God knew I was in deep need.

CHARLES G. FINNEY

# I Claim Salvation for My Own

*Ye shall go and pray unto me,*
*and I will hearken unto you.*
*And ye shall seek me, and find me,*
*when ye shall search for me with all your heart.*
JEREMIAH 29:12–13 KJV

I wrestled with the enemy of my soul for hours. He warned that my hope for God was unfounded. I cried at the top of my voice and exclaimed that I would not leave that place until I had the hope of my salvation. Finally after hearing God in the words of Jeremiah 29:13, I seized Him like a drowning man. I cried out to Him, "Lord, I take thee at thy Word. I have searched with all my heart."

I know not how long I prayed. I recollect saying with great emphasis, "If I am ever converted, I will preach the gospel." All my feelings seemed to rise and flow out, and the utterance of my heart was, "I want to pour my whole soul out to God." The rising of my soul was so great that I rushed into the room back of the front office to pray.

There was no fire and no light in the room; nevertheless it appeared to me as if it were perfectly light. It seemed as if I met the Lord Jesus face-to-face. No words can express the wonderful love that was shed abroad in my heart. I was converted!

*And preach he did. Charles Finney, according to his biographer, was a firebrand for his Master. Men and women, boys and girls, left his services with a whole galaxy of hope lighting up their souls.*

CHARLES G. FINNEY

# Mother's Prayers

*I thank God, whom I serve,*
*as my forefathers did,*
*with a clear conscience,*
*as night and day I constantly*
*remember you in my prayers.*

2 TIMOTHY 1:3 NIV

A synonym dictionary expands the word hope to mean "expectation, desire, longing." How keenly those synonyms describe a mother's prayer for her son. . .and so it was when pioneer missionary Hudson Taylor's mother prayed for his conversion.

❧

Let me tell you how God answered the prayers of my dear mother for my conversion. On a day which I shall never forget, when I was about fifteen years of age, my mother being absent from our home, I looked through my father's library to find some book to read. I turned over a basket of pamphlets and selected a gospel tract that looked interesting.

Little did I know what was going on in the heart of my dear mother, seventy or eighty miles away. She arose from the table where she was dining with an intense yearning for the conversion of her boy. She went to her room and turned the key in the door, resolving not to leave that spot until her prayers were answered. Hour after hour did that dear mother plead for me, until she could pray no longer but was constrained to praise God for what had already been accomplished—the conversion of her only son.

I, in the meantime, had been led to take up a little tract and while reading it was struck with the sentence, "The finished work of Christ." Immediately the words "It is finished" suggested themselves to my mind. What was finished?

HUDSON TAYLOR

# Answered Prayer

*God answered prayer.*

2 SAMUEL 21:14 NIV

Hudson Taylor's mother's hope and faith knew no bounds. The way was prepared for her intercession by God helping her son find a salvation tract and reading it in her absence. What was finished?

❧

Then it came to my mind, "If the whole work of salvation was finished and the whole debt paid, what is there left for me to do?" With this dawned the joyful conviction, as light flashed into my soul by the Holy Spirit, that there was nothing in the world to be done but to fall down on one's knees and, accepting this Savior and His salvation, to praise Him forevermore. Thus while my dear mother was praising God on her knees in her chamber, I was praising him in the old warehouse to which I had gone alone to read this little book at my leisure.

My dear mother assured me that it was not from any human source that she had learned about the value of hope and the power of prayer.

HUDSON TAYLOR

# The Hope of Something Better

*Truly, if they had been mindful of that country*
*from whence they came out,*
*they might have had opportunity to have returned.*
*But now they desire a better country,*
*that is, an heavenly. . .city.*

HEBREWS 11:15–16 KJV

Abraham left his country at God's command, and he never went back again, the proof of faith and hope that lies in perseverance. There is a sort of faith that runs well for a while, but it is soon ended, and it does not obey the truth.

The writer of Hebrews tells us, however, that the people of God were not forced to continue, because they could not return. Had they been mindful of the place from which they came out, they might have found opportunities to return.

Frequent opportunities came their way. There was communication between them and the old family home. They had news concerning the family house. More than that, there were messages exchanged; servants were sometimes sent. There was also a natural relationship kept up. They had many opportunities to return to their old home, to settle back down comfortably. But they continued to follow the uncomfortable life of wanderers of the weary foot, who dwell in tents, who own no plot of land. They were aliens in the country that God had given them by promise.

Our position is very similar, as many of us who have believed in Christ Jesus have been called out. We have been separated ourselves; we are strangers and sojourners. We are passing through to reach the Canaan, which is to be the land of our perpetual inheritance. That is the bright star of hope.

CHARLES H. SPURGEON

# Hope at the Crossroads

*We preach Christ crucified:*
*a stumbling block to Jews and foolishness to Gentiles.*
1 CORINTHIANS 1:23 NIV

Right where two roads through life diverge, God has put Calvary. There He put up a cross, the stumbling block over which the love of God said, "I'll touch the heart of man with the thought of father and son." He thought He that would win the world to him, but for nineteen hundred years men have climbed the Mount of Calvary and trampled into the earth the tenderest teachings of God.

Are you on the devil's side? How are you going to cross over?

So you cross the line, and God won't issue any extradition papers. Some of you want to cross. If you believe, then say so and step across. I'll bet there are countless who are on the edge of the line and many straddling it. But that won't save you. You believe in your heart—confess Him with your mouth. With his heart man believes and with his mouth he confesses. Then confess and receive salvation full, free, perfect, and external.

A man isn't a soldier because he wears a uniform or carries a gun or wears a canteen. He is a soldier when he makes a definite enlistment. All of the military accoutrements can be bought without enlisting. It's the oath that makes him a soldier. Going to church doesn't make you a Christian any more than going into a garage makes you an automobile. Definite enlistment for Christ makes you a Christian. *That's where hope is found.*

WILLIAM "BILLY" SUNDAY

# *Perfect Peace*

*Jesus said to the woman,*
*"Your faith has saved you; go in peace."*
LUKE 7:50 NIV

When the many tears from her eyes fell upon His feet, He did not withdraw them. When those feet were wiped with the tresses of her hair, still He did not withdraw them; and when she ventured upon a yet closer familiarity and not only kissed His feet but did not cease to kiss them, He still did not withdraw them but quietly accepted all that she did. And when the precious ointment was poured in lavish abundance upon His precious feet, he did not chastise her; neither did He refuse her gifts but tacitly accepted them, although without a word of acknowledgement just then.

It us a very blessed thing for any one of us to be accepted before God, even though no word has come from His lips assuring you that you are. When your tears and cries and secret love and earnest seeking—when your confession of sin, your struggle after faith, and the beginning of your faith are just accepted by the Lord, although He has not yet said to you, "Your sins are forgiven," it is a very blessed stage for you to have reached, for the Lord does not begin to accept anyone and then draw back, even by a silence which seems constant. He accepted this woman's love and gifts, though for a time, He gave her no assurance of that acceptance, and that fact must have greatly encouraged her.

CHARLES H. SPURGEON

# Seven Wondrous Words, Part 1

*"Father, forgive them,*
*for they do not know*
*what they are doing."*
LUKE 23:34 NIV

Last words are precious words; how we cling to them and let them gently stir through our memory and persist through the years. Human men build about the departed's final words little-read sentimental poems and songs. They will show up on dusty library shelves in never-read tomes.

The last words of Jesus, matchless for pathos and forgiveness and trust, provide a bouquet of hope that will never fade. There are three words spoken before the darkness, one during, and three after the darkness.

The first is the word of intercession: "Father, forgive them. . . they know not what they do" (Luke 23:34). These hired soldiers who drove the nails and raised the cross, He forgave.

The second word is a word of hope for beyond death, spoken to the young thief on a cross: "This day shall you be with Me in paradise."

The third word is one of loving provision: "Woman, behold your son." One of the most tender acts in all history, Jesus did not forget His mother; He was a Son as well as a Savior; a Son to the last.

These first three words were spoken for others. He brought hope by caring for others before He thought of Himself.

A. E. GREGORY

# Seven Wondrous Words, Part 2

*"My God, my God,
why have you forsaken me?"*
MATTHEW 27:46 NIV

Silhouetted against the darkening Middle Eastern sky stood a cross—an upright that is a symbol of Jesus' relationship to His Father in heaven and a horizontal cross piece that represents us. From that cross came what we today call "The Seven Last Words of Jesus Christ."

The fourth word from the cross: "Why have You forsaken Me?" spoken in terrible darkness. Words that we will never understand. It is a word of loneliness. While the first three words were spoken for others, this fourth word exposes His personal feelings, beginning with, "My God!" He lost His sense of God, but not His trust.

When the darkness passes, Jesus speaks three more words. The fifth is "I thirst," the word of humanity. Believers must never forget He was every bit human and every bit divine.

The sixth word, "It is finished," is the word of victory. The act of redemption had been performed. Not only was His life temporarily over, the plan of God was made complete.

The seventh word from the cross is the word of trust: "Father, into Your hands." *Father* is the precious word for God. The word of supreme confidence, hope, assurance, and victory!

To born-again Christians who read these seven last words of Christ, there is a message of hope and glory for yesterday, today, and forever. We, too, will be with Him in paradise.

A. E. GREGORY

# He Exceeds My Hopes

*"No eye has seen, no ear has heard,
no mind conceived what God has prepared
for those who love him."*

1 CORINTHIANS 2:9 NIV

An Australian sheep farm has to be seen to be believed. One of my good friends has had business with the owners of such a farm on numerous occasions. He has often told me about watching sheep farmers handling stock. My friend told a rather poignant story about this one particular farmer and a lamb.

On the morning of his story, he saw the farmer take a small lamb and place it in a huge enclosure where there were several thousand complaining sheep whose bleating, together with the profane shouting of the sheepshearers, was deafening.

The shaky lamb was terribly bewildered by all the noise, so he uttered his feeble cry. At the farthest end of the enclosure, a mother sheep looked up, flicked her ears, and responded to youngster's cry by searching every square foot of the pen until she found her lamb.

Do not imagine that you are beyond the reach of the Good Shepherd. He sees you; He hears you. He knows your every good desire and every secret longing for better things. He sees you as if there were no other child in the whole wide world. Oh, how He loves you and me!

HENRY HAZELETT FORSYTH

# Only Once

> *"Today, if you hear his voice do not harden your hearts."*
>
> HEBREWS 3:15 NIV

We live but once. The years of childhood, when once they pass, are gone forever. It matters not how ardently we may wish to live them over; it avails us nothing. What is gone is gone.

So it is with other stages of life. The past is no longer ours. It has gone beyond our reach. Regardless of our social standing, bank accounts and investments, education, or anything else— we cannot reach back. What we have made of our past days shall remain. There is no power in heaven or on earth that can change our yesterdays. The record of our past stands forth in bold and ineffaceable characters, open to the all-seeing eyes of God. There it stands, and one day we shall give an account of it.

The present moment alone is ours. Today is a day that we never had before, which we shall never have again. It rose from the great ocean of eternity and again sinks into its unfathomable depths.

The urgency of the day is expressed in the framed motto often seen hanging in homes across our great nation: "Only one life, 'twill soon be past; only what's done for Christ will last." Do it today.

> For yesterday is but a dream,
> And tomorrow is only a vision;
> But today, well lived,
> Makes every yesterday
> A dream of happiness,
> And every tomorrow a vision of hope.

THOMAS DeWITT TALMAGE

# Be of Courage!

*Be on your guard; stand firm in the faith;*
*be men of courage; be strong.*
1 CORINTHIANS 16:13 NIV

Mr. Moody was the teacher in the school I attended as a boy. One day during our geography lesson, he asked Bob Henderson a question about the great state of Tennessee. The boy quickly answered the question, and then the teacher did something quite strange. He seemed to be troubled by the boy's answer and loudly cried out with vexation, "Sit down, Robert!" The abashed boy sat abruptly down.

Several boys were asked the same question and gave the same answer; then they promptly became confused when Mr. Moody voiced his unexplained disapproval and shouted for them to sit down, too.

Finally I was called to stand and was given the same question, to which I responded with the same answer as the other boys. "Sit down!" roared the teacher. But I held my ground and insisted that the answer was correct. For a few moments our teacher stormed at me, but seeing that I was convinced and refused to move, he smiled and said, "Well, boys, you were all correct, but Beecher here was the only one sure enough to stand up for his answer."

For the man of principle, it is important not only to give the right answer but to stick to it through thick and thin.

HENRY WARD BEECHER

# *Hope Needed*

*Whoever comes to me*
*I will never drive away.*
JOHN 6:37 NIV

Cast out! My soul, how often might this have been your history. You have cast off your God—might He not often have cast you out? Yes, cast you out as fuel for the fire of His wrath. And yet, notwithstanding all your ungrateful requital for His unmerited forbearance, He is still declaring, "As I live, says the Lord, I have no pleasure in the death of him that dies." Your sins may be legion—the sand of the sea may be their befitting type—the thought of their vileness and aggravation may be ready to overwhelm you; but be still! Your patient God waits to be gracious. Oh, be deeply humbled and softened because of your guilt, and resolve to dedicate yourself anew to His service—and so coming, "He will by no means cast you out!"

Despond not by reason of former shortcomings. Your sins are great, but your Savior's merits are greater. He is willing to forget all the past and sink it in oblivion, if there be present love and the promise of future obedience.

"Simon, son of Jonah, do you love me?" Ah, how different is God's verdict from man's. After such sins as yours, man's sentence would have been, "I will in nowise receive." But "it is better to fall into the hands of God than into the hands of man"; for He says, "I will in nowise cast out."

JOHN MACDUFF

# Reward for Righteousness

*Knowing that of the Lord ye shall receive*
*the reward of the inheritance:*
*for ye serve the Lord Christ.*
COLOSSIANS 3:24 KJV

That we are justified in the sight of the Divine Majesty from the whole lump of our sins, both past, present, and to come; by free grace through that one offering of the body of Jesus Christ; once for all, I bless God. I believe it and that we shall be brought to glory by the same grace, through the same most blessed Jesus. I thank God by His grace I believe for their works of faith and love, whether in a doing or a suffering way—and that not principally to be enjoyed here, but hereafter: "great is your reward in heaven."

If this reward had been an impairing or derogation to the free grace of God that saves us, He would never have mentioned it for our encouragement unto good works, would not have added a promise of reward for them that do them, nor have counted Himself unfaithful if He should not do it.

The same may be said concerning Jesus Christ, who doubtless loves and tenders the honor of His own merits as much as any who are saved by Him can do, whether they be in heaven or earth; yet He hath promised a reward to a cup of cold water or giving of any other alms; and further told us, they that do these things, they do lay up treasure in heaven.

JOHN BUNYAN

# *The Risen Christ*

*Blessed be the God and Father of our Lord Jesus Christ,*
*which according to his abundant mercy*
*hath begotten us again unto a lively hope*
*by the resurrection of Jesus Christ from the dead.*

1 PETER 1:3 KJV

"He is risen." And blessed be God it is so. For if it were not, then the gospel would be in vain (1 Corinthians 15:14), seeing it hangs the whole weight of our faith, hope, and salvation upon Christ as risen from the dead. If this were not so, then could the holy and divinely inspired apostles be found false witnesses (1 Corinthians 15:15). For they are believers yet in their sins (1 Corinthians 15:17). For our justification is truly ascribed to the Resurrection of Christ (Romans 4:25). While Christ was dying, and continued in the state of the dead, the price of our redemption was all that while but in paying; the payment was completed when He revived and rose again.

Therefore, for Christ to have continued always in the state of the dead had been never to have completely satisfied; hence the whole force and weight of our justification depends upon His Resurrection. If you are regenerated creatures, brought forth in a new nature to God, for we are "begotten again to a lively hope, by the resurrection of Jesus Christ from the dead." Christ's Resurrection is the ground work of our hope. And the new birth is our title or evidence of our interest in it.

JOHN FLAVEL

APRIL 16

# *Hope for Chief Sinners*

*I am not come to call the righteous,*
*but sinners to repentance.*
MATTHEW 9:13 KJV

Christ came to his own, and His own received Him not (John 1:11). Those that had heads in heaven by some kind of resemblance to God in moral righteousness, being undefiled with the common pollution of the world—those received him not, when publican and harlots started ahead of them and ran before them to catch hold of offers of grace. "Publicans and harlots go into the kingdom of heaven before you" (Matthew 21:31). Just as travelers who have loitered away their time in an alehouse, being sensible how the darkness of the night creeps upon them, spur on, and outstrip those that were many miles on their way and get to their stage before them. So these publicans and harlots which were at a great distance from heaven, arrived there before those who were not far off from it.

Great sinners are most easily convinced of the notorious wickedness of their lives and are more inclinable to endeavor an escape from the devil's slavery and are frightened and shaken by their consciences into a compliance with the doctrine of redemption; whereas those that that do by nature the things contained in the law are so much a law to themselves, that it is difficult to persuade them of the necessity to part with this self-law in regard to justification. Cassianus speaks very peremptorily in this case; that is, often have we seen the cold and carnal warmed into a spiritual fervor, the dainty and the brutish never.

STEPHEN CHARNOCK

## Victory in Battle

*Some trust in chariots, and some in horses:*
*but we will remember*
*the name of the Lord our God.*
PSALM 20:7 KJV

The Lord was pleased to visit me with a slight illness in my late journey. The Lord gave me much peace in my soul, and I was enabled to hope He would bring me safe home, in which I was not disappointed. I have reason to speak much of His goodness, for it was sweetened with abundant mercies. I thought that had it been His pleasure I should have continued sick at Oxford, or even have died there. I had no objection. Though I had that joy and sensible comfort which some are favored with, yet I was quite free from pain, fear, and care, and felt myself sweetly composed to His will, whatever it might be. Thus He fulfills His promise in making our strength equal to our day; and every new trial gives us a new proof how happy it is to be enabled to put our trust in Him.

Take it for granted upon the warrant of His word, that you are His, and He is yours; that He has loved you with an everlasting love, and therefore in loving-kindness has drawn you to himself—that He will surely accomplish that which He has begun and that nothing which can be named or thought of shall ever be able to separate you from Him. This persuasion will give you strength for the battle. Be strong therefore, not in yourself, but in the grace that is in Christ Jesus.

JOHN NEWTON

# Hope in Hard Times

*Thou has shewed thy people hard things.*
PSALM 60:3 KJV

I have always been glad that the psalmist said to God that some things were hard. There is no mistake about it; there are hard things in life. Some beautiful pink flowers were given me this summer, and as I took them I said, "What are they?" And the answer came, "They are rock flowers; they grow and bloom only on rocks where you can see no soil." Then I thought of God's flowers growing in hard places; and I feel, somehow, that He may have a peculiar tenderness for His "rock flowers" that He may not have for His lilies and roses.

MARGARET BOTTOME

# *Hope in Christ Alone*

*But now in Christ Jesus ye who sometimes were far off are made nigh by the blood of Christ.*

EPHESIANS 2:13 KJV

There is no coming to the Father but by Christ. He is the way. The apostle says in 1 Corinthians 3:21–22, "All things are your's, whether Paul, or Apollos, or Cephas, or the world, or life, or death, or things present, or things to come, all are your's." Mark it: All are yours, and you are Christ's, and Christ is God's. There is such a distance between you and God that, were not Christ in the middle, you would never come together. But Christ has come between and joined you together so that all is yours because you are Christ's and Christ is God's. We have a notable expression of this mystery in Ephesians 2:12. Paul has told them that they had been without hope and without God in the world, but he says in verse 13, "Ye who sometimes were far off are made nigh by the blood of Christ."

It is by the blood of Christ that you have anything to do with God, "In whom we have boldness and access with confidence by the faith of him" (Ephesians 3:12). In Christ we come to have boldness and access. There is no coming to the Father except by Christ, and Christ takes a believer by the hand and leads him to the Father.

JEREMIAH BURROUGHS

# From a Missionary Journal, Part 1

*What a wretched man I am!*
*Who will rescue me from this body of death?*
*Thanks be to God—through Jesus Christ our Lord!*
ROMANS 7:24–25 NIV

David Brainerd [1718–1747] responded to God's call to minister to American Indians; yet much of his prayer time was consumed with wrestling over "the hope that lieth within" him. He had great hope for his ministry, but his diary reveals spiritual struggles, many of which stayed with him through the twenty-nine years of his life.

Tuesday, April 20 [1742]: This day I am twenty-four years of age. O how much mercy have I received the years past! How often has God caused His goodness to pass before me! And how poorly have I answered the vows I have made this time, to be wholly the Lord's, to be forever devoted to His service! The Lord help me to live more to His glory for the time to come.

This has been a sweet, a happy day to me: blessed be God. I think my soul was never so drawn out in intercession for others, as it has been this night. Had a most fervent wrestle with the Lord tonight for my enemies; and I hardly ever so longed to live to God and to be altogether devoted to Him; I want to wear out my life in His service and for His glory. This is the great hope of my heart and soul.

DAVID BRAINERD

# From a Missionary Journal, Part 2

> *"I looked for a man among them who*
> *would build up the wall and stand before me*
> *in the gap on behalf of the land."*
>
> EZEKIEL 22:30 NIV

Felt much calmness and resignation, and God again enabled me to wrestle for numbers of souls, and had such fervency in the sweet duty of intercession. I enjoyed of late more sweetness in intercession for others than in any other part of prayer. My blessed Lord really let me come near to Him and plead with Him.

> Lord, I'm a stranger here alone;
> Earth no true comforts can afford;
> Yet, absent from my dearest one,
> My soul delights to cry, my Lord.
> Jesus, my Lord, my only love,
> Possess my soul, nor thence depart;
> Grant me kind visits, heavenly Dove;
> My God shall then have all my heart.

DAVID BRAINERD

# From a Missionary Journal, Part 3

*I have been crucified with Christ*
*and I no longer live,*
*but Christ lives in me.*
GALATIANS 2:20 NIV

New Haven, Connecticut: I think I scarce ever felt such hope in my life; I rejoiced in resignation and giving myself up to God, to be wholly and entirely devoted to Him forever.

I had much of the presence of God in family prayer and had some comfort in secret. I was greatly refreshed from the Word of God this morning, which was exceeding sweet to me: Some things that appeared mysterious were opened to me.

Lord's day: Spent much time alone. My soul longed to be holy and reached after God. I hungered and thirsted, but was not refreshed. My soul hung on God as my only portion. O that I could grow in grace more abundantly every day!

Tuesday: This morning I spent about two hours in prayer and meditation, with considerable delight. I had divine assistance in my studies, felt a surge of power, was optimistic in my hope with fervency and comfort in prayer.

My secret retirement was very refreshing to my soul; it appeared such a happiness to have God for my life, that I had rather be any other creature in this lower creation, than not enjoy God. I had rather be a beast, than a man without God.

DAVID BRAINERD

# *From a Missionary Journal, Part 4*

> *They go from strength to strength,*
> *every one of them in Zion appeareth before God.*
> PSALM 84:7 KJV

Lord's day: This morning I spent about two hours in secret duties [quiet time devotions] and was enabled more than ordinarily to agonize for immortal souls; though it was early in the morning and the sun scarcely shined at all, yet my body was quite wet with sweat.

At night I was exceedingly melted with divine love and great hope and had some feeling sense of the blessedness of the upper world [heaven]. Those words [text] hung upon me, with much divine sweetness. O the near access that sometimes gives us in our addresses to Him! This may well be termed "appearing before God": It is true indeed in the spiritual sense and in the sweetness sense.

I think I have not had such power of intercession these many months, both for God's children and for sinners, as I have had this evening. I hoped and longed for the coming of my Lord: I longed to join the angelic hosts in praises, wholly free from imperfection. All I want is to be more holy.

Farewell, vain world; my soul can bid adieu;
My Savior's taught me to abandon you.

Your charms may gratify a sensual mind;
Not please a soul wholly for God designed.

DAVID BRAINERD

# From a Missionary Journal, Part 5

*Above all, love each other deeply.*
1 PETER 4:8 NIV

The David Brainerd journal contains hundreds of entries describing his faith and struggle with feelings of spiritual infirmity. Underlying it all is a deep love for the Indians he is attempting to reach.

✧

Rode from Danbury to Southbury; preached there from 1 Peter 4:8. I had much of the comfort of the power of God in the service. I seemed to have power with God in prayer and power to get hold of the hearts of the people in preaching.

I felt comfortable in secret prayer; my soul was refreshed with hope—the hope that the heathen will be coming home to Christ. It was a sweet and comfortable hour unto my soul, while I indulged with freedom to plead, not just for myself, but also for the souls of Indians. I scarce ever enjoyed more of God in any one prayer. O it was a blessed season indeed to my soul. This has been a sweet and comfortable day to my soul. Blessed be God. I long to be totally transformed into His image.

I also felt more compassion for souls. I feel much more kindness, meekness, gentleness, and love toward the heathen than ever. I wonder how God can reach more of their poor souls. This is my anticipation and hope. God give us the desire to "love each other deeply."

DAVID BRAINERD

# Bliss in Dying

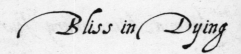

*Blessed are the dead which die in the Lord.*

REVELATION 14:13 KJV

My soul, is this blessedness yours in prospect? Are you ready, if called this night to lie down on your death pillow, sweetly to fall asleep in Jesus? What is the sting of death?—It is sin. Is death, then, to you, robbed of its sting by having listened to the gracious accents of pardoning love? Be of good cheer, your sins, which are many, are all forgiven. If you have made your peace with God, resting on the work and atoning blood of His dear Son, then is the last enemy divested of all his terror, and you can say, in sweet composure, of your dying couch and dying hour— "I will both lay down in peace and sleep, because You, Lord, make me to dwell in safety."

Reader, ponder that solemn question, "Am I ready to die? Am I living as I should wish I had done when that last hour arrives?"

And when shall it arrive? Tomorrow is not yours. "Truly, there may be but a step between you and death." Oh, solve the question speedily—risk no doubts and no peradventure. Every day is proclaiming anew the lesson, "The race is not to the swift, nor the battle to the strong" (Ecclesiastes 9:11). Seek to live, so that that hour cannot come upon you too soon, or too unexpectedly. Live a dying life! How blessed to live—how blessed to die, with the consciousness, that there may be but a step between you and glory.

JOHN MACDUFF

# Practicing the Presence of God

*A man of many companions may come to ruin,*
*but there is a friend who sticks closer than a brother.*
PROVERBS 18:24 NIV

I cannot understand how religious people can remain content without the practice of the presence of God. As for me, I keep myself recollected in Him in the depth and center of my soul as much as possible, and when I am thus with Him, I fear nothing; the least deviation is perdition for me.

This exercise does not hurt the body. It is nonetheless appropriate to deprive the body occasionally, and even with some frequency. God will not permit your soul desirous of being entirely His to find consolation other than with Him, and that is more than reasonable.

I do not say we must put ourselves to a great deal of trouble. No, we must serve God in a holy freedom; we must do our business faithfully, without stress or tension; reminding ourselves of God mildly and with tranquillity, as often as we find our minds wandering from Him.

BROTHER LAWRENCE

# Abundant Pardon

*Let the wicked forsake his way,*
*and the unrighteous man his thoughts:*
*and let him return unto the LORD,*
*and he will have mercy upon him;*
*and to our God, for he will abundantly pardon.*

ISAIAH 55:7 KJV

Every natural man has a way by which he hopes to be saved.

God's way of justifying a sinner is by the death and obedience of His Son. It is by casting yourself under the doing and dying of His Son. I say, then, it is not your way. You are groping in the dark, but God's way is in the light. And then it is a more glorious way; just as there is a greater glory spread over the bespangled heaven than there is over this poor earth, so is there over God's way. God's is high up, a perfect, righteous way. Your sins may be covered by this way as completely as the waters of the flood covered the earth.

"He will abundantly pardon," or He will multiply pardon. The meaning is twofold; it is either He will pardon great sinners or He will pardon pardoned ones. Those of you who are unregenerate men, He will pardon you. Then the other meaning is, He will pardon upon pardon. When you go away and sin and come back again, He will pardon you, if only you will give over your own way and follow God's way of righteousness. If only you will give over that way and return to Christ, then God swears by Himself that He will receive you, and will multiply pardon to you.

ROBERT MURRAY MCCHEYNE

# Refreshment in Christ

*A man shall be. . .as rivers of water in a dry place,*
*as the shadow of a great rock in a weary land.*
ISAIAH 32:2 KJV

[Christ] shall be the safety of His people, to which they shall flee for protection in the time of danger.

He shall be as "rivers of water in a dry place." This is an allusion to the deserts of Arabia. One may travel there many days and see no sign of a river, so that travelers are ready to be consumed with thirst, as the children of Israel were in the wilderness.

Now when a man finds Jesus Christ, he is like one who has been traveling in those deserts till he is almost consumed with thirst, and who at last finds a river of cool clear water. And Christ was typified by the river of water that issued out of the rock for the children of Israel in this desert. He is compared to a river, because there is such plenty in Him.

He is the "shadow of a great rock in a weary land." It is not said, as the shadow of a tree, because in some places of that country, there is nothing by dry sand and rocks, and the sun beats exceedingly hot upon the sand; all the shade to be found is under some great rock. They who come to Christ find such rest and refreshment as the weary traveler in that hot and desolate country finds under the shadow of a great rock.

JONATHAN EDWARDS

# The Nearness of God

*One cried unto another, and said,*
*Holy, holy, holy, is the LORD of hosts:*
*the whole earth is full of his glory.*
ISAIAH 6:3 KJV

It is said the whole earth is full of God's glory. You and I would be prepared to admit that where the glory of God shines is like the spray above Niagara Falls, or like when morning is seen coming upon the Matterhorn and the evening glow upon the Jungfrau. But to be told that the whole earth is full of the glory of God—that startles us.

We must understand that when the heart is full of God, you will find God anywhere and everywhere; it's as the miner wears a light on his helmet through the dark cavity of the earth and lights his step.

Oh, men and women, that is what we may rely on here! It is not that I can do anything, but God, heaven, and eternity are near. It is the Spirit of God, who is as much in this assembly as He was in the upper room on the Day of Pentecost. Can you not detect the movement of God's Spirit at this moment upon your heart? The whole earth is full of God. It is because God is here, and there is as much of the Holy Spirit in this place as there was in the upper room on the Day of Pentecost. The mighty river of God, which is full of water and flowing through this place, is why you and I are certain of His blessing.

F. B. MEYER

# Being an Overcomer

*I am the root and the offspring of David,*
*and the bright and morning star.*
REVELATION 22:16 KJV

There are two very important principles presented in Revelation 3, verses three and eleven, which are profoundly interesting, but clear, simple, easily grasped, and full of power, when understood—two distinct things which characterize the overcomer. The first is the truth that has been communicated, and the second, the hope that is set before us.

We are apt to be discouraged and disheartened by the state of things around us and may want to surrender everything. Because of the condition of our world, we can become spiritually paralyzed. But, if we get hold of truth and hope, we are able to stem the tide and to be an overcomer.

We belong to the region of light. Our proper hope is the Morning Star, which is only seen by those who are watching through the night.

He is coming for me, and I have to watch for the Bright and Morning Star. Now let my heart rise up and overcome the condition of things around. Build on what God has given us and on the hope that is set before you. Hold fast to the standard of the truth of God, and do not accept anything less, even though you may be alone. If a regiment were cut to pieces and only one man left, if he holds the colors, the dignity of the regiment is maintained.

C. H. MACINTOSH

# *Hope Made Real*

*"Blessed are the dead who die in the Lord."*
REVELATION 14:13 NIV

When I was a boy I had one huge hope. I hoped that heaven was the glorious golden city with jeweled walls and gates of pearl that I'd seen pictured in my Bible storybook. And I hoped that there was no one there I knew but the angels, and they were all strangers to me.

But after a while my little brother died; then I thought of heaven as the great city, full of angels, with just one little fellow in it—my brother. He was the only one I knew there. Then another brother died, and there were two in heaven that I knew.

Then my friends and acquaintances began to die, and their number grew larger all the time. But it was not until one of my own little ones was taken that I began to feel that I had a personal interest in heaven. It almost seemed as if I had more friends and loved ones in heaven than here.

In some strange way, my hope for everlasting life in a place God has prepared has become more real. It's no longer something that I hope about, but it has become an assured hope.

AUTHOR UNKNOWN

# Hope Building

*We will have confidence on the day of judgment,*
*because in this world we are like him.*
1 JOHN 4:17 NIV

I rejoice in the hope of that great glory to be revealed, for it is no uncertain glory that we look for. Our hope is not hung upon such an untwisted thread as, "I imagine so," or "It is likely," but it is hung upon the cable, the strong tow cable of our fastened anchor; it is the oath and promise of Him who is eternal verity. Our salvation is fastened with God's own hand, and with Christ's own strength, to the strong stake of God's unchangeable nature. To us hope does not mean, "I hope so"; our hope is, "I know so!"

And those of you bypass that strong stake of God's unchangeable nature? It was the Italian poet Dante who best pictures what awaits those of you who are hopeless. Who can ever forget his description of the entrance to hell, with its inscription above the smoldering gate, "Leave behind all hope, you who enter here."

Thank God for His Divine Providence in that He has provided a way of escape from the road to hell, through the blood of His Son Jesus Christ. That is the basis of our hope, the strong stake of God's unchanging nature.

SAMUEL RUTHERFORD

# *Hope in Victory*

*Thou art my King, O God:*
*command deliverances for Jacob.*

PSALM 44:4 KJV

There is no foe to your growth in grace, no enemy in your Christian work, which was not included in your Savior's conquests.

You need not be afraid of them. When you touch them, they will flee before you. God has promised to deliver them up before you. Only be strong and very courageous. Fear not, nor be dismayed. The Lord is with you, O mighty men of valor— mighty because you are one with the Mightiest. Claim victory.

Whenever your enemies close in upon you, claim victory! Whenever heart and flesh fail, look up and claim victory!

Be sure that you have a share in that triumph which Jesus won, not for Himself alone, but for us all; remember that you were in Him when He won it, and *claim victory!*

Reckon that it is yours, and gather spoil. Neither the Anakim nor fenced cities need daunt or abash you. You are one of the conquering legion. Claim your share in the Savior's victory.

F. B. MEYER

# The Hope of Heaven

*In keeping with his promise we are looking to*
*a new heaven and a new earth,*
*the home of righteousness.*
2 PETER 3:13 NIV

The Christian's hope of heaven is not of an undiscovered country. It cannot be compared with anything we know on earth. Perhaps nothing but the shortness of our range of sight keeps us from seeing the celestial gates all open to us, and nothing but the deafness of our ears prevents our hearing the joyful ringing of the bells of heaven. There are constant sounds around us that we cannot hear, and the sky is studded with bright worlds that our eyes have never seen. Little as we know about this bright and radiant land, there are glimpses of its beauty that comes to us now and then.

It is said by travelers, that in climbing the Alps, the houses of far distant villages can be seen with great distinctness. The distance looks so short that the place seems almost at hand, but after hours and hours of climbing, it looks no nearer yet. This is because of the clearness of the atmosphere. By perseverance, however, the place is reached at last, and the tired traveler finds rest. So, sometimes we dwell in high altitudes of grace; heaven seems very near, and the hills of Beulah are in full view. At other times, the clouds and fogs that come through suffering and sin, cut off our sight. We are just as near heaven in the one case as we are in the other, and we are just as sure of gaining it if we keep in the path that Christ has trod.

DWIGHT L. MOODY

# The Best Hope

> "I am going away and
> I am coming back to you."
>
> JOHN 14:28 NIV

Christ's Second Coming is our best hope. Andrew Fuller's verse on the excellency and utility of the grace of hope speaks to this.

> O hope all hope surpassing
> Forever more to be,
> O Christ, the church's Bridegroom,
> In Paradise with Thee:
> For soon shall break the day, and shadows flee away.

Hope holds up a period, even within the limits of time, a heaven compared with the present state of things, when "holiness to the Lord shall be written as upon the belts of the horses, and a time when Zion shall become a quiet habitation. But you say, that we have but little hope of living to see this come to pass. Perhaps so: still you live in prospect of a better life—a blessed society where purity and amity forever reign. Yes, brethren, immediately on entering this quiet habitation, you will "enter into peace," and each one of you will walk forever in His uprightness.

> For soon shall break the day,
> And shadows flee away.

THOMAS GOODWIN

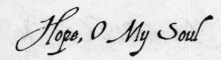

# Hope, O My Soul

*"Keep watch because you do not know
when the owner of the house will come back."*
MARK 13:35 NIV

Hope, O my soul, hope. You know neither the day nor the hour. Watch carefully, for everything passes quickly, even though your impatience makes doubtful what is certain and turns a very short time into a long one.

Let nothing trouble you, let nothing make you afraid. All things pass away. God never changes. Patience obtains everything. God alone is enough.

Even with hope, the more you struggle, the more you prove the love that you bear for your God, and the more you will rejoice one day with your Beloved in a happiness and rapture that can never end.

Our true friend, whom alone we can trust, is Jesus Christ. When I depend upon Him, I feel so strong that I think I could stand firm against the whole world.

There is more value in a little study of humility and in a single act of it than in all the knowledge in the world.

There is no such thing as bad weather. All weather is good because it is God's.

The person without hope is missing joy; he is like one who cannot see a star in the heavens or the flower in a weed patch. While to the person with hope. The world opens up to great wonder and beauty.

TERESA OF AVILA

# You've Still Got It

*Hope in God,*
*who richly provides us with*
*everything for our enjoyment.*
1 TIMOTHY 6:17 NIV

Learn from yesterday, live for today, hope for tomorrow. If you can look at a sunset and smile and realize that God painted that picture, then you still have hope. If you can find some good in other people, then you still have hope. If you meet new people with a trace of excitement and optimism, then you still have hope. If you still give people the benefit of the doubt, then you still have hope.

If the suffering of others still fills you with pain, then you still have hope. If you still like happy endings to your stories, then you still have hope. If you can look to the past and find it in yourself to smile, you still have hope. If you can recall the blessings of God in your life and share them with someone else, then you still have hope.

If when faced with bad and told everything is futile and you are able to look up at the end of the conversation and say, "Yeah, but. . ." then you still have great quantities of hope. If you can still offer your hand of friendship to those who have touched your life, then you still have hope.

If you refuse to let a friendship die  or accept that it must end, then you still have hope. Hope sees the invisible, feels the intangible, and achieves the impossible. Hope is from God.

ATTRIBUTED TO REV. SILAS MUELLER
OF BETHLEHEM, PENNSYLVANIA

# A Heavenly City

*For he looked for a city*
*which hath foundations,*
*whose builder and maker is God.*
HEBREWS 11:10 KJV

A heavenly country, where there is a heavenly Father, a heavenly host, heavenly things, heavenly visions, heavenly places, a heavenly kingdom, and the heavenly Jerusalem. This is a country to be desired, and therefore no marvel if any, except those that have lost their wits and senses refuse to choose themselves an habitation here.

Here is the "mount Sion. . .the general assembly and church of the firstborn. . .God the Judge of all, and the spirits of just men made perfect, and. . .Jesus" (Hebrews 12:22–24).

Who would not be here? This is the country that the righteous desire a habitation: "but now they desire a better country, that is, an heavenly: wherefore God is not ashamed to be called their God: for he hath prepared for them a city" (Hebrews 11:16).

Mark, they desire a country, and God prepares for them a city; He goes beyond their desires, beyond their apprehensions, beyond what their hearts could conceive to ask for. There is none that are weary of this world from a gracious disposition that they have to an heavenly, but God will take notice, will own them, and not be ashamed to own them; yea, such shall not lose their longing. And all this is, that the promise to them might be fulfilled, "The desire of the righteous shall be granted."

JOHN BUNYAN

# Knowing God Through Faith

*I know whom I have believed,*
*and am convinced that he is able.*

2 TIMOTHY 1:12 NIV

For I know well the spring that flows and runs,
Although it is night.

That eternal spring is hidden, for I know well where
it has its rise,
Although it is night.

I do not know its origin, nor has it one, but I know that
every origin has come from it,
Although it is night.

I know that nothing else is so beautiful, and that the
heavens and the earth drink there,
Although it is night.

I know that is bottomless, and no one is able to cross it,
Although it is night.

I know well the stream that flows from this spring is
mighty in compass and power,
Although it is still night.

This living stream that I long for, I see this bread of life,
Although it is night.

JOHN OF THE CROSS

# The Spiritual Essence

*Love the LORD your God. . .*
*walk in all His ways. . .*
*hold fast to Him.*
DEUTERONOMY 11:22 NKJV

Practicing the presence of God; this is, in my opinion, the essence of the spiritual life, and it seems to me that by practicing it properly you become spiritual in no time.

I know that to do this your heart must be empty of all other things because God desires to possess it exclusively without first emptying it of everything other than Himself; neither can He act within it nor do there what He pleases.

There is no way of life in the world more agreeable or delightful than continual conversation with God; only those who practice and experience it can understand this. I do not suggest, however, that you do it for this reason. We must not seek consolation from this exercise, but must do it from a motive of love, and because God wants it.

If I were a preacher, I would preach nothing but the practice of the presence of God; and if I were a spiritual director, I would recommend it to everyone, for I believe there is nothing so necessary or so easy.

This is the devotion I have practiced since I entered religious life. Although I have practiced it feebly and imperfectly, I have nonetheless received many advantages. I certainly know this is due to the Lord's mercy and goodness—and this must be acknowledged—since we can do nothing without Him.

BROTHER LAWRENCE

# The Growing Soul

*"Whoever wants to save his life will lose it,
but whoever loses his life for me will save it."*

LUKE 9:24 NIV

Sadhu Sundar Singh has been called the St. Paul of India. His conversion to Christ is one of the great stories of the faith.

༚

The material body cannot keep company forever with the spirit. After fulfilling its purpose for some time as an instrument of the soul for its work in the world, the body begins to refuse, through weakness and old age, to go along with the spirit any further. This is because the body cannot keep pace with the eternally growing soul.

Although the soul and body cannot live together forever, the fruits of the work which they have done together will remain forever. So it is necessary to lay carefully the foundation of our eternal life. Unfortunately, by the misuse of freedom, we can lose it forever. Freedom means the capacity to do either good or bad deeds. By constantly choosing to do bad deeds, we become slaves of sin and destroy our freedom and life (John 8:21, 34).

By giving up our sins, on the other hand, and by following truth, we are made free forever (John 8:32). The works of those who are thus made free and spend all their life in God's service, that is, who die in the Lord, will follow them (Revelation 14:13). To die in the Lord does not mean death, for the Lord is "the Lord of the living and not of the dead," but to die to die in the Lord means losing oneself in His work (Luke 9:24).

SADHU SUNDAR SINGH

# Hope in a Burden Bearer

*"Come to me,*
*all you who are weary and burdened,*
*and I will give you rest."*
MATTHEW 11:28 NIV

Many Christians love God's will in the abstract but carry great burdens in connection with it. From this also there is deliverance in the wonderful life of faith. For in this way of life no burdens are carried, no anxieties felt. The Lord is our burden-bearer, and upon Him we must lay off every care. He says, in effect, "Be careful for nothing, but make your requests known to me, and I will attend to them all" (Philippians 4:6).

Be careful for *nothing*, he says, not even your service. Why? Because we are so utterly helpless that no matter how careful we were, our service would amount to nothing! What have we to do with thinking whether we are fit or unfit for service? The Master-workman surely has the right to use any tool He pleases for His own work, and it is plainly not the business of the tool to decide whether it is the right one to be used or not. He knows; and if He chooses to use us, of course we must be fit.

In truth, if we only knew it, our chief fitness is in our utter helplessness. His strength is made perfect, not in our strength, but in our weakness. Our strength is only a hindrance.

HANNAH WHITALL SMITH

# God's Way of Working

*May he work in us what is pleasing to him,*
*through Jesus Christ,*
*to whom be glory for ever and ever.*

HEBREWS 13:21 NIV

Nothing could possibly be conceived more effectual than this. How often have we thought, when dealing with our children, "Oh, if I could only get inside them and make them want to do just what I want, how easy it would be to manage them then!"

How often in practical experience we have found that to deal with cross-grained people we most carefully avoid suggesting our wishes to them but must in some way induce them to suggest the thing themselves, sure that then there will be no opposition with which to contend. And we, who are by nature stiff-necked people, always rebel more or less against a law from outside of us, while we joyfully embrace the same law springing up from within.

God's way of working, therefore, is to get possession of the inside of us, to take the control and management of our will, and to work it for us. Perhaps this is the war that many of us have experienced; God and our will striving to get the upper hand. But when He does, then obedience is easy and a delight, and service becomes perfect freedom, until the Christian is forced to explain, "This happy service! Who could dream that earth had such liberty?"

HANNAH WHITALL SMITH

# A Due Reaping

*In due season we shall reap,*
*if we faint not.*
GALATIANS 6:9 KJV

Believer! All the glory of your salvation belongs to Jesus—none to yourself; every jewel in your eternal crown is His—purchased by His blood and polished by His Spirit. The confession of time will be the ascription of all eternity: "By the grace of God I am what I am" (1 Corinthians 15:10). But though "all be grace," your God calls you to personal strenuousness in the work of your high calling—to labor, to fight, to wrestle, to agonize; and the heavenly reaping will be in proportion to the earthly sowing: "He which soweth sparingly shall reap also sparingly; and he which soweth bountifully shall reap also bountifully" (2 Corinthians 9:6). What an incentive to holy living and increased spiritual attainments.

My soul! Would you be a star shining high and bright in the firmament of glory? Would you receive the ten-talent recompense? Then be not weary. Put on your armor for fresh conquests. Be gaining daily some new victory over sin. Deny yourself. Be a willing cross-bearer for your Lord's sake. Do good to all men as you have opportunity; be patient under provocation, "slow to wrath," resigned in trial. Let the world take knowledge of you that you are wearing Christ's uniform and bearing Christ's spirit and sharing Christ's cross. So, when the reaping time comes, He who has promised that the cup of cold water cannot go unrecompensed will not allow you to lose your reward.

JOHN MACDUFF

# À Kempis on Spiritual Reading

*"Do you understand what you are reading?"*
ACTS 8:30 NIV

Read to despise exterior things and to give thyself to the interior.

Assign some stated time every day for the employment of spiritual reading. So far as you possibly can, keep this exercise in inviolable.

Prepare yourself for reading, by purity of intention and by fervent prayer to God, that He would enable you to see His will and give you a firm resolution to perform it.

Be sure to read, not cursorily or hastily, but leisurely, seriously, and with great attention, with proper pauses and intervals, and that you may allow time for the enlightening of the divine grace. To this end, recollect, every now and then, what you have read, and consider how to reduce it to practice.

Further, let your reading be continued and regular, not rambling and desultory. To taste of many things, without fixing upon any, shows a vitiated palate and feeds the disease which makes it pleasing. Whatsoever book you begin, read, therefore, through in order.

Labor to work yourself up into a disposition correspondent with what you read; the reading is useless which only enlightens the understanding, without warming the affections. And therefore intersperse earnest aspirations to God, for His heat as well as His light. Select also any remarkable sayings or advices, and treasure them in your memory.

Conclude all with a short prayer to God that from your reading He might sow seeds in your heart and that it may bring forth fruit.

THOMAS À KEMPIS, ADAPTED BY JOHN WESLEY

# Nothing but the Hope

*I am the LORD your God;*
*sanctify yourselves therefore,*
*and be holy, for I am holy.*
LEVITICUS 11:44 NRSV

Persons who indulge the Christian hope, do not know how holy God is, have no just appreciation of His character, and therefore do not strive to become like God in this respect. Under this delusion they live, and thus die, with no suspicion of their mistake. I have before my mind another case—that of a man who was altogether a leader in his church.

On one occasion, as I was at his home for supper, he asked me what I should think of a man who, day after day, prayed for the Holy Spirit in his life, yet he never believed he had Him in his life. Why, I concluded that he prayed from the wrong motives. His motive was to be happy.

What motive should he have? My answer, the same that David had when he prayed for pardoning and restoring grace: "Then will I teach transgressors thy ways; and sinners shall be converted unto thee" (Psalm 51:13). My friend turned suddenly away—said nothing; but several hours afterward, he came to me and confessed that he had turned away, mad at the truth I had presented and deeply offended that God should require such self-renunciation. He saw himself as he was, but felt for sometime that he had rather die than let it be known that he had been deceived.

At length, though, he passed safely over that point where so many make shipwreck and are lost. Praise the Lord!

CHARLES G. FINNEY

# The Waiting Soul

*Those who wait for the LORD*
*shall renew their strength.*

ISAIAH 40:31 NRSV

Breathe from the gentle south, O Lord,
And cheer me from the north;
Blow in the treasures of Thy word,
And call the spices forth.

I wish, Thou knowest, to be resign'd,
And wait with patient hope;
But hope delay'd fatigues the mind,
And drinks the spirits up.

Help me to reach the distant goal;
Confirm my feeble knee;
Pity the sickness of a soul
That faints for love of Thee!

I seem forsaken and alone,
I hear the lion roar;
And every door is shut but one,
And that is Mercy's door.

There, till the dear Deliverer come,
I'll wait with humble prayer;
And when He calls His exile home,
The Lord shall find him there.

JOHN NEWTON

# The Brief Gospel

*Only believe.*
MARK 5:36 KJV

The briefest of the words of Jesus, but one of the most comforting. They contain the essence and epitome of all saving truth.

Reader, is Satan assailing you with tormenting fears? Is the thought of your sins, the guilty past, surfacing in terrible memorial before you? Is it almost tempting you to give way to hopeless despondency? Fear not! A gentle voice whispers in your ear, "Only believe." Your sins are great, but My grace is greater. "Only believe" that I died for you, and that I'm living for you and pleading for you.

Are you a backslider? Did you once run well? Has your own guilty apostasy alienated and estranged you from that face which was once all love? "Only believe" the word of Him whose ways are not as man's ways; "Return, O backsliding children, and I will heal your backsliding."

Are you beaten down with some heavy trial? Have your fondest schemes been blown upon, your fairest blossoms been withered in the bud? Has wave after wave been rolling upon you? Has the Lord forgotten to be gracious? Listen, hear the word of Jesus saying, "Believe, only believe." There is an infinite reason for the trial—a lurking thorn that requires removal; a gracious lesson that requires teaching.

Are you fearful and agitated in the prospect of death? Through fear of the last enemy, have you been all your lifetime subject to bondage? "Only believe." Remember, "As your days, so shall your strength be" (Deuteronomy 33:25).

E. M. BOUNDS

# A Fruitful Harvest

*He that reapeth receiveth wages,*
*and gathereth fruit unto life eternal.*

JOHN 4:36 KJV

I want to call your attention to our text [above]. I want you to get those words in your heart. I can speak from experience; I have been in the Lord's service for twenty-one years, and I want to testify that He is a good paymaster—that He pays promptly. I believe I saw faces light up at these words. You have been out in the harvest fields of the Lord, and you know this to be true. To go out and labor for Him is a thing to be proud of: to guide a poor, weary soul to the way of life, and turn the person's face toward the golden gates of Zion. The Lord's wages are better than silver and gold. The loyal soul shall receive a crown of glory.

As I was on the street today I thought that if I could only impress upon you that we have come here as to a vineyard, to reap and to gather, we shall have a glorious harvest. There is work for you to do, and by-and-by the harvest shall be gathered, and what a scene will be on the shore when we hear the master on the throne shout, "Well done! Well done!" May the blessing of God fall upon us, and may every man and woman be up and doing.

DWIGHT L. MOODY

# Christ on His Throne

*You will fill me with joy in your presence.*
PSALM 16:11 NIV

A throne is to be approached with devout joyfulness. If I find myself favored by divine grace to stand among those favored ones who frequent His courts, shall I not feel glad? I might have been in His prison, but I am before His throne. I might have been driven from His presence forever, but I am permitted to come near to Him, even into His royal palace, into His secret chamber for a gracious audience. Shall I not then be thankful? Shall not my thankfulness ascend into joy. And shall I not feel that I am honored, that I am made the recipient of great favors when I am permitted to pray?

Why then is your countenance sad when you stand before the throne of grace? If you were before the throne of justice to be condemned for your iniquities, your hands might well be at your sides; but now you are favored to come before the King in His robes of love. Let your face shine with sacred delight. If your sorrows are heavy, tell them to Him, for He can ease them. If your sins are multiplied, confess them, for He can forgive them.

O ye courtiers in the hall of such a Monarch, be ye exceedingly glad and mingle praises with your prayers.

CHARLES H. SPURGEON

# Submitting to God

*Therefore submit to God.*
JAMES 4:7 NKJV

A throne, whenever it is approached, should be so with complete submission. We do not pray to God to instruct Him as to what He ought to do, neither for a moment must we presume to dictate the line of the divine procedure. We are permitted to say to God, "Thus and thus would we have it," but we must furthermore add, "But seeing that we are ignorant and may be mistaken—seeing that we are still in the flesh, and therefore, may be actuated by carnal motives, we must say, not as we will, but as You will.

Who shall dictate to the throne? No loyal child of God will for a moment imagine that he is to occupy the place of the King, but he bows before Him who has the right to be Lord of all. And though he utters his desire earnestly, vehemently, importantly, and pleads again, yet it is evermore with this needful reservation: "Your will be done, my Lord. And if I ask anything that is not in accordance with it, my inmost will is that You would be good enough to deny Your servant. I will take it as a true answer if You refuse me, if I ask that which seems not good in Your sight."

If we constantly remember this, we should be less inclined to push certain issues before His throne. We should feel, "I am here in seeking my own ease, my own comfort, my own advantage, and perhaps, I may be asking for that which would dishonor God; therefore will I speak with the deepest submission to the divine decrees."

CHARLES H. SPURGEON

# No Condemnation

*Therefore, there is now no condemnation for*
*those who are in Christ Jesus,*
*because through Christ Jesus the law of the Spirit of life s*
*et me free from the law of sin and death.*

ROMANS 8:1–2 NIV

Condemnation is a word of tremendous importance, and the better we understand it, the more shall we appreciate the wondrous grace that has delivered us from its power. In the halls of a human court this is a term which falls with a fearful toll upon the ear of the convicted criminal and fills the spectators with sadness and horror.

But in the court of Divine Justice it is vested with a meaning and content infinitely more solemn and awe-inspiring. To that Court every member of Adam's fallen race is cited. "Conceived in sin, shaped in iniquity," each one of us enters this world under arrest—an indicted criminal, a rebel manacled. How, then, is it possible for such a one to escape the execution of the dreaded sentence? There was only one way, and that was by the removal from us of the sentence, namely sin.

Let guilt be removed and there can be "no condemnation." Has guilt been removed, removed, we mean, from the sinner who believes? Let the scriptures answer: "As far as the east is from the west, so far hath he removed our transgressions from us" (Psalm 103:12).

A. W. PINK

# *Hope in God*

*Why art thou cast down, O my soul?*
*and why art thou disquieted in me?*
*hope thou in God:*
*for I shall yet praise him for the help of his countenance.*

PSALM 42:5 KJV

A believing confidence in God is a sovereign antidote against prevailing despondency and a disquieted spirit. When the soul embraces itself, it sinks; if it catches hold on the power and promise of God, it keeps the head above water.

Hope in God, that He shall have glory from us. I shall experience such a change in my state that I shall not want matter for praise. It is the greatest desire and hope of every good man to be unto God for a name and a praise. What is the crown of heaven's bliss but this, that there we shall be forever praising God?

We shall have comfort in Him. We shall praise Him for the help of His countenance, for His favor, the support we have by it, and the satisfaction we have in it. Those who know how to value and improve the light of God's countenance will find in that a suitable, seasonable, and sufficient help, in the worst of times, and that which will furnish them with constant matter for praise.

David's believing expectation of this kept him from sinking; nay, it kept him from drooping; his harp was a palliative cure of Saul's melancholy, but his hope was an effectual cure of his own.

MATTHEW HENRY

# The Hope of a Warmed Heart

*[There] are given unto us exceeding*
*great and precious promises,*
*that by these ye might be*
*partakers of the divine nature.*

2 PETER 1:3 KJV

The Reverend John Wesley was almost in despair. He did not have the faith to continue to preach. He felt dull within and little motivated even to pray about it. The following is what he entered in his journal in 1738.

❧

On this day, May 24, 1738, I opened my Bible at about five in the morning and came across these words, "There are given unto us exceeding great and precious promises, even that ye should be partakers of the divine nature." I read similar words in other locations.

That evening I reluctantly attended a meeting in Aldersgate. Someone read from Luther's *Preface to the Epistle to Romans*. About 8:45 p.m. while he was describing the change which God works in the heart through faith in Christ, I felt my heart strangely warmed. I felt I did trust in Christ, Christ alone for salvation; and an assurance was given me that He had taken away my sins, even mine, and saved me from the law of sin and death.

JOHN WESLEY

## Hope and Glory

*The LORD will give grace and glory.*
PSALM 84:11 KJV

Do not forsake hope! Oh, happy day, when this toilsome warfare will all be ended. Jordan crossed, Canaan entered, the multitude of enemies of the wilderness no longer dreaded—sorrow, sighing, death, and worst of all, sin, no more either to be felt or feared. Here is the terminating link in the golden chain of the everlasting covenant. It began with predestination; it ends with glorification. It began with sovereign grace in eternity past, and no link will be lacking until the ransomed spirit is presented faultless before the throne.

Grace and glory! If the pledge is so sweet, what must be the glories of the eternal banqueting house? O my soul, make sure of your saving interest in the one as the blessed prelude to the other.

"Having access by faith into this grace, you can rejoice in hope of the glory of God"; for "whom he justifies, them he also glorifies."

Has grace begun in you? Can you mark—though it should be but the tiny drops of a streamlet which will terminate in such an ocean—the tiny grains which are to accumulate and issue in such "an exceeding weight of glory"? Do not delay this momentous question. No grace, no glory.

JOHN MACDUFF

# Twenty-Five Years Ago

*"Everyone who believes in him
may have eternal life."*
JOHN 3:15 NIV

When I was converted twenty-five years ago I had unspeakable hope and faith in God; but five years later my hope and faith increased a hundred fold, and five years ago I had more than ever. Why? Because I became better acquainted with Him in whom I have anchored my hope and faith. I have read up His word, and I see that the Lord has done so and so, and then I have turned to where He has promised to perform it, and when I see this I have reason to have hope in Him and the future.

"But," a man said to me, "no one has come back from the future, and we don't know what's out there. It is all dark. How can we be sure?" My answer: Thank God, Christ came down from heaven, and I would rather have Him coming as He does right from the bosom of the Father, than anyone else. We can rely on what Christ says, and He says, "He that believeth on me shall not perish, but have everlasting life."

My hope and faith are firmly established in that promise—for now, as well as in the future.

DWIGHT L. MOODY

# Our Shield

*The LORD God is a sun and shield:*
*the LORD will give grace and glory:*
*no good thing will he withhold*
*from them that walk uprightly.*

PSALM 84:11 KJV

In the days when David wrote this Psalm, fighting was mostly done man to man, at close range, sometimes toe touching toe, the sword of one clashing against that of the other—a struggle that could not end until one of the two was bathed in his own blood.

Of course, in such a struggle the shield was one's very life. Without a shield, while in hand-to-hand combat with another who had a shield, one of those who fought had to be lost.

A shield was a cover for the body, which mark you, was not held in front of the combatant by another but, even in most extreme danger, was handled by the man himself.

"The Lord is my shield" does not say that God protects us from afar off, and covers us without any effort on our part. "The Lord is my shield" is the language of faith. It sprang from the sense that God is close at hand, that our faith lay hold of Him, that we use Him as a defense against the assailant, and thus by faith, we become one with God. We know and feel that we are covered with His Almightiness. Praise the Lord!

FRANKLIN P. WISE

# Christ as King

*To the King eternal,*
*immortal, invisible, the only God,*
*be honor and glory for ever and ever.*
1 TIMOTHY 1:17 NIV

If we should always regard prayer as an entrance into the courts of the royalty of heaven; if we are to behave ourselves as a courtiers should in the presence of an illustrious majesty, then we are not at a loss to know the right spirit in which to pray. If in prayer we come to a throne, it is clear that our spirit should, in the first place, be one of lowly reverence. It is expected that the subject in approaching the king should pay him homage and honor. The pride that will not recognize the king, the treason that rebels against the sovereign will, if it be wise, avoid any shortcut to the throne. Let pride bite the curb at a distance, let treason lurk in corners, for only lowly reverence may come before the king himself when he sits clothed in his royal robes.

In our case, the king before whom we come is the highest of all monarchs; the King of Kings, the Lord of Lords. Emperors are but the shadows of His imperial power. They call themselves kings by right divine, but what divine right have they? Common sense laughs and scorns at their pretensions. The Lord alone has divine right, and to Him only does the kingdom belong. He is the blessed and only potentate. They are but nominal kings, to be set up and put down at the will of men or the decree of providence. He is Lord alone. He is the Prince of the kings of the earth.

CHARLES H. SPURGEON

# The Lord, Our Hope

*His delight is in the law of the LORD,*
*and on his law he meditates day and night.*
*He is like a tree planted by streams of water,*
*which yields its fruit in season and*
*whose leaf does not wither.*
*Whatever he does prospers.*

PSALM 1:2–3 NIV

The duty required of us is to make the Lord our hope, His favor the good we hope for and His power the strength we hope in. He that does so shall be as a tree planted by the waters, a choice tree, which great care has been taken to set it in the best soil.

He shall be like a tree that spreads out its roots, and firmly fixed, spreads them out by the waters, whence it draws abundance of sap. Those who make God their hope are easy and enjoy a continual security and serenity of mind. A tree thus planted, thus watered, shall not see when heat comes, shall not sustain any damage from the most scorching heats of summer; it is so well moistened from its roots that it shall be sufficiently guarded against draught.

They shall flourish like a tree that is always green, whose leaf does not wither; they shall be cheerful to themselves and beautiful in the eyes of others. They shall be fixed in an inward peace and satisfaction: They shall not be careful in a year of drought, when there is want of rain; for, as the tree has seed in itself, so it has its moisture. Those who trust in God and by faith derive strength and grace from Him, shall not cease from yielding fruit.

MATTHEW HENRY

# The Sure Afterward

*No discipline seems pleasant at the time, but painful.*
*Later on, however, it produces a harvest of righteousness*
*and peace for those who have been trained by it.*
HEBREWS 12:11 NIV

There are some promises which we are apt to reserve for great occasions and thus lose the continual comfort of them. Perhaps we read this one with a sigh and say, "How beautiful this is for those whom the Lord is really chastening! I almost think I should not mind that, if such a promise might then be mine. But the things that try me are only little things that turn up every day to trouble and depress me."

Does the Lord specify what degree of trouble, or what kind of trouble, is great enough to make up a claim to the promise? And if He does not, why should you? He only defines it as "not joyous, but grievous." And though you feel ashamed of feeling them so much and hardly like to own to their having been so trying and would not think of signifying them as "disciplining," yet, if they come under the Lord's definition, He not only knows all about them, but they were, every one of them, disciplining from His hand; neither to be despised and called "just nothing" when all the while they did "grieve" you; nor are they to be wearied of because they are working out blessing to you and glory to Him. Every one of them has been an unrecognized token of His love and interest in you, for "whom the Lord loveth he chasteneth [disciplines]."

FRANCES RIDLEY HAVERGAL

# The Johnstown Flood

*"Blessed are those who are invited to
the wedding supper of the lamb!"*
REVELATION 19:9 NIV

A pretty, pale woman told this true story today to our newspaper. When the Johnstown Flood was coursing toward the home of this mother and her seven children, the dear lady reported gathering her children in the parlor and telling them not to be afraid, as God was there and would guard them.

As the water rose, the family moved to the second, then third floor of the house. When the flood waters filled the room they were in, the little mother fought her way to the window and opened it, caught a piece of floating plank, and put the eldest child on it, with a hasty kiss and a prayer. Then she let it float way into the roar of the waves. Six times more she did this. The children were frightened, but hope and courage were what they were taught, and obedience was part of their creed.

Just before the last child was released, she asked her mother, "You said God would take care of me always, mamma. Will he take care of me now?"

"I told her He would, and then a thirty-five-foot wall of water carried her out of my sight, but I heard her cry out, 'I'm not afraid, Mamma!' "

"That's all the story, except the roof was torn off and I floated off with it. I was rescued at Kernville, sixteen miles from here. The children? Oh, they were lost, but a hope burns within my bosom; I will see them again!"

*Philadelphia Times* Newspaper
MAY 31, 1889

# The Bosom of Christ Jesus

*We do not want you to be ignorant about those who fall asleep,*
*or to grieve like the rest of men who have no hope.*
1 THESSALONIANS 4:13 NIV

You cannot find in the New Testament any of those hateful representations of dying which humankind has invented, by which death is portrayed as a ghastly skeleton with a scythe and black hood.

The representations of death in the New Testament are very different. There are two of them which I think are exquisitely beautiful. One is that of falling asleep in Jesus. When a little child has played all day long and becomes tired out, and the twilight has sent him in weariness to his mother's knee, where he thinks he has come for further games, then, almost in the midst of their frolicking, the little boy falls back into his mother's arms and nestles close to the sweetest and softest couch that ever a cheek has pressed. In no time at all sleep overtakes him and she wraps her arms around him.

So we fall asleep in Jesus. We have played long enough at the games of life. We become tired out and we lay our head back on the bosom of Christ and quietly fall asleep. Friend in Christ, this is your hope.

HENRY WARD BEECHER

## *For a Soldier Friend*

*Endure hardships with us like
a good soldier of Christ Jesus.*

2 TIMOTHY 2:3 NIV

We have a faithful God who is infinitely gracious and knows all our wants. I always thought that He would reduce you to extremity. He will come in His own time and when you least expect Him. Hope in Him more than ever; thank Him for His favors, particularly for the fortitude and patience which He gives you in your afflictions; it is a plain mark of the care He takes of you; comfort yourself then with Him, and give thanks for all.

I also admire your bravery and courage. God has given you a good disposition and a good will; but there is still in you a little of the world and a great deal of youth. A little lifting up of the heart suffices; a little remembrance of God, one act of inward worship, though upon a march and sword in hand, are prayers which, however short, are nevertheless very acceptable to God; and far from lessening a soldier's courage in occasion of danger, they best fortify it and kindle hope.

Think of God the most you can; accustom yourself by degrees to this small but holy exercise; nobody perceives it, and nothing is easier to repeat it [brief prayers] often in the day. Think of God the most you can in the manner here directed; it is very fir? and most necessary for a soldier, who is daily exposed to dangers of life, and often of his salvation.

BROTHER LAWRENCE

# Hoping and Praying, Part 1

*My son, be strong in the grace*
*that is in Christ Jesus.*
2 TIMOTHY 2:1 NIV

Prayers often reflect the hope of the one praying. Thomas More prayed the following in the shadow of his beheading for opposing the divorce of King Henry the VIII from Catherine of Aragon.

Good and gracious Lord, as You give me grace to acknowledge my sins, so give me grace in both my words and heart to repent them and utterly forsake them. Glorious God, give me Your grace to turn my back on the things of this world and fix my heart solely on You.

Give me Your grace to amend my life, so that I can approach death without resentment knowing in You it is the gateway to eternal riches. Take from me all sinful fear, all sinful sorrow and self-pity, all sinful hope and all sinful desire. Instead give me such fear, such sorrow, such pity, such hope, and such desire as may be profitable for my soul.

Good Lord, give me this grace, in all my fear and agony, to find strength in that great fear and agony which You had on the Mount of Olives before Your passion. Take from me all desire for worldly praise and all emotions of anger and revenge. Give me a humble, lowly, quiet, peaceable, patient, generous, kind, tender, and compassionate mind.

Grant me, good Lord, a full faith, a firm hope, and a fervent love, that I may desire only that which gives You pleasure and conforms to Your will. And above all, look upon me with Your love and Your favor.

THOMAS MORE

# Hoping and Praying, Part 2

*Prepare your minds for action.*
1 PETER 1:13 NIV

It's a risky thing to pray and the danger is that our very prayers get between God and us. The great thing is not to pray but to go directly to God. There is no such thing as a kind of prayer in which you do absolutely nothing. If you are doing nothing you are not praying.

Prayer is the movement of trust, of gratitude, of adoration, or of sorrow, that places us before God, seeing both Him and ourselves in the light of His infinite truth, and moves us to ask Him for the mercy, the spiritual strength, the material help that we all need.

The man [or woman] whose prayer is so pure that he never asks God for anything does not know who God is, and does not know who he is himself: for he does not know his own need of God.

All true prayer somehow confesses our absolute dependence on the Lord of life and death. It is, therefore, a deep and vital contact with Him whom we know not only as Lord but as Father. It is when we pray truly that we really are. Our being is brought to a high perfection by this.

THOMAS MERTON

# Hoping and Praying, Part 3

*Even though I walk through*
*the valley of the shadow of death,*
*I will fear no evil, for you are with me.*
PSALM 23:4 NIV

When hope is shaky:

❧

My Lord God, I have no idea where I am going.

I do not see the road ahead of me.

I cannot know for certain where it will end.

Nor do I really know myself, and the fact that I think that I am following your

Will does not mean that I am actually doing so.

But I believe that the desire to please you does in fact please you.

And I hope I have that desire in all that I am doing.

I hope that I will never do anything apart from that desire.

And I know that if I do this you will lead me by the right road though I may know nothing about it.

Therefore will I trust you always though I may seem to be lost and in the shadow of death.

I will not fear, for you are ever with me, and you will never leave me to face my perils alone.

THOMAS MERTON

# Hoping and Praying, Part 4

*Faith by itself,
if it is not accompanied by action, is dead.*

JAMES 2:17 NIV

The London-based missionary to Africa, David Livingstone, kept a
journal throughout his ministry preaching, teaching, researching,
praying, and sharing hope.

❧

1816: It is well known that if one of a troop of lions is killed,
the others take the hint and leave that part of the country. So,
the next time the herds were attacked of lions, I went with the
people, in order to give them hope and encourage them to rid
themselves of the annoyance by destroying one of the maraud-
ers. We found the lions on a small hill about a quarter of a mile
in length.

A circle of men was formed around the hill. Being down
below on the plain with a native schoolmaster named Mebalwe,
I saw one of the lions sitting on rock within the now closed circle of men. Mebalwe fired at him and the ball struck the rock on
which the lion was sitting. The men were afraid to attack him,
perhaps on account of their belief in witchcraft. When the circle was reformed, we saw two other lions in it; but we were
afraid to fire lest we should strike the men, so they allowed the
beasts to burst through and escape.

*Later in the journal Livingstone tells the reader that the Bechuana
men have lost face in a maneuver of this sort. While the Bechuanas
have no word for "hope," their language reflects that Christian
quality with the legendary characteristics of the lion, king of thesa-
vannah—that is, focused, keen, clear eyed, and anticipatory.*

DAVID LIVINGSTONE

# Hoping and Praying, Part 5

*There is hope only for the living.*
*For as they say,*
*"It is better to be a live dog than a dead lion!"*
ECCLESIASTES 9:4 NLT

Livingstone's optimism and clear-eyed hope was tested in this "missionary story" found in his journal.

✌

1816: I heard a shout. Startled, I looked half around and saw the lion just in the act of springing on me. I was upon a little raised spot; he caught my shoulder as he sprang, and we both came to the ground below together. Growling horribly close to my ear, he shook me as a terrier dog does a rat.

Turning around to relieve myself of the weight—he had one paw on the back of my head—I saw his eyes directed to teacher Mebalwe, who was trying to shoot the lion from a distance of ten or fifteen yards. His flint gun misfired in both barrels; the lion immediately left me, and attacking the teacher, bit his thigh. Another man attempted to spear the lion while he was biting Mebalwe. He left Mebalwe and caught this man by the shoulder, but at that moment, the bullets he had received took effect, and he fell down dead. That carcass was declared to be the largest lion they had ever seen.

And me? Besides crunching the bone into splinters, he left eleven teeth wounds on my upper arm. As the men came to express their pity for me, I quoted Ecclesiastes 9:4.

DAVID LIVINGSTONE

# Hoping and Praying, Part 6

> "A farmer went out to sow his seed.
> As he was scattering the seed,
> some fell along the path. . . .
> Some fell on rocky places. . . .
> Still other seed fell on good soil,
> where it produced a crop."
>
> MATTHEW 13:3–8 NIV

Hope and optimism are splashed over every page of David Livingstone's journal. The conversion of one Sechele, a tribal chief, consumes many pages of the missionary's notebooks.

When he at last applied for baptism, I simply asked him how he, having the Bible in his hand and able to read it, thought he ought to act. He went home, gave each of his superfluous wives new clothing and all his own goods which they kept in their huts for him, and sent them to their parents with an intimation that he had no fault to find with them, but that in parting with them he wished to follow the will of God.

On the day Sechele and his children were baptized, great numbers came to see the ceremony. All the friends and families of the divorced wives became the opponents of our religion. The attendance at school and church diminished to very few besides the chief's own family. They all treated us with respectful kindness, but to Sechele himself they said things which, if they had said in former days, would have cost them their lives.

It was trying, after all we had done, to see our labors so little appreciated; but we had sown the good seed and have every hope it will yet spring up.

DAVID LIVINGSTONE

# Notes of Hope

*He hath put a new song in my mouth,*
*even praise unto our God.*
PSALM 40:3 KJV

Besides theology, music is the only art capable of inducing hope and affording peace and joy of the heart like that introduced by the study of the science of divinity. The proof of this is that the Devil, the originator of despondency, anxieties, and restlessness, flees before the sound of music almost as assuredly as he does before the Word of God.

This is why the prophets preferred music before all the other arts, proclaiming the Word in psalms and hymns. My heart, which is full to overflowing, has often been solaced, encouraged, and refreshed by music when discouraged, sick, and weary.

From deepest woe I cry to Thee; Lord hear me,
 I implore Thee!
Bend down Thy gracious ear to me; I lay my sins
 before Thee.
If Thou remembrest every sin, if naught but just
 reward we win,
Could we abide Thy presence?

And thus my hope is in the Lord, and not in my own merit;
I rest upon His faithful word to them of contrite spirit,
That He is merciful and just; here is my comfort and
 my trust:
His help I wait with patience.

MARTIN LUTHER

# Matter of the Heart

*If from there you seek the LORD your God,
you will find him if you look for him with all your heart
and with all your soul.*

DEUTERONOMY 4:29 NIV

"I searched the world over for God and found Him in my heart," said Augustine. In the heart of the believer, a still small voice speaks in clearest accents, bearing "witness with our spirits that we are the children of God." That is the believer's hope. It is what gives man his vision of eternal life. It is a matter of the heart.

Nothing on earth is so heavenly as that—so like "the voices of angels singing in the silence." It is as clear as bells at eventime. It is assuring like the familiar voice of a friend beloved. The Holy Spirit speaking in the secret chambers of the heart is the climax of God's revelation to us. It is what gives us hope.

None but God can satisfy the longing of the immortal soul: The heart was made for Him. He only can fill it.

RICHARD TRENCH

# To Be Like Christ

*But we all,*
*with open face beholding as in*
*a glass the glory of the Lord,*
*are changed into the same image from glory to glory,*
*even as by the Spirit of the Lord.*

2 CORINTHIANS 3:18 KJV

I have a desire to be with Him, to see myself with Him; this is more blessed still; for, for a man to see himself in glory, this is a sight worthy seeing. Sometimes I look upon myself, and say, "Where am I now?" and do quickly return to myself again. Why am I in an evil world, a great way from heaven; in a sinful body, among devils and wicked men; sometimes benighted, sometimes beguiled, sometimes fearing, sometimes hoping, sometimes breathing, sometimes dying, and the like.

But then I turn the tables and say: "But where shall I be shortly? Where shall I see myself anon, after a few times more have passed over me?" And when I can but answer this question thus I shall see myself with Jesus Christ; this yields glory, even glory to one's spirit now: no marvel, then, if the righteous desire to be with Christ.

I have a desire to be with Christ. A sight of Jesus in the Word, some know how it will change them from glory to glory (2 Corinthians 3:18), but how then shall we be changed and filled, when we shall see him as he is? "When he shall appear, we shall be like him; for we shall see him as he is" (1 John 3:2).

JOHN BUNYAN

# The Presence of God

> *My presence shall go with thee,*
> *and I will give thee rest.*
>
> EXODUS 33:14 KJV

God's presence is the safety of a man. If God be with one, who can hurt one? As He said, "If God be for us, who can be against us?" Now, if so much safety flows from God, how safe are we when God is with us? "The beloved of the Lord," said Moses, "shall dwell in safety by him, and the Lord shall cover him all day long, and he shall dwell between his shoulders" (Deuteronomy 33:12). God's presence keeps the heart awake to joy and will make a man sing in the night (Job 35:10).

What shall I say? God's presence is renewing, transforming, seasoning, sanctifying, commanding, sweetening, and enlightening to the soul! Nothing like it in all the world; His presence supplies all wants, heals all maladies, saves from all dangers; is life in death, heaven in hell, all in all. No marvel, then, if the presence of, and communion with, God, is become the desire of the righteous man. To conclude this, by the presence of God being with us, it is known to ourselves, and to others, what we are. They are then best known to themselves. They know they are His people. Because God's presence is with them. Therefore he saith, "My presence shall go with thee, and I will give thee rest."

JOHN BUNYAN

# Duty!

*Freely you have received, freely give.*
MATTHEW 10:8 NKJV

There is perhaps, no part of Christian experience where a greater change occurs upon entering into his life hid with Christ in God, than in the matter of service.

In all the ordinary forms of Christian life, service is apt to have more or less of bondage in it; that is, it is done purely as a matter of duty, and often as a trial and a cross. Certain things, which at the first may have been a joy and a delight, become after a while weary tasks, performed faithfully, perhaps, but with much secret disinclination.

The soul finds itself saying, instead of the "May I?" of love, the "Must I?" of duty. The yoke, which was at first easy, begins to gall, and the burden feels heavy instead of light.

This may seem to some like a strong statement; but does it not present a vivid picture of some of your own experiences, dear Christian? Have you never gone to work as a slave to his daily task, believing it to be your duty and that therefore you must do it? You have known of course that this was the wrong way to feel and have been thoroughly ashamed of it.

What you need to do, then, dear Christian, is put your will over completely into the hands of your Lord. Say, "Yes, Lord, *Yes!*" and trust Him to bring your whole wishes and affections into conformity with His sweet will.

HANNAH WHITALL SMITH

# The Circle of Eternity

*The LORD my God has given me rest on every side.*

1 KINGS 5:4 NIV

Meister Eckhart is read today not for his theological content but for his mystical vision of God. He underscores maturity in the Christian life.

❧

Pay attention to what the "circle of eternity" is. The soul has three ways to God. One of them is to seek God in all creatures through multiple "pursuits" and through burning love. This is what King David of the Old Testament meant when he said, "In all things I have found rest." That is, Jesus and you, embraced once by the eternal light—that is *one thing* in the embrace of the eternal light.

The second way is a wayless way that is free and yet bound. On it we are raised up and carried without will and without form above ourselves and all things. . . This is what Christ meant when He said: "You are a happy man, Peter! Flesh and blood do not enlighten you (Matthew 16:17).

The third way is indeed called a "way," yet it means being "at home": seeing God directly in His own being. Our dear Christ says, "I am the Way, the Truth, the Life" (John 14:6).

Listen then to this wonder! How wonderful it is to be both outside and inside, to seize and to be seized, to see and at the same time too be what is seen, to hold and to be held—that is the goal where the spirit remains at rest, united with eternity.

MEISTER ECKHART

# The Chief End of Prayer

*Father. . .glorify thy Son,*
*that thy Son also may glorify thee.*
*I have glorified thee on the earth.*
*Glorify thou me with thine own self.*
JOHN 17:1, 4–5 KJV

This was Jesus' goal when He was on earth: "I seek not mine own honor: I seek the honor of Him who sent me." In such words we have the keynote of His life. The first words of His High-priestly prayer voice it: "Father glorify Thy Son, that Thy Son may glorify Thee. I have glorified Thee on earth: glorify me with thyself." His reason for asking to be taken up into the glory He had with the Father.

Let us make His aim ours. Let the glory of the Father be the link between our asking and His doing!

Jesus' words come indeed as a sharp two-edged sword, dividing the soul and the spirit, and quickly discerning the thoughts and intents of the heart. In His prayers on earth, His intercession in heaven, and His promise of an answer to our prayers, Jesus makes His first object the glory of His Father. Is this our object, too? Or are self-interest and self-will the strongest motives urging us to pray? A distinct, conscious longing for the glory of the Father must animate our prayers.

For the sake of God's glory, let us learn to pray well. When we seek our own glory among men, we make faith impossible. The surrender to God and the expectation that He will show His glory in hearing us are essential. Only he who seeks God's glory will see it in the answer to his prayer.

ANDREW MURRAY

# Contentedness

*I have learned, in whatsoever state I am,*
*therewith to be content.*

PHILIPPIANS 4:11 KJV

The story is told of a king who went into his garden one morning and found everything withered and dying. He asked the oak tree that stood near the gate what the trouble was. The old oak replied that he was sick of life and was determined to die, because he was not tall and beautiful like the pine. The pine was all out of heart because it could not bear grapes like the vine. The vine was going to throw its life away because it could not stand erect and have as fine fruit as the peach tree; and so on through the garden.

Coming to a little purple violet, the king found its bright face lifted as cheery as ever. "Well, violet, I'm glad amidst all this discouragement to find one brave little flower. You do not seem to be the least disheartened."

"No. I'm really not an important flower, but I believe that if you wanted an oak or a pine or a peach tree or a lilac, you would have planted one; but since I know you wanted a violet, I am determined to be the best violet that I can be."

They who are God's without reserve are in every situation content, for they will do only what He wills and desire to do for Him whatever He desires them to do and be. They strip themselves of everything and in this nakedness find all things restored one hundred fold.

CHARLES H. SPURGEON

# The Fullness of Joy

*You show me the path of life.*
*In your presence there is fullness of joy:*
*in your right hand are pleasures forevermore.*
PSALM 16:11 NRSV

Just as the simple presence of the mother makes the child's joy, so does the simple fact of God's presence with us make our joy. The mother may not make a single promise to the child nor explain any of her plans or purposes, but she is, and that is enough for the child. The child rejoices in the mother; not in her promises, but in herself. And to the child, there is, behind all that changes and can change, the one unchangeable joy of mother's existence. While the mother lives, the child will be cared for; and the child knows this instinctively if not intelligently and rejoices in knowing it.

And to the children of God as well, there is, behind all that changes and can change, the one unchangeable joy that God is. And while He is, His children will be cared for, and they ought to know it and rejoice in it. For what else can God do, being what He is? Neglect, indifference, forgetfulness, ignorance are all impossible to Him. He knows everything. He cares about everything. He can manage everything, and He loves us! Surely this is enough for a "fullness of joy" beyond the power of words to express; no matter what else may be missed besides.

HANNAH WHITALL SMITH

# *God Cares*

*So do not worry, saying,*
*"What shall we eat?" or*
*"What shall we drink?" or*
*"What shall we wear?". . .*
*Your heavenly Father knows that you need them.*

MATTHEW 6:31–32 NIV

In this and the previous selections, Hannah Smith (1832–1911) writes with the tenderest of pens and hearts. Every believer ought to read *The Christian's Secret of a Happy Life*.

Who is the best cared for in every household? Is it not the little children? And does not the least of all, the helpless baby receive the largest share? We all know that the baby toils not, neither does he spin; and yet he is fed and clothed and loved and rejoiced in more tenderly than the hardest worker of them all.

This life of faith, then, consists in just this—being a child in the Father's house. And when this is said, enough is said to transform every weary, burdened life into one of blessedness and rest.

Let the ways of childish confidence and freedom from care, which so please you and win your hearts in your own little ones, teach you what should be your ways with God; and, leaving yourself in His hands, learn to be literally "careful for nothing"; and you shall find it to be a fact that the peace of God which passes all understanding shall keep your heart and mind through Christ Jesus.

HANNAH WHITALL SMITH

# All for Good

*We know that in all things
God works for the good of those who love him,
who have been called according to his purpose.*

ROMANS 8:28 NIV

How wonderful is the providence of God in overruling things most disorderly and in turning to our good things which in themselves are most pernicious! We marvel at His mighty power, which holds the heavenly bodies in their orbits. We wonder at the continually recurring seasons and the renewal of the earth. But this is not nearly so marvelous as His bringing good out of evil in all the complicated occurrences of human life and making even the power and malice of Satan with the naturally destructive tendency of His works to minister good for His children.

"All things work together for good." This must be so for three reasons. First, because all things are under the absolute control of the Governor of the universe. Second, because God desires our good, and nothing but our good. Third, because even Satan himself cannot touch a hair of our heads without God's permission, and then only for our good.

Not all things are good in themselves, not in their tendencies; but God makes all things work for our good. Nothing enters our life by blind chance, nor are there any accidents. Everything is being moved by God, with this end in view—our good. Everything being subservient to God's eternal purpose works blessing to those marked out for conformity to the image of the Firstborn. All suffering, sorrow, and loss are used by our Father to minister to the benefit of believers.

A. W. PINK

# *Enjoying God*

> *If then you were raised with Christ,*
> *seek those things which are above, where Christ is,*
> *sitting at the right hand of God.*
> *Set your mind on things above, not on things on the earth.*
> *For you died, and your life is hidden with Christ in God.*
> *When Christ who is our life appears,*
> *then you also will appear with Him in glory.*
>
> COLOSSIANS 3:1–4 NKJV

God is the highest good of the reasonable creature; and the enjoyment of Him is the only happiness with which our souls can be satisfied. To go to heaven to enjoy God is infinitely better than the most pleasant accommodations here. Fathers and mothers, husbands, wives, or children, or the company of earthly friends, are but shadows; but the enjoyment of God is the substance.

These are but scattered beams, but God is the sun. These are streams, but God is the fountain. These are but drops, but God is the ocean. Therefore it becomes us to spend this life only as a journey toward heaven, as it becomes us to make the seeking of our highest end and proper good—the whole work of our lives, to which we should subordinate all other concerns of life.

Why should we labor for or set our hearts on anything else but that which is our proper end and true happiness?

A traveler is not wont to rest in what he meets with, however comfortable and pleasing the road. If he passes through pleasant places, flowery meadows, or shady groves, he does not take up his contentment in these things, but only takes a transient view of them as he goes along his way. He is not enticed by fine appearances to put off the thought of what is ahead in life.

JONATHAN EDWARDS

# Hope in God's Will

*I have come to do your will, O God.*
HEBREWS 10:7 NIV

That is what we are here for—to do God's will. That is the object of your life and mine—to do God's will. Our purpose here is not to be happy or to be successful or famous or to do the best we can and get on honestly in the world. It is something far higher than this—to do God's will. There at the very outset, is the great key to life. Any one of us can tell in a moment whether our lives are right or not. Are we doing God's will? We do not mean we are doing God's work—preaching or teaching or collecting money, but God's will.

People may think they are doing God's work, when they are not even doing God's will. And a man may be doing God's work and God's will every bit by hewing stones or sweeping streets, as by preaching or praying.

So the question is just this: Are we working out our common everyday life on the great lines of God's will? This is different from the world's modeled life, which is; "I came to push my way." This is the world's way of doing it. "Not my way, not my will, but Thine be done." This is the Christian's way.

HENRY DRUMMOND

# An Unplugged Life, Part 1

*Do not put out the Spirit's fire.*
1 THESSALONIANS 5:19 NIV

Out in Colorado they tell of a little town nestled down at the foot of some hills—a sleepy-hollow village. Because rainfall is very slight out there, they depend upon irrigation. But some enterprising citizen ran a pipe up the hills to a lake of clear, sweet water. As a result the town enjoyed a bountiful supply of water the year round without being dependent upon the doubtful rainfall. And the population increased and the place had quite a western boom.

One morning the housewives turned the water spigots, but no water came. The men climbed the hill. There was the lake as full as ever. They examined the pipes, but could find no break. Try as they might, they could find no cause for the stoppage. As the days moved into weeks, people began moving away again; grass grew in the streets, and the prosperous town was returning to its sleepy condition.

One day the town officials received a note. It was poorly written, with bad spelling and poor grammar. It said in effect, "Ef you'll jes pull the plug outta the pipe jes eight inches from the top, you'll git your water back."

Up they went to the top of the hill and examined the pipe. They found the plug, which some vicious tramp had inserted. Not a very big plug—just big enough to fill the pipe.

(To be continued)

S. D. GORDON

# An Unplugged Life, Part 2

*Do not put out the Spirit's fire.*
1 THESSALONIANS 5:19 NIV

When the village fathers found the small plug, one of them commented, "It's surprising how a large reservoir of water can be held back by this small plug." Out came the plug and down came the water and by-and-by back came the people, and prosperity once again reigned.

Why is there such a lack of power in our lives? The reservoir up yonder is full to overflowing with clear, sweet, life-giving water. And here all around us the earth is so dry, so thirsty, cracked open. And the connecting pipes between the reservoir above and the parched plain below are all in place.

Why then do not the refreshing waters come rushing down? The answer is very plain. You know why? *There is a plug in the pipe.* Something in us is clogging up the channel and nothing can get through. How shall we have power, abundant, life-giving, sweetening our own lives, and changing those whose lives we touch?

The answer is easy for me to give—it will be much harder for us all to do—*pull out the plug.* Get out the things that you know is hindering.

S. D. GORDON

# The Promise of Hope

*But if we hope for what we do not yet have,*
*we wait for it patiently.*

ROMANS 8:25 NIV

We are expecting that one of these days, if the chariot and horses of fire do not stop at our door, our dear Lord and Savior will fulfill His promise to us, "If I go and prepare a place for you, I will come again, and receive you unto myself; that where I am, there ye may be also" (John 14:3).

To a true believer in Jesus, the thought of departing from this world and going to be "forever with the Lord," has no gloom associated with it. Heaven is our home. We are longing for the great reunion with our beloved Lord, from whom we shall then never be separated.

I cannot attempt to depict the scene when He introduces us to the principalities and powers in heavenly places and invites us to sit with Him. Surely then, the holy angels, who have never sinned, will unite in exclaiming, "Behold, how He loved them!" It is a most blessed thought, to my mind, that we may be up there before the hands of that clock complete another round. If not that soon, it will not be long before all of us who love the Lord will be with Him where He is. Then the last among us shall know more of His love than the greatest of us can ever know while here below.

CHARLES H. SPURGEON

# *Pure Hope*

*Everyone who has this hope in him purifies himself,*
*just as he is pure.*
1 JOHN 3:3 NIV

The apostle urges the engagement of these sons of God to the prosecution of holiness: "Everyone who has this hope in him purifies himself, just as he is pure." The sons of God know their Lord is holy and pure. He is pure, heart and eyes, and will not permit any pollution or impurity to dwell within Him.

Those who hope to live with Him must turn their backs on the absolute impurity from the world and flesh and sin. They must grow in grace and holiness. Not only does their Lord command them to do so, but their new nature inclines them so to do. Yes, their hope of heaven will dictate and constrain them to do so.

The sons of God know that their High Priest is holy, harmless, and undefiled. They know that their God and Father is the High and Holy One, that His people are pure and holy, that their inheritance is an inheritance of saints. It is a contradiction to such hope to indulge in sin and impurity.

Therefore, as we are sanctified by faith, we must be sanctified by hope. So that we may be saved by hope, we must be purified by hope.

MATTHEW HENRY

# God's Provision

*"Therefore I tell you, do not worry about your life,*
*what you will eat or drink;*
*or about your body, what you will wear.*
*Is not life more important than food,*
*and the body more important than clothes?*
*Look at the birds of the air;*
*they do not sow or reap or store away in barns,*
*and yet your heavenly Father feeds them.*
*Are you not much more valuable than they?"*

MATTHEW 6:25–26 NIV

Does not God provide for all the birds and beasts and fishes? Do not the sparrows fly from their bush and every morning find meat where they laid it not? Do not the young ravens call to God, and He feeds them? And were it reasonable that the sons of the family should fear the father would give meat to the chickens and the servants, his sheep and his dogs, but none to them? He would be a very ill father that should do so; or he would be a very foolish son who would think his father would do so.

Besides the reasonableness of this faith and this hope, we have infinite experience of it. How innocent, how careless, how secure, is infancy. And yet how certainly provided for. We have lived at God's charges all the days of our life, and hitherto He has not failed us. We have no reason to be wary about the future. God has given us His Holy Spirit; He has promised heaven to us; He has given us His Son; and we are taught from the scriptures.

Our lesson is this: How should not He with Him give us all things else?

JEREMY TAYLOR

# Rules to Govern Our Hope

*The man who plants and the man who waters*
*have one purpose, and each will be rewarded*
*according to his own labor.*
*For we are God's fellow workers;*
*you are God's field, God's building.*

1 CORINTHIANS 3:8–9 NIV

Let your hope be moderate, proportioned to your state, person, and condition—whether it be gifts or graces or temporal favors. It is an ambitious hope for persons, whose diligence is like them that are least in the kingdom of heaven, to believe themselves endeared to God as the greatest saints. That they shall have a throne equal to St. Paul or the Virgin Mary.

A stammer cannot, with moderation, hope for the gift tongues; or a peasant to become learned as Origen. Or if a beggar desires to become a king or asks for a wealthy stipend, we call him impudent or less than reasonable.

God will crown your endeavors with hope, the reward that He freely gives according to our proportions. Hope is given for good success according to the efficacy of the causes and the instrument. Let the husbandman hope for a good harvest, not for a rich kingdom or a victorious army.

Therefore, let your hope be patient, without tediousness of spirit or hastiness of prefixing time. Make no limits on God. Let your prayers and endeavors continue with a constant belief in the providence of God. Continue going forward with hope.

JEREMY TAYLOR

# Invitations

*I am the gate;*
*whoever enters through me will be saved.*
*He will come in and go out, and find pasture.*

JOHN 10:9 NIV

There are many sweet invitations to sinners in the Bible; I have often felt these words to be the sweetest. There are some invitations addressed to those who are thirsty. It is said in Isaiah, "Ho, every one who thirsts, come to the waters" (Isaiah 55:1). There are some invitations to those who have a burden, "Come to me all you that labor and are heavy laden, and I will give you rest" (Matthew 11:28). There are some invitations to prisoners; "I have given you a covenant: to bring out the prisoners from the dungeons" (Isaiah 42:6–7).

But the sweetest invitation of all is; "If any man. . ." (note, it does not say, any thirsty man, any weary man, any burdened man), but it does say, if *any* man enters in, he shall saved. I have seen some rich men's doors, where none could enter unless he is wealthy. But Christ's door is open to the poor—to any man, whatever your life, whatever your character may be.

Christ is not like the door to some churches, where none can enter but the socially elite. Christ's door is wide open to the poor. "To the poor the gospel is preached." Some, perhaps, can say, "I am the most vile one in this congregation," yet Christ says, "Enter in." Someone may say, "I have been the worst of sinners"; and what does Jesus Christ say?—"Enter in."

ROBERT MURRAY MCCHEYNE

# Exceeding Fruitfulness

*And God Almighty bless thee,*
*and make thee fruitful,*
*and multiply thee,*
*that thou mayest be a multitude of people.*
GENESIS 28:3 KJV

Years ago you thought you could effect something in your life. You had energy, genius, the grace of oratory, the power of personal attraction, and fascination. You used to be able to sway people; people gathered around you and recognized their born leader. Perhaps you could organize effectively and efficiently. Beneath your word and deft hand all rabble would fall into rank and become a disciplined army. You had the facility of selection—intrepid courage, wise counsel, quick sympathy.

But all this is over now. You are compelled reluctantly to confess that the total residue is disappointing, so you are coming to think that the remainder of your life will never rise above the dead levels of the past, will never achieve any large success for God, will never be fruitful.

"But, I will do my best," you say, "building up believers. If I am unable to perform great feats of winning the ungodly, I can train children, I can share my faith, I can be a channel of love."

To people like this, God comes with His assurance; "I am able to make thee exceeding fruitful."

"Walk before Me, and be thou perfect" (Genesis 17:1).

This is the one prime and irreversible condition for the life which shall become fruitful.

Have we conformed to it?

Then take heart, for it is to such that God says, "I will make thee exceeding fruitful" (Genesis 17:6).

F. B. MEYER

# *Peace Within*

*You will keep in perfect peace
him whose mind is steadfast,
because he trusts in you.*

ISAIAH 26:3 NIV

If you sometimes fall, do not lose heart or cease striving to make progress, for even out of your fall, God will bring good; just as a man selling an antidote will drink poison before he takes it in order to prove its power.

If nothing else could show us what wretched creatures we are and what harm we do to ourselves by dissipating our desires, this war that goes on within us would be sufficient to do so and lead us back to recollection. Can any evil be greater than the evil we find in ourselves? What hope can we have of being able to rest in others, if we cannot rest in ourselves?

None of our friends and relatives are as near to us as our own personal selves. Whether we like it or not, there are times when even our personal faculties seem to be making war upon us, as if they were resentful of the war made upon them by our personal vices.

"Peace, peace," said the Lord; words He spoke many times to His apostles. Unless we are at peace and strive for peace within ourselves, we shall not find it in others. Let this war cease. By the blood that Christ shed for us, I beg this of those who have not begun to enter within themselves. Those who have begun to do so must not allow such warfare to turn them back. Let them place their trust, not in themselves, but in the mercy of God.

TERESA OF AVILA

# Some Serious Questions

*Your attitude should be the same as
that of Christ Jesus.*
PHILIPPIANS 2:5 NIV

What is your hope? Some of you hope for an education, some of you for fame, some for respectable connections in society; but have you the Christian's hope? If you have, then your heart is set upon being like Christ. Is it so? Is your heart thus set? Does your hope beget most earnest strivings to be like Christ? You have some religious hope of some sort—but is it a true Christian's hope? Many people are so in the dark, they hold on to a hope, supposing it all right, when in the light of the Bible, there is not the first element of a Christian hope in it. Their hope is their curse and their ruin.

No good hope can be kept secret. Some people talk of having a secret hope and speak of others as having a secret hope. The fact is, a hope that can be kept secret, shows itself to be poor and vain. For if it were a good hope, it would lead its professor to purify himself. No man can throw the energies of his being into the struggle after Christian purity and still keep his faith a secret. The world will know him; Christian brethren will feel the warmth of his heart.

CHARLES G. FINNEY

# No Hope-So Witness

> Jesus replied, "Blessed are you,
> Simon son of Jonah,
> for this was not revealed to you by man,
> but by my Father in heaven."
>
> MATTHEW 16:17 NIV

We believe in salvation *here* and *now*. There are *think-so* Christians, and there are *hope-so* Christians, and there are *know-so* Christians. My brethren, if you have salvation, you are sure of it.

Our work is salvation. We believe in salvation and we have salvation. We are not mere sentimentalists or theory people. We publish what we have heard and seen and handled and experienced in the world of life and the power of God. We aim at salvation. We hold out hope. Soul-saving is our vocation, the great purpose and business of our lives. Look at this. Clear your vision. Halt, stand still and fully comprehend your calling. *You* are to be a worker together with God for the salvation of your fellow men. What is the business of your life? Not merely to save your soul and make yourself ready for Paradise.

No, you are to be a redeemer, a savior, a copy of Jesus Christ Himself. So consecrate every awakened power to the great end of saving men. Rescue the perishing. They are all around you, everywhere, crowds upon crowds, multitudes. Be skillful. Improve yourself. Study your business. Be self-sacrificing. Remember the Master. What you lose for His sake, you shall find again. Stick to it. Having put your hand to the salvation plough, don't look behind you.

WILLIAM BOOTH

# Hope for You in Pain

*By His stripes we are healed.*
ISAIAH 53:5 NKJV

To one who is in great pain, God is the Physician of body and of soul. I do not pray that you may be delivered from your pains; but I pray to God earnestly that He would give you strength and patience to bear them as long as He pleases. Comfort yourself with Him who holds you. He will relive you when He sees fit. Happy are those who suffer with Him. Accustom yourself to suffer in that manner, and seek from Him the strength to endure.

The people of the world do not understand the truth of suffering, since they suffer like what they are, and not like Christians. They consider sickness as a pain to their natural body, and not as a favor from God. The world finds nothing in it but grief and distress, but we who know God consider our sickness as a condition understood by God. I wish I could convince you that God is often (in some sense) nearer to us and more effectually present with us, in sickness than in health. Then put all your trust in Him, and you will soon find the effects of it in your recovery, which we often retard by putting greater confidence in a physician than in God.

Comfort yourself with the sovereign Physician both of soul of body.

BROTHER LAWRENCE

# The Spirit of Expectation

*"Yes, I am coming soon."*
REVELATION 22:20 NIV

The believer who abides closely in Christ will share with Him in this spirit of expectation. Not so much for the increase of personal happiness, but from the spirit of enthusiastic allegiance to his King. He longs to see Him come in His glory, reigning over every enemy, the full revelation of God's everlasting love. "Till He come," is the watchword of every truehearted believer. "Christ shall appear and we shall appear with Him in glory."

There may be very serious differences in the exposition of the promises of His coming. To one it is plain as day that He is coming very speedily in person to reign on earth, and that speedy coming is his hope and his stay. To another, loving his Bible and his Savior not less, the coming can mean nothing but the judgment day—the solemn transition from time to eternity, the close of history on earth, the beginning of heaven; and the thought of that manifestation of his Savior's glory is no less his joy and his strength. It is Jesus, Jesus is coming again; Jesus is taking us to Himself. Jesus, who is adored as Lord of all.

It is by abiding in Christ that the believer will be quickened to that truly spiritual looking for His coming.

ANDREW MURRAY

# In the Evil Day

*Thou art my hope in the day of evil.*
JEREMIAH 17:17 KJV

The path of the Christian is not always bright with sunshine; he has his seasons of darkness and of storm. True, it is written in God's Word, "Her ways are ways of pleasantness, and all her paths are peace." That is a great truth. Since religion is calculated to give a man happiness here as well as bliss above, but experience tells us that if the course of the just be "as the shining light that shines more and more unto the perfect day," sometimes that light is eclipsed.

At certain periods clouds cover the believer's sun, and he walks in darkness and sees no light. There are many who have rejoiced in the presence of God for a season; they have basked in the sunshine in the earlier stages of their Christian career; they have walked along the "green pastures" by the side of the "still waters," but suddenly they find the sky is clouded. The best of God's saints must drink the wormwood; the dearest of His children must bear the cross. No Christian has enjoyed perpetual prosperity.

Perhaps the Lord allotted you at first a smooth and unclouded path, because you were weak and timid. He tempered the wind for the little lamb, but now that you are stronger in your spiritual life, you must enter into the rougher experience of God's full-grown children. We need winds and tempests to exercise our faith to root us more firmly in Christ. The day of evil reveals to us the value of our glorious hope.

CHARLES H. SPURGEON

# Hope in Our Mediator

*There is one God and one mediator
between God and men,
the man Christ Jesus.*
1 TIMOTHY 2:5 NIV

We could not be redeemed, even though the one Mediator between God and man is Man himself, Christ Jesus, and He is also God! When Adam was created, being made an upright man, there was no need for a mediator. Once sin entered, however, it widely separated the human race from God, it was necessary for a mediator, who alone was born, lived, and was put to death without sin, to reconcile us to God and provide even for our bodies a resurrection to life eternal—and all this in order that man's pride might be exposed and healed through God's humility.

Thus, it might be shown man how far he had departed from God, when by the incarnate God he is recalled to God that man in his will resistance might be furnished an example of obedience by the God-Man, that the fount of grace might be opened up, that even the resurrection of the body—itself promised to the redeemed—might be previewed in the Resurrection of the Redeemer Himself, that the devil might be vanquished by that very nature he was rejoicing over having deceived. All this, however, with giving man ground for glory in himself, lest pride spring up anew.

AUGUSTINE

# Some Tough Words

*Our prayer is for your perfection.*
2 CORINTHIANS 13:9 NIV

Some of you have a hope, which, instead of leading to a holy life, makes you quiet and easy in your sins. It does not tend at all to make you purify yourselves from sin, but to the contrary, it makes you careless and dead in your sins. You know you live in sin, yet you have a hope that you shall be saved at last. Is it not a fact on the very face of it, that your hope is bad, and that your soul is on its way to hell? It has precisely the opposite influence to what it should have; it works more sin rather than more holiness; it fits you for hell—not for heaven; yet you hold on to it as if it were your very life. Do you not see that it must inevitably drown your soul in destruction?

It helps you to live careless and prayerless. It impels you after everything else but Christ. Surely you must see that it is leading down to hell! Unless you abandon it, you can never be saved! What good can this false hope do for you? You may just as well have a good hope, in a glorious gospel—a hope that shall purify your heart and lift you upward to heaven. Why will you have the counterfeit, while the good coin can be had just as well and as cheap? Why cleave to delusion and death, when the truth is free, and eternal life in Christ comes without money and without price?

CHARLES G. FINNEY

# Ark of Salvation

*The LORD then said to Noah,*
*"Go into the ark, you and your whole family,*
*because I have found you righteous in this generation."*
GENESIS 7:1 NIV

Suppose that after the ark was completed God said to Noah, "Now, get eight spikes of iron and drive them into the side of the ark." So Noah procured the spikes and did as he was bidden. The word came to him, "Come, you and all your household, and hang on to these spikes." So Noah and his wife, and the three sons and their wives, each held on to a spike. And the rains descended and the flood came, and as the ark was borne up on the waters their muscles were strained to the uttermost.

Imagine God saying to them, "If you hang on till the deluge is over you will be saved!" Can you even think of such a thing as any one of them going safely through?

But, oh, how different the simple Bible story. "And the Lord said to Noah, come thou and all thy house into the ark." That is a very different thing than holding on! Inside the ark they were safe as long as the ark endured the storm. And every believer in Christ is as safe as God can make him. Look away then from all self-effort and trust Him alone. Rest in the ark and rejoice in God's great salvation.

HARRY IRONSIDE

# *Exploits*

*And such as do wickedly
against the covenant
shall he corrupt by flatteries:
but the people that do know
their God shall be strong,
and do exploits.*

DANIEL 11:32 KJV

The scantiness or the fullness of your life all depends upon how large a God you have! The God of most Christians is not much larger than the dumb idol of wood or stone the heathen worships and then takes down from its pedestal and scolds if it does not answer his prayers or meet his expectations.

The God of Paul was a very glorious and mighty Being, and it was the greatness of his God that gave greatness to his character and life. He was but a vessel to receive and reflect the glory of God. "The people that do know their God shall be strong, and do exploits." The people who have learned to clothe themselves with His Almightyness are the people of enlarged vision and victorious faith. Human heroes are honored for the measure in which they have dropped out of sight and simply magnify Him. It is not Elijah, but Elijah's God that we remember. It is not Paul, but Paul's Christ who we want.

A. B. SIMPSON

# *Prisoners of Hope*

> *Turn you to the strong hold,*
> *ye prisoners of hope:*
> *even today do I declare that*
> *I will render double unto thee.*
>
> ZECHARIAH 9:12 KJV

The Jews that had returned out of captivity into their own land were, in effect, but prisoners, yet prisoners of hope or expectation, for God had given them a little reviving in their bondage. Those that yet continued in Babylon, detained by their affairs there, yet lived in hope some time or other to see their own land again.

Now both these are directed to turn their eyes upon the Messiah, set before them in the promise as their stronghold, to shelter themselves in Him and stay themselves upon Him, for the perfecting of the mercy which by His grace and for His sake, was so gloriously begun. The promise of the Messiah was the stronghold of faith long before His coming.

The prophets directed them still to turn to Christ and to comfort themselves with the joy of their King coming to them with salvation. But as their deliverance was typical of our redemption by Christ, so this invitation to the stronghold speaks the language of the gospel call.

Sinners are prisoners, but they are prisoners of hope; their case is sad, but it is not desperate. Christ is the stronghold for them, a strong tower, in whom they may be safe and quiet from the fear of the wrath of God, the curse of the law, and the assaults of the spiritual enemies. To Him they must turn by a lively faith; to Him they must flee and trust in His name.

MATTHEW HENRY

# The Little Flock

*Fear not, little flock;*
*for it is your Father's good pleasure*
*to give you the kingdom.*
LUKE 12:32 KJV

The music of the shepherd's voice. A comforting word, and how tender. His flock, a little flock, a feeble flock, a fearful flock, but a beloved flock, loved of the Father, enjoying His "good pleasure," and soon to be a glorified flock, safe in the fold, secure within the kingdom. How does He quiet their fears and misgivings? As they stand panting on the bleak mountainside, He points His crook upward to the bright and shining gates of glory and says, "It is your Father's good pleasure to give you these." What gentle words! What a blessed consummation! Gracious Savior, Your gentleness has made me great.

Believers, think of this: "It is your Father's good pleasure." The Good Shepherd, in leading you across the intervening mountains, shows you signals and memorials of paternal grace. Let the melody of the Shepherd's voice fall gently on your ear— "It is your Father's good pleasure." *I have given you,* He seems to say, *the best proof that it is mine. In order for you to have that kingdom, I died for you!*

"As a shepherd seeks out his flock in the day that He is among his sheep that are scattered," says God, "so I will seek out my sheep and will deliver them out of all places where they have been scattered in the cloudy and dark day."

JOHN MACDUFF

# Faith and Hope

*Faith is the substance of things hoped for,
the evidence of things not seen.*

HEBREWS 11:1 KJV

Faith and hope go together; and the same things that are the object of our hope are the object of our faith. It is a firm persuasion and expectation that God will perform all that He has promised to us in Christ. This persuasion is so strong that it gives the soul a kind of possession and presents the fruit of those things. It gives them a subsistence in the soul.

Christ dwells in the soul by faith, and the soul is filled with the fullness of God, as far as his present measure will admit. He experiences a substantial reality in the objects of faith. Faith demonstrates to the mind's eye the reality of those things that cannot be discerned by the body's eye.

Faith is the firm assent of the soul to the divine revelation, and every part of it sets to its seal that God is true. It is a full approbation of all that God has revealed as holy, just, and good. It helps the soul to make application of all to itself with suitable affections and endeavors; and so it is designed to serve the believer instead of sight and to be to the soul all that the senses are to the body.

MATTHEW HENRY

# The Pure Heart

*Who may ascend the hill of the LORD?*
*Who may stand in his holy place?*
*He who has clean hands and a pure heart.*
PSALM 24:3–4 NIV

If your desire and aim is to reach the destination of the path and home of true happiness, of grace and glory by a straight and safe way, then earnestly apply your mind to seek constant purity of heart, clarity of mind, and calmness of the senses. Gather up your heart's desire and fix it continually on the Lord God above. To do so, you must withdraw yourself as far as you can from friends and from everyone else and from the activities that hinder you from such a purpose. Grasp every opportunity when you can find the place, time, and means to devote yourself to silence and contemplation and gathering the secret fruits of silence, so that you can escape the shipwreck of this present age and avoid the restless agitation of the noisy world.

Simplify your heart with all care, diligence, and effort so that, still and at peace, you can remain always in the Lord within, as if your mind were already in the now of eternity. In this way you will be able to commit yourself completely and fully to God in all difficulties and eventualities and be willing to submit yourself patiently to His will and good pleasure at all times.

There can be no greater happiness than to place one's all in Him who lacks nothing. Cast yourself, all of yourself, with confidence into God and He will sustain you, heal you, and make you safe.

ALBERT THE GREAT

# The Foundation of Hope

*For you have been my hope,*
*O Sovereign LORD,*
*my confidence since my youth.*
*From birth I have relied on you.*

PSALM 71:5–6 NIV

Let your hope be well-founded, relying upon just confidence; that is, upon God, according to His revelation and promises. For it is possible for a man to have a vain hope in God. And in matters of religion, it is presumptuous to hope that God's mercies will be poured forth upon lazy persons who do nothing toward holy and strict walking.

Rely not in temporal things based upon uncertain prophecies and astrology, not upon our own wit or industry, not upon gold or friends, not upon armies and princes. Expect not health from physicians who cannot cure their own breath, much less than their mortality.

Use all lawful instruments, but expect nothing from them above their natural or ordinary efficacy, and, in the use of them, from God expect a blessing. A hope that is easy and creditable is an arm of flesh, an ill support without a bone.

"O Sovereign Lord, my confidence since my youth. . .I have relied on you."

JEREMY TAYLOR

# Walk Close to Christ

*So walk in Him.*
COLOSSIANS 2:6 NKJV

If we have received Christ in our inmost hearts, our new life will manifest its intimate acquaintance with Him by a walk of faith in Him. Walking implies action. Our religion is not to be confined to our closet; we must carry it out into practical effect that which we believe. If a man walks in Christ, he then acts as Christ would act; for Christ being in him, his hope, his love, his joy, his life—he is the reflection of the image of Jesus, causing people to say, "He is like his Master."

Walking signifies progress. Proceed from grace to grace; run forward until you reach the uttermost degree of knowledge about our beloved Lord that a person can attain. Walking implies continuance. There must be a perpetual abiding in Christ. How many Christians think that in the morning and evening they ought to come into the company of Jesus and may then give their hearts to the world all day; but this is poor living. We should always be with Him, treading in His steps and doing His will.

Walking also implies habit. When we speak of a person's walk and conversation, we mean habits—the constant tenor of his life. Now, if we sometimes enjoy Christ and then forget him through the day; sometimes we call Him ours, and then we lose our hold. That is not a habit; we are not walking in Him. We must keep to Him, cling to Him, never let Him go. That is, live and have our being in Him.

CHARLES H. SPURGEON

# The Vision

*Blessed are the pure in heart;*
*for the shall see God.*

MATTHEW 5:8 KJV

Here is heaven! This word of Jesus represents the future state of the glorified to consist not in locality, but in character; the essence of its bliss is the full vision and fruition of God. Our attention is called from all vague and indefinite theories about future happiness. The one grand object of contemplation—the glory which excels—is the sight of God himself. The one grand practical lesson enforced on His people is the cultivation of that purity of heart without which no one can enjoy God—now and in the future life.

Reader, have you attained any of this heart purity? It has been beautifully said that "the openings of the streets of heaven are on earth." Even here we may enjoy, in the possession of holiness, some foretaste of coming bliss. Who has not felt that the happiest moments of their lives were those of close walking with God—nearness to the mercy seat—when self was surrendered and the eye was directed to the glory of Jesus, with most single, unwavering, undivided aim?

What will heaven be but the entire surrender of the soul to Him, without any bias to evil, without the fear of corruption within echoing to temptation without; every thought brought into captivity to the obedience of Christ; no contrariety to His mind; all in blessed unison with His will; the whole being impregnated with holiness. That means the intellect purified and ennobled, consecrating all its powers to His service.

JOHN MACDUFF

# A Hoped-For Reunion

*"I will come again,*
*and receive you to Myself;*
*that where I am,*
*there you may be also."*
JOHN 14:3 NKJV

If the meeting of a long-absent friend or brother on earth is a joyous event, what, my soul, must be the joy of your union with this Brother of brothers, our Friend of friends! "I will come again!" What an errand of love, what a promised honor and dignity it is. His saints will share not His heaven only but His immediate presence.

"Where I am, there you shall be also!" and "Father, I will that those whom you have given me, be with Me where I am." Happy reunion! Blessed Savior, if Your presence be so sweet on a sin-stricken earth, and when known only by the eye of faith, what must be that presence in a sinless heaven, unfolded in all its unutterable loveliness and glory.

Happy reunion! It will be a meeting of the whole ransomed family of God—the Head with all its members—the Vine with all its branches—the Shepherd with all His flock—the Elder Brother with all His Kinsmen. Oh, the joy, too, of mutual recognition among the death-divided, ties snapped asunder on earth, severed friendships all reunited through the triumph of love. That is love binding brother with brother and friend with friend and all to the Elder Brother.

My soul, what do you think of this heaven? Remember who it is that Jesus says shall sit with Him upon the throne—"He who overcomes."

JOHN MACDUFF

# Hope Considerations

*Satisfies your desire with good things.*
PSALM 103:5 NIV

The great Christian virtues are radiant with happiness. Faith, hope, and charity [love] have no sadness in them; and if penitence makes the heart sad, penitence belongs to the sinner, not to the saint.

We do not please God more by eating bitter aloes than by eating honey. A cloudy, foggy rainy day is not more heavenly than a day of sunshine. A funeral march is not so much like the music of the angels as the song of birds on a May morning. There is no more religion in the gaunt, naked forest in winter than in the laughing blossoms of the spring and the rich ripe fruits of autumn. It was not the pleasant things in the world that came from the devil and the dreary, dull things from God.

It was "sin brought death into the world and all our woe"; as the sin vanishes the woe will vanish, too. God Himself is the ever-blessed God. He dwells in the light of joy as well as of purity, and instead of becoming more like Him as we become more miserable, and as all the brightness and glory of life are extinguished, we become more like God as our blessedness becomes more complete.

The great Christian graces are radiant with happiness. Faith, hope, love—there is no sadness in them. Penitence makes the heart sad. Penitence belongs to the sinner, not to the saint: As we become more saintly, we have less sin to sorrow over.

R. W. DALE

# An End of Weeping

*The days of your mourning shall be ended.*
ISAIAH 60:20 NKJV

Christ's people are often a weeping band, even though there be much in this lovely world to make them joyous and happy. Yet when they think of their past and their sins—their own sins and the unblushing sins of a world in which their God is dishonored—need we wonder at their tears? Or that they should be called "mourners" and their home a "valley of tears"? Bereavement and sickness and poverty and death following the track of sin add to their mourning experience. And, with many of God's best beloved, one tear is scarce dried when another is ready to flow.

Mourners, rejoice! When the reaping time comes, the weeping time ends. When the white robes and golden harps are bestowed, every remnant of the sackcloth attire is removed. The moment the pilgrim whose forehead is here furrowed with woe, bathe it in the crystal river of life—that moment the pangs of a lifetime of sorrow are eternally forgotten. Reader, if you are one of these careworn ones, the days of your mourning are numbered. A few more throbbings of this aching heart and then the angel who proclaims "time" shall proclaim, also, sorrow and sighing and mourning to be "No more!"

Seek now to mourn your sins more than your sorrows; reserve your bitterest tears for forgetfulness of your dear Lord. The saddest and sorest of all bereavements is when the sins which have separated you from Him, evoke the anguished cry, "Where is my God?"

JOHN MACDUFF

# Imitation

*Let this mind be in you,*
*which was also in Christ Jesus.*

PHILIPPIANS 2:5 KJV

To be in Christ is to live out His ideas, character, and spirit as the atmosphere of your being. People everywhere are living in the ideas and character of others. He who lives in the spirit of Raphael becomes a painter; he who is lives in the spirit of Milton becomes a poet; he who lives in the spirit of Bacon becomes a philosopher; he who lives in the spirit of Caesar becomes a warrior. He who lives in the spirit of Jesus Christ becomes a mature person.

In the spirit of Christ, live for something outside of yourself. Do good and leave behind you a monument of virtue that the storm of time can never destroy. Write your name in kindness, love, and mercy on the hearts of thousands you come in contact with year by year; you will never be forgotten. No, your name, your deeds will be as legible on the hearts you leave behind as the stars on the brow of evening. Good deeds will shine as the star of heaven.

Is life worth living? Yes, so long as there is wrong to right, so long as lingers gloom to chase or streaming tears to dry, so long as a tale of anguish swells the heart and eyes grow wet and, at the sound God's Word, we pardon and forget. Is life worth living? Only when we are living in Christ and let Him shine through us.

THOMAS CHALMERS

# Willing Service

*Whatever you do, work at it with all your heart,*
*as working for the Lord, not for men.*
COLOSSIANS 3:23 NIV

A musician is not recommended for playing long, but for playing well; it is obeying God willingly that is accepted. The Lord hates that which is forced; it then becomes a tax instead of an offering. Cain served God grudgingly. He brought his sacrifice, not his heart.

To obey God's commandments unwillingly is like the devils who came out of the possessed man at Christ's command, albeit with reluctance and against their will. Good duties cannot be pressed and beaten out of us as the waters were beaten out of the rock when Moses smote it with the budding rod. Good duties must freely drop from us, as myrrh from the tree or honey from the comb.

If a willing mind be wanting, there wants that flower which should perfume our obedience and make it a sweet-smelling savor unto God. Someone has said that a noble deed for someone else is a step toward God.

The avaricious man is like the barren sandy ground of the desert which sucks in all the rain and dew with greed, but yields no fruitful herbs or plants for the benefit of others.

Only one life will soon be past. Only what's done for Christ will last.

THOMAS WATSON

# Hope over Discouragement

> *Why art thou down, O my soul?*
> *and why art thou disquieted within me?*
> *hope thou in God:*
> *for I shall yet praise him,*
> *who is the health of my countenance,*
> *and my God.*
>
> PSALM 42:11 KJV

If I am asked how we are to get rid of discouragement, I can only say, as I have had to say of so many other wrong spiritual habits, we must give it up. It is never worthwhile to argue against discouragement. There is only one argument that can meet it, and that is the argument of God.

When David was in the midst of what were perhaps the most discouraging moments of his life, he found his city burned and his wives stolen. He and his men wept together until they had no more power to weep; and when his men, exasperated at their misfortunes, spoke of stoning him, then we are told, "But David encouraged himself in the Lord his God." The result was a magnificent victory in which all that they had lost was more than restored to them. This always will be, and always must be, the result of a courageous faith, because faith lays hold of the omnipotence of God.

The psalmist does not analyze his disquietude or try to argue it away, but he turns at once to the Lord. Then by faith David began to praise his Lord. It was the only way. Discouragement flies where faith appears. And in the same way, faith flies when discouragement appears. We must choose between them, for they will not be mixed.

HANNAH WHITALL SMITH

# God Is Enough

*[Nothing] will be able to separate us from
the love of God that is in Christ Jesus our Lord.*
ROMANS 8:39 NIV

O doubting and sorrowful Christian hearts, in the face of all we have learned concerning the God of all comfort, consider Job and David and Paul and the saints of all ages; nothing else was needed to quiet their fears. They realized God *is*. His simple existence is all the warrant your need requires for its certain relieving.

Nothing can separate you from His love, absolutely nothing; neither death, nor life, nor angels, nor principalities, nor powers, nor things present, nor things to come, nor height, nor depth, nor any other creature. Every possible contingency is provided for here; and not one of them can separate you from the love of God that is in Christ Jesus our Lord.

After such a declaration as this, how can any of us dare question or doubt God's love? Since He loves us, He cannot exist and fail to help us. Do we not know by our own experience what an imperative necessity it is for love to pour itself out in blessing on the ones it loves; and cannot we understand that God, who is love, simply cannot help blessing us.

We do not need to beg Him to bless us. He simply cannot help it. Therefore God is enough! God is enough for time. God is enough for eternity. *God is enough!*

HANNAH WHITALL SMITH

# There's Hope in Service

*His servant will serve him.*
*They will see his face,*
*and his name will be on their foreheads.*
REVELATION 22:3–4 NIV

They shall see His face. Where? In the city. When? In eternity? No, tomorrow. Those who serve in any city cannot help but continually see Jesus. He is there with them. He is there before them. They cannot but meet face-to-face. No gentle word is ever spoken that Christ's voice does not speak also; no meek deed is ever done that the unsummoned vision does not see there and then appear. Whoever, in whatever place, receives a little child in My name receives Me.

This is how men and women and boys and girls get to know God—by doing His will. And there is no other way. This is how men become like God; how God's character becomes written upon people's character. An act reacts upon a soul. A good act makes a good person; a just act, a just person; a kind act, a kind person; a divine act, a divine person. There is no other way of becoming good, just, kind, divine. And there is no heaven for those who have not become these. For these are heaven.

When John's heaven faded from his sight and the prophet woke to the desert wastes of Patmos, did he grudge to exchange the heaven of his dreams for the common tasks around him? Was he not glad to be alive and there? Traveler to God's last city, be glad that you are alive. Be thankful for the city at your door and for the chance to build its walls a little nearer heaven before you go.

HENRY DRUMMOND

# The Unchangeable God

*Very, verily, I say unto you,*
*Before Abraham was, I am.*
JOHN 8:58 KJV

Christ adopts this name of "I am" as His own. These simple words, I am, express therefore eternity and unchangeableness of existence, which is the very first element necessary in a God who is to be depended upon. No dependence could be placed by any one of us upon a changeable God. He must be the same yesterday, today, and forever if we are to have any peace or comfort.

But is this all His name implies, simply "I am"? "I am what?" we ask. What does this "I am" include? I believe it includes everything the human heart longs for and needs. This unfinished name of God seems to me like a blank check signed by a rich friend given to us to be filled in with whatever sum we may desire. The whole Bible tells us what it means. Every attribute of God, every revelation of His character, every proof of His undying love, every declaration of His watchful care, every assertion of His purposes of tender mercies, every manifestation of His loving kindness—all are the filing out of this unfinished "I am."

God tells us through all the pages of His Book what He is. "I am," He says, "all that my people need": "I am their strength"; "I am their wisdom"; "I am their righteousness"; "I am their peace"; "I am their salvation"; "I am their life"; "I am their all in all."

HANNAH WHITALL SMITH

# *False Hope*

*If I have made gold my hope,*
*or have said to the fine gold,*
*Thou art my confidence. . .*
*this also were an iniquity to be punished by the judge:*
*for I should have denied the God that is above.*

JOB 31:24, 28 KJV

Our wealth is either advantageous or pernicious to us according as we stand affected to it. If we make it our rest and our ruler, it will be our ruin; if we make it our servant, and an instrument of righteousness, it will be a blessing to us. Job here tells us how he stood affected to his worldly wealth. He put no great confidence in it; he did not make gold his hope. They are very unwise who do and are enemies to themselves—those who depend on gold as sufficient to make them happy, who think themselves safe and honorable and sure of comfort in having an abundance of this world's goods.

Some people make gold their hope and confidence for another world, as if it were a certain token of God's favor; and those who have so much sense as not to think so, yet promise themselves that it will be a portion for them in this life, whereas the things themselves are uncertain and our satisfaction in them is much more so. The way to *weep as though we wept not is to rejoice as though we rejoiced not.* The less pleasure the enjoyment is the less pain the disappointment will be.

MATTHEW HENRY

# Hope in Times of Temptation

*God is faithful,*
*who will not allow you to be tempted beyond what you are able,*
*but with the temptation will provide the way of escape also,*
*that you may be able to endure it.*

1 CORINTHIANS 10:13 NASB

Although temptations are troublesome and grievous, yet they are often profitable to us, for by them we are humbled, cleansed, and instructed. All saints endure many trials and temptations and profit by them.

No man can be entirely free from temptation as long as he lives; for the source of temptation lies within our own nature, since we are born with an inclination toward evil. When one temptation or trial draws to a close, another takes its place; and we shall always have something to fight, for man has lost the blessing of original happiness. Many try to escape temptations, only to encounter them more fiercely, for no one can win victory by flight alone; it is only by patience and true humility that we can grow stronger than all our foes.

Little by little and by patience endurance, you will overcome by God's help, better than by your own violence and importunity. Some people undergo their heaviest temptations at the beginning of their conversion; some toward the end of their course; others are greatly troubled all their lives; while there are some whose temptations are but light.

We must not despair, therefore, when we are tempted, but earnestly pray God to grant us help in every need. So, let us humble ourselves under the hand of God in every trial and trouble, for He will save and raise up the humble in spirit.

THOMAS À KEMPIS

# Strength in Weakness

*"My strength is made perfect in weakness."*

2 CORINTHIANS 12:9 NKJV

There is almost no word that is so imperfectly understood in the Christian life as the word *weakness*. Sin and shortcoming, sluggishness and disobedience are given as the reason for our weakness. With this interpretation of weakness, the true feeling of guilt and the sincere endeavor after progress are impossible. How can I be guilty when I do not do what it is not in my power to do? The Father cannot demand of His child what he can certainly do independently. That, indeed, was done by the law under the Old Covenant. He requires nothing more of us than what He has prepared for us to do in His Holy Spirit. The new life is a life in the power of Christ through the Spirit.

Whenever the young Christian acknowledges and admits to his weakness, then he learns to understand the secret of the power of Jesus. He then sees that he is not to wait and pray to become stronger or to feel stronger. No, in his inability, he is to have the power of Jesus. By faith he is to receive it. He is to believe that it is for him and that Jesus Himself will work in him and by him.

It is wonderful how glorious that life of faith becomes for him who is content to have nothing. How glorious to feel nothing in himself and to always live on the power of his Lord. He learns to understand what a joyful thing it is to know God as his strength.

ANDREW MURRAY

# Kept in God

*The Lord is faithful,*
*who shall stablish you, and keep you.*
2 THESSALONIANS 3:3 KJV

Will our God, in His tenderhearted love toward us, not keep us every moment when He has promised to do so? Oh! If we can get hold of the thought, our whole spiritual life is to be God's doing. "It is God which worketh in you both to will and to do his pleasure" (Philippians 2:13). Once we get faith to expect that from God, God will do all for us.

The keeping is to be continuous. Every morning God will meet you as you wake. It is not a question: If I forget to wake in the morning with the thought of Him, what will come of it? If you trust your waking to God, God will meet you in the mornings as you wake with His divine sunshine and life. He will give you the consciousness that through the day you have God to continually take charge of you with His almighty power. And God will meet you the next day and every day. Never mind if, in the practice of fellowship, failure sometimes comes. If you maintain your position and say, "Lord, I am going to expect You to do Your utmost, and I am going to trust You day by day to keep me absolutely," your faith will grow stronger and stronger. You will know the keeping power of God in unbrokenness.

ANDREW MURRAY

# Faith in Christ

*Dear friends, build yourselves up in your most holy faith*
*and pray in the Holy Spirit.*
*Keep yourselves in God's love as you wait for the mercy*
*of our Lord Jesus Christ to bring you to eternal life.*

JUDE 20–21 NIV

When we firmly trust in His person and commit our souls to Him by an unwavering act of confidence in Him for all that He is affirmed to be to us in the Bible, this is faith. We trust Him upon the testimony of God. We trust Him for what the doctrines and facts of the Bible declare Him to be to us. This act of trust unites our spirit to Him in a union so close that we directly receive from Him a current of eternal life.

Faith, in consciousness, seems to complete the divine galvanic circle, and the life of God is instantly imparted to our souls. God's life and light and love and peace and joy seem to flow to us as naturally and spontaneously as the current from a battery. We then, for the first time, understand what Jesus meant by our being united to Him by faith; as the branch is united to the vine, Christ is then and thus revealed to us as God.

We are conscious of direct communion with Him and know Him as we know ourselves, by His direct activity within us. We then know directly, in consciousness, that He is our life, and that we receive from Him, moment by moment, as it were, an impartation of eternal life.

CHARLES G. FINNEY

# Blessed Assurance

*We are more than conquerors through him who loved us.*
ROMANS 8:37 NIV

In 1820, the two great blind poets of history, Homer and Milton, were joined by a third, Fanny J. Crosby of New York. Losing her sight as an infant, Fanny Crosby's greatest regret was not that she was blind; it was that she would never have a proper education. Yet, over eight thousand of her poems were set to music. A childhood statement to her mother sums up Fanny's life, "Mother, if I had a choice, I'd still choose to be blind. For when I die, the first face I'll ever see is my Savior's face." Fanny Crosby died a month short of her ninety-fifth year.

❧

Blessed assurance, Jesus is mine! O what a foretaste
    of glory divine!
Heir of salvation, purchase of God, born of His spirit,
    washed in His blood.

Perfect submission, perfect delight! Visions of
    rapture now burst on my sight!
Angels descending, bring from above echoes
    of mercy, whispers of love.

Perfect submission, all is at rest. I in my Savior
    are happy and blest.
Watching and waiting, looking above, filled with
    His goodness, lost in His love.

This is my story, this is my song,
Praising my Savior all the day long;
This is my story, this is my song,
Praising my Savior all the day long.

FANNY J. CROSBY

# A Cathedral Builder

*Whatever you do, work at it with all your heart,*
*as working for the Lord, not for men.*

COLOSSIANS 3:23 NIV

Three men, all engaged at the same employment, were asked what they were doing. One said he was making five dollars a day. Another replied he was cutting stone. The third said he was building a cathedral. The difference was not in what they were actually doing, although, the spirit of the third might quite possibly have made him the more expert at his task. They were all earning the same wage; they were all cutting stone; but only one held it in his mind that he was helping build a great edifice. Life meant more to him than to his mates; he saw further and clearly. He had a vision of hope in his task.

The farmer may be only planting seed, but if he opens his eyes, he is feeding the world. The railroad man, the factory hand, the clerk in the store, likewise, are building their cathedrals. The investors in stocks and bonds, the executives of great corporations—they are building cathedrals likewise, if only they can catch the vision. The homemaker does not count the dollars she receives for her exertions. If she did, her life might be unhappy indeed.

The rest of us, the great and the humble, are thinking too much about such things as cutting stone and making profits. Stop! Realize the beauty of life. Stir up the hope that lies within you.

*The Omaha Bee* NEWSPAPER

# Your Treasure

*Where your treasure is,*
*there your heart will be also.*
MATTHEW 6:21 NIV

I was standing in Tiffany's great jewelry store in New York, and I heard a salesman say to a lady who had asked him about some pearls, "Madam, this pearl is worth $17,000." I was interested at once. I said, "Let me see the pearl that is worth $17,000." The sales clerk put it on a piece of black velvet, and I studied it quite carefully. "I suppose Tiffany stock is very valuable," I observed.

As I looked around that beautiful shop, I imagined them bringing their entire inventory to my house and saying, "We want you to take care of these diamonds and emeralds and sapphires and golden trinkets tonight." What do you think I would do? I would go as quickly as I could to the telephone and call the chief of police and say, "I have all of Tiffany's jewelry inventory in my house, and it's too great of a responsibility. Will you please send over some of your most trusted officers to help me?" You would do the same, wouldn't you?

But I have a little boy in my house, upon whom I have pinned my hopes for the future. I am responsible for him. I have had him for nine years. I turn to the old Book and I read these words: "What shall it profit a man if he gain the whole world and lose his own soul." It is as if he had all the jewels in the world and held them in one hand and just put all his dreams and hopes for a little boy in the other. Which hand held the most valuable commodity?

J. WILBUR CHAPMAN

# Hope for the Home, Part 1

> The men said to Lot,
> "Have you anyone else here?
> Sons-in-law, sons, daughters,
> or anyone you have in the city—
> bring them out of the place."
>
> GENESIS 19:12 NRSV

The setting for this scripture is the old city of Sodom. It deals with those who are bound to us affectionately by ties of flesh and blood and marriage.

❧

The people of Sodom had sown to the flesh. A center of wickedness was that city and, despite all warnings to change their ways, they went from bad to worse. The destruction of the city was inevitable; for as all men sow, so must they reap. In the midst of all this we see grand old Abraham praying for his nephew Lot and his family, beseeching God to have mercy upon him and his household. God sent two messengers to warn Lot and his family of the doom coming to Sodom and urged them to flee for their lives.

Is it any wonder Jesus wept over the ancient city of Jerusalem [Luke 19:41]? Oh, the pathos in the lives of families who reside in the city. I should like to stand in the door of every household in this city and pour out my heart for those dwelling under each roof. The chief human institution in the city is the home. As goes the home, so will go the city.

In Lot's day God was concerned about the home life of His people. Let this meditation for us today to which surely we would do well to give our most earnest heed.

GEORGE W. TRUETT

# Hope for the Home, Part 2

*"I prayed for this child,*
*and the LORD granted me what I asked of him.*
*So now I give him to the LORD."*
1 SAMUEL 1:27–28 NIV

The highest dignity that God gives to humanity is parenthood. The most glorious sight that one ever sees is the sight of worthy motherhood. Many are the times when I have seen tears on the cheeks of manly men in this city as they whispered those reverent words: "A little baby boy, or a darling little girl, came to our house last night." The most interesting object in the world that God ever sent to a family is a little baby.

"Take this child and rear it for me," says God in His divine commission in the gift of every child in every home, and if parents forget that and if they fail at this point, then down the road of life there are heartbreaks too sad for words to describe.

Here is the piercing cry for all our homes. Is it well with the head of the house there? Is that father behaving as he should? Is that husband in that home behaving worthily as the head of the house? Is that mother behaving like Hannah, who gave her best for the little Samuel who became one of God's chief prophets?

How can parents be comfortable and satisfied when the children are not anchored to our Savior and Lord? Oh, you parents, are you willing to talk about success and achievement and honors and attainments with the boy or girl lost? Such a scene as this provokes our most faithful efforts in behalf of our home.

GEORGE W. TRUETT

# Hope for the Home, Part 3

*"As for me and my household,*
*we will serve the LORD."*
JOSHUA 24:15 NIV

You remember the awful doom that came to Lot's wife because of her disobedience. And you recall that his two single daughters, who went with him from the doomed city, became mothers of two of the wickedest tribes told in the entire Bible. It is no wonder that the old man sat alone at his tent door as the sun went down and nightfall came on. For a father to fail, for a mother to fail, for a home to fail—this is a failure so terrible that demons must laugh at the frailty of man. Put crepe on the door of your heart if things are wrong in the family.

Now, what about your home? Is Christ Master there? He alone can enable you to be all that parents ought to be. He is the one who can give the highest victories to you and your loved ones, even those children of your heart. Let the highest welfare of your home be a major interest in life for you. Let Christ rule in your heart and do your best to win each member of your family to the side and service of Christ who is the only Savior and the one rightful Lord and Master of all.

GEORGE W. TRUETT

# A Father's Hope

*My son, do not despise the LORD's discipline*
*and do not resent his rebuke,*
*because the LORD disciplines those he loves*
*as a father the son he delights in.*
PROVERBS 3:11–12 NIV

The following is a digest of a letter written in 1685 when absent from his family due to persecution.

My dear children, since in this my absence from you, it is the desire of one of you (that is, my eldest son) to have a line of counsel from his father, I shall write in general terms for all of you.

First, I charge you frequently to read the holy scriptures; and that not as a task or burden laid on you, but get your hearts to delight in them. Secondly, consider, seriously and often, of the sinfulness and miserable estate you are in by nature, from the guilt of original sin. Thirdly, learn to know God according to the revealing He hath made of Himself in and by His word, in all His glorious attributes and infinite perfections.

Fourth, remember that God is your Creator, from whom you received life and being; and as such, you are bound to worship Him. Fifth, know this, that as you worship God, so it must be in His own way, with true worship and in a right manner, according to the rules of the gospel. Sixth, do not entertain any hard thoughts of God or of His ways, because His people are persecuted. Jesus Himself was persecuted to death by wicked men.

Lastly, I charge you to be dutiful and obedient to all your superiors—to your grandfather and both grandmothers and all other relations and friends that are over you, but in an especial manner to your mother. Your very loving father,

ISAAC WATTS

# Hope in Providence

*You gave me life and showed me kindness,*
*and in your providence watched over my spirit.*

JOB 10:12 NIV

John Paton went to minister in the South Pacific in 1887, a day when so-called cannibals inhabited the islands. In his journal Paton writes, "Hope was what goaded me on through the vicissitudes of ministry."

One morning at daybreak I found my house surrounded by armed men, and the chief intimated that they had assembled to take my life. Seeing that I was entirely in their hands, I knelt down and gave myself away body and soul to the Lord Jesus, for what seemed my last time on earth.

Rising, I went out to them and began calmly talking about their unkind treatment of me and contrasting it with all my conduct toward them. . . . At last some of the chiefs, who had attended the worship, rose and said, "Our conduct has been bad; but now we will fight for you and kill all those who hate you."

Once when natives in large numbers were assembled at my house, a man furiously rushed on me with his axe, but a Kaserumini chief snatched a spade with which I had been working and dexterously defended me from instant death.

Life in such circumstances led me to cling very near to the Lord Jesus. As my courage increased, Divine Providence increased my deliverances.

JOHN G. PATON

# Courage in Joy

*The joy of the LORD is your strength.*
NEHEMIAH 8:10 NIV

Oh, that the pleasure-seeking men and women of the world could only taste and feel the real joy of those who know and love the true God—a heritage which the world cannot give to them, but which the poorest and humblest followers of Jesus inherit and enjoy!

When will men's eyes at home be opened? When will the rich and the learned renounce their shallow frivolities and go to live amongst the poor, the ignorant, the outcast, and the lost? Those who have tasted the highest joy, "the joy of the Lord," will never ask, "Is life worth living?"

Let me record my immovable conviction that this is the noblest service in which any human being can spend or be spent. If God gave me back my life to be lived over again, I would without one quiver of hesitation lay it on the altar to Christ, that He might use it as before in similar ministries of love, especially amongst those who have never yet heard the name of Jesus.

Nothing that can now befall me makes me tremble; on the contrary, I deeply rejoice! Why? My joy comes from this everlasting hope: "Lo, I am with you always."

JOHN G. PATON

# A Hope for Others

*He has sent me. . .*
*to proclaim freedom for the captives.*
ISAIAH 61:1 NIV

Chief Sechele was one of David Livingstone's early converts in the faith. The English missionary recorded the following in his journal.

Seeing me anxious that his people should believe the words of Christ, he once said, "Do you imagine these people will ever believe by you merely talking to them? I can make them happy to embrace Christianity." During the space of two years and a half he continued to profess to his people his full conviction of the truth of Christianity.

In the hope that others would be induced to join him in his attachment to Christianity, he asked me to begin family worship with him in his house. I did so and by-and-by was surprised to hear how well he conducted prayer in his own simple and beautiful style, for he was quite a master of his own language.

Sechele continued to make a consistent profession for about three years. I had no desire that he should be in any hurry to make a full profession by baptism, and by putting away all his wives but one. When he at last applied for baptism, I simply asked him how the Bible declared he ought to act. He went home, gave each of his superfluous wives new clothing and all his own goods, which they had kept in their huts for him, and sent them to their parents with the word that he had found no fault with them, and that in parting, he wished to follow the will of God.

DAVID LIVINGSTONE

# The Hope of Home

*I go to prepare a place for you.*
JOHN 14:2 KJV

The burning question with every man and woman who has thought about life in those days was, "Where is this life leading?" The present, alas, was dim and inscrutable enough, but the future was a fearful and unsolved mystery. So Christ put that right before He went away.

He gave this unknown future form and color. He told us—and it is only because we are so accustomed to it that we do not wonder more at the magnificence of the concept—that when our place in this world is finished there would be another ready for us. We do not know much about that place, but the best thing we do know—He prepares it. No eye has seen, nor has an ear heard, neither has it entered into the heart of any of us what the Lord has prepared for those of us who love Him. It is better to think of this, to let our thoughts rest on this, that He prepares it than to fancy details of our own.

But that truth does not exhaust the matter. Consider the alternative; if Christ had not gone away, what then? We should not either. The circumstances of our future life depended upon Christ's going away. The fact of our going away depended upon His going away. We could not follow Him, unless He went first. He had to be the Resurrection and the life.

HENRY DRUMMOND

# The Hope of Grace

*It is by grace you have saved, through faith—*
*and this not from yourselves, it is the gift of God—*
*not by works, so that no one can boast.*

EPHESIANS 2:8–9 NIV

It was of mere grace that God gave us His only begotten Son. The grace is great in proportion to the excellency of what is given. The gift was infinitely precious because it was of a person infinitely worthy, a person of infinite glory; and also because it was of a person infinitely near and dear to God.

The grace is great in proportion to the benefit we have given us in Him. The grace is doubly infinite, in that in Him we have deliverance and we receive eternal joy and glory. The grace in bestowing this gift is great in proportion to our unworthiness. Instead of deserving such a gift, we merited infinitely ill from God's hands. The grace is great according to the manner of giving or in proportion to the humiliation and expense of the means by which a way is made for having the gift. The Father gave Him to dwell amongst us; He gave Him to us incarnate, or in our nature; and in the like, though sinless, infirmities. He gave Him to us in a low and inflicted state; and not only so, but as slain, that He might be a feast for our souls.

The grace of God, in bestowing this gift, is most free. It was what God was under no obligation to bestow.

JONATHAN EDWARDS

# Growing in Grace

*Grow in grace,*
*and in the knowledge of*
*our Lord and Savior Jesus Christ.*

2 PETER 3:18 KJV

By trusting in Christ, we receive an inward influence that stimulates and directs our activity; by faith we receive His purifying influence into the very center of our being; through and by His truth revealed directly to the soul, He quickens our whole inward being into the attitude of a loving obedience. This is the way, and the only practical way, to overcome sin.

God works in us to will and to do; and we, accepting by faith His working, will and do according to His good pleasure. Faith itself is an active and not a passive state.

A passive holiness is impossible and absurd. Let no one say that when we exhort people to trust wholly in Christ, we teach that anyone should be or can be passive in receiving and cooperating with the divine influence within. This influence is moral and not moral. It is purgation and not force. It influences the free will, and consequently does this by truth, not by force. Oh, that it could be understood that the whole of spiritual life that is in any man is received directly from the Spirit of Christ by faith, as the branch receives its life from the vine.

Oh, that men would learn to look directly at Christ through the gospel and to close in with Him by an act of loving trust as to involve a universal sympathy with His state of mind. This, and this alone, is sanctification.

CHARLES G. FINNEY

# The Good Shepherd

> *The LORD is my shepherd;*
> *I shall not want.*
>
> PSALM 23:1 KJV

Perhaps no aspect in which the Lord reveals Himself to us is fuller of genuine comfort than the aspect set forth in the Twenty-third Psalm and in its corresponding passage in the tenth chapter of John. The psalmist tells me that the Lord is my Shepherd, and the Lord himself declares that He is the *good* shepherd. Can we conceive of anything more comforting? Repeat these familiar words to yourself, "The Lord is my Shepherd; I shall not want."

Who is your shepherd? The Lord! Oh, my friends, what a wonderful announcement. The Lord God of heaven and earth, the Almighty Creator of all things, He who holds the universe in His hand as though it were a very little thing, He is your Shepherd and has charged Himself with the care and keeping of His sheep.

If your hearts will only take in this thought, I can promise you that your religion will from henceforth be full of the profoundest comfort, and all your old uncomfortable religion will drop off forever, as the mist disappears in the blaze of the summer sun.

HANNAH WHITALL SMITH

# The Goodness of God

*How great is your goodness,*
*which you have stored up for those who fear you,*
*which you bestow in the sight of men*
*on those who take refuge in you.*

PSALM 31:19 NIV

The will inclines to love one in whom it has seen so many acts and signs of love, some of which it would like to return. In particular, the will shows the soul how this true Lover never leaves it, but goes with it everywhere and gives it life and being. Then the understanding comes forward and makes the soul realize that, for however many years it may live, it can never hope to have a better friend—for the world is full of falsehood, and these pleasures which the devil pictures to it are accompanied by trials and cares and annoyances—and tells it to be certain that outside this castle it will find neither security nor peace. Let it refrain from visiting one house after another when its own house is full of good things, if it will only enjoy them. How fortunate it is to be able to find all that it needs, as it were, at home, especially when it has a Host who will put all good things into its possession.

TERESA OF AVILA

# Jehovah-Shammah: "The Lord Is There"

*The name of the city from that time on shall be
[Jehovah-shammah], The LORD is There.*

EZEKIEL 48:35 NRSV

The name Jehovah-shammah means "the Lord is there." To me
this name includes all the others. Wherever the Lord is, all must
go right for His children. Where the good mother is, all goes
right, up to the measure of her ability, for her children. (And how
much more God! His presence is enough.) We can all remember
how the simple presence was enough for us when we were children. All that we needed was comfort, rest, and deliverance,
assured to us by the mere fact of mother as she sat in her accustomed chair with her work or her book or her writing, and we
would burst in on her with our doleful budget of childish woes.

If we could but see that the presence of God is the same
assurance of comfort and rest and deliverance, only infinitely
more so. He would cause a wellspring of joy to be opened up in
our religious lives that would drive out every vestige of discomfort and distress.

All through the Old Testament the Lord's one universal
answer to all the fears and anxieties of the children of Israel were
the simple words, "I will be with thee." He did not need to say anything more. His presence was to them a perfect guarantee that
all their needs would be supplied; and the moment they were
assured of it, they were no longer afraid to face the fiercest foe.

HANNAH WHITALL SMITH

# *Scriptural Hope*

*For everything that was written in the past
was written to teach us,
so that that through endurance and the encouragement
of the Scriptures we might have hope.*

ROMANS 15:4 NIV

Hope in God, and in the promises of His Word, is often spoken of in the scriptures as a very considerable part of true religion. It is mentioned as one of the three great qualities of which religion consists (1 Corinthians 13:13). Hope in the Lord is also frequently mentioned as the characteristic of the saints: Psalm 146:5, "Happy is he that hath the God of Jacob for his help, whose *hope* is in the Lord his God"; Jeremiah 17:7, "Blessed is the man that trusteth in the Lord, and whose *hope* the Lord is"; Psalm 31:24, "Be of good courage, and he shall strengthen your heart, all yet that *hope* in the Lord." And the like in many other places.

Hope is so great a part of true religion that the apostle says we are saved by *hope* (Romans 8:24). Hope is spoken of as part of the Christian soldier's armor: 1 Thessalonians 5:8, "And for the helmet, the *hope* of salvation"; and the sure and steadfast anchor of the soul, which preserves it from being cast away by the storms of this evil world; Hebrews 6:19, "Which *hope* we have as an anchor of the soul, both sure and steadfast, and which entereth into that within veil."

JONATHAN EDWARDS

# All Comfort

*The God of all comfort. . .*
2 CORINTHIANS 1:3 NIV

Among all the names that reveal God, this, the "God of all comfort," seems to me one of the loveliest and most absolutely comforting. The words *all comfort* admit of no limitation and no deductions; and one would suppose that, however full of discomforts the outward life of the followers of such a God might be, their inward religious life must necessarily be always under all circumstances a comfortable life.

But, as a fact, it often seems as if exactly the opposite were the case, and the religious life of large numbers of the children of God are full, not of comfort, but of the utmost discomfort. This discomfort arises from anxiety as to their relationship to God and doubts as to His love. They torment themselves with the thought that they are too good-for-nothing to be worthy of His care, and they suspect Him to be indifferent to their trials and of forsaking them in times of need.

They are anxious and troubled about everything in their religious life, about their disposition and feelings, their indifference to the Bible, their want of fervency in prayer, their coldness of heart. They are tormented with unavailing regret over their past and with devouring anxieties for their future. They feel unworthy to enter God's presence and dare not believe that they belong to Him.

They can be happy and comfortable with their earthly friends, but they cannot be happy or comfortable with God. And although He declares Himself to be the God of all comfort, they continually complain that they cannot find comfort anywhere; and their sorrowful look and the doleful tones of their voice shows that they speak the truth.

HANNAH WHITALL SMITH

# Blessed Adoption

*Having predestinated us unto the adoption of*
*children by Jesus Christ to himself,*
*according to the good pleasure of his will.*
EPHESIANS 1:5 KJV

The moment you become a child, the Father loves you. This is shown in what Christ said to Mary, "I ascend unto my Father and to your Father, to my God and your God." Christ here intimated that we have the same love that He had. We have not got so much of the love of the Father as Christ, because He has got an infinite capacity; but it is the same love. Christ plainly shows you that in the seventeenth chapter of John, where He prays that the same love may be in us that was in Him. Oh, how much better is it, then, to be under the love of God, than under the wrath of God!

Let me mention to you a second part of the blessedness we get. *The Spirit of the Son dwells in us.* You will see this in Galatians 4:6, "Because ye are sons, God hath sent forth the Spirit of his Son into your hearts, crying, Abba, Father."

Brethren, when Christ comes, the first thing He does is to redeem you from under the curse of the law, and then He makes you a son. It is sweet to get the love of Christ, but I will tell you what is equally as sweet, that is, to receive the Spirit of Christ. Has He given you the Spirit? He will do it if you are a son, that you may be made to cry, "Abba, Father."

ROBERT MURRAY MCCHEYNE

# Waiting on God

> *It is good that a man should both
> hope and quietly wait for
> the salvation of the LORD.*
>
> LAMENTATIONS 3:26 KJV

Those who deal with God will find it is not in vain to trust Him; for, one, He is good to those who do. His tender mercies are over all his works; all His creatures taste of His goodness. But He is in a particular manner good to those who wait for Him. Note, while trouble is prolonged and deliverance is deferred, we must patiently wait for God and His gracious return to us.

While we wait for Him by faith, we must seek Him by prayer; our souls must seek Him, else we do not seek so as to find. Our seeking will help to keep up our waiting. To those who thus wait and seek, God will be gracious. He will show them His marvelous loving-kindness.

And, two, those who do so will find it good for them. It is good to hope and quietly wait for the salvation of the Lord; to hope that it will come, through the difficulties that lie in the way. To wait till it does come, though it be long delayed; and while we wait, to be quiet and silent, not quarreling with God, nor making ourselves uneasy.

If we call to mind, "Father, thy will be done," we may have hope that all will end well at last.

MATTHEW HENRY

# There Is Hope in Prayer

*This is the confidence that we have in him, that,*
*if we ask any thing according to his will,*
*he heareth us.*
1 JOHN 5:14 KJV

The prayer that is answered is the prayer after God's will. And the reason for this is plain. What is God's will is God's wish. And when a man does what God wills, he does what God wishes done. Therefore God will have that done at any cost, at any sacrifice.

Thousands of prayers are never answered, simply because God does not wish them answered. If we pray for any one thing, or any number of things, we are sure God wishes to come to pass, we may be sure our prayers will be gratified. For our wishes are only the reflection of God's. And the wish in us is almost equivalent to the answer. It is the answer casting its shadow backwards. Already the thing is done in the mind of God. It casts two shadows: one backward, one forward. The backward shadow—that is the wish before the thing is done which sheds itself in prayer. The forward shadow—that is the joy after the thing is done which sheds itself in praise.

Oh, what a rich and wonderful life this ideal life must be. Asking anything, getting everything, willing with God, praying with God, praising with God. Surely it is too much. How can God trust us with a power so deep and terrible? Ah, He can trust the ideal life with anything. "If I ask anything." Well, if he does, he will ask nothing amiss. It will be God's will if it is asked. It will be God's will if it is not asked.

HENRY DRUMMOND

# Moody on the Book

*The word of God is living and active.*
*Sharper than any double-edged sword,*
*it penetrates even to dividing*
*soul and spirit, joints and marrow;*
*it judges the thoughts and attitudes of the heart.*

What can botanists tell you of the Lilly of the Valley? You must study the Book for that. What can geologists tell you of the Rock of Ages, or mere astronomers about the Bright and Morning Star? In the Bible we find all knowledge unto salvation. Here we read of the ruin of man by nature, redemption by the blood, and regeneration by the Holy Ghost. These three—ruination, redemption, and regeneration—run all through this Book.

I believe hundreds of Christian people are being deceived by Satan now on this one point: that they have not gotten the assurance of salvation just because they are not willing to take God at His word, as spoken in this Book!

There was never a sermon that you have listened to but in it Christ was seeking you. I contend that a man cannot but find on every page of this Book that Jesus Christ is seeking him through His blessed Word. This is what the Bible is for—to seek out the lost.

I hold to the doctrine of sudden conversion, as taught in the Bible, as I do my life, and I would as quickly give up my life as give up this doctrine, unless it can be proved that it is not according to the Word of God.

DWIGHT L. MOODY

# Befriended Orphans

*No, I will not abandon you as orphans—*
*I will come to you.*
JOHN 14:18 NLT

Does the Christian's path lie all the way through to our Promised Land? No, he is forewarned it is to be one of "much tribulation." He has his Marahs as well as Elims—his valleys of Baca, as well as the grapes of Eschol. Often is he left unbefriended to bear the brunt of the storm—his gourds fading when most needed. His sun going down while it is yet day. His happy home and happy heart darkened in a moment with sorrows with which a stranger cannot understand.

But, there is a Brother "born for adversity" who can understand. How often has that voice broken the muffled stillness of the sick-chamber. "I will not leave you comfortless. The world may, friends may, the desolation of bereavement and death may; but I will not. You will be alone, yet not alone; for I your Savior and your God will be with you."

Jesus seems to have an especial love and affection for His orphaned and comfortless people. A father loves his sick and sorrowing child most. Of all his household, he occupies most of his thoughts on them. Christ seems to delight to lavish His deepest sympathy on "Him that has no helper." It is in the hour of sorrow His people have found Him most precious. It is in "the wilderness" He speaks most "comfortably to them." He gives them their vineyards in the places they least expect; wells of heavenly consolation break forth.

JOHN MACDUFF

# My Soul Has Found a Resting Place

*He has reconciled you. . .*
*through death to present you holy in his sight. . .*
*free from accusation.*

COLOSSIANS 1:22 NIV

Those of an evangelical faith have always sung experiential hymns and gospel songs that give expression to the hope they have in Jesus Christ.

My faith has found a resting place—not in device nor creed:
I trust the ever-living One—His wounds for me shall plead.

*Refrain*
I need no other argument; I need no other plea.
It is enough that Jesus died, and that He died for me.

Enough for me that Jesus saves—this ends my fear and doubt;
A sinful soul, I come to Him—He'll never cast me out.

My heart is leaning on the Word—the written Word of God;
Salvation by my Savior's name—salvation through His blood.

My great Physician heals the sick—the lost He came to save;
For me His precious blood He shed—for me His life He gave.

LIDIE H. EDMUNDS

# Hope in an Unchanging Lord

*He who began a good work in you*
*will carry it on to completion*
*until the day of Christ Jesus.*
PHILIPPIANS 1:6 NIV

The joy of the Lord in the spirit springs from an assurance that all the future, whatever it may be, is guaranteed by divine goodness, that being children of God, the love of God toward us is not of a mutable character, but abides and remains unchangeable. The believer feels an entire sanctification in leaving himself in the hands of eternal and immutable love. However happy I may be today, if I am in doubt concerning tomorrow, something is eating at the root of my peace; although the past may now be sweet in retrospect and the present fair in enjoyment, yet if the future be grim with fear, my joy is not mine, and deep peace is still out of my reach.

But when I know that He whom I have rested in has power and grace enough to complete that which He has begun in me and for me; when I see the work of Christ to be no halfway redemption, but a complete and eternal salvation; when I perceive that the promises are established upon an unchangeable basis and are in Christ Jesus, ratified by oath and sealed by blood, then my soul hath perfect contentment.

CHARLES H. SPURGEON

# *Hope in the Cross*

> *God. . .has saved us and called us to a holy life—*
> *not because of anything we have done*
> *but because of his own purpose and grace.*
> *This grace was given us in Christ Jesus*
> *before the beginning of time.*
>
> 2 TIMOTHY 1:8–9 NIV

I will confess to you that over and over I am personally driven to do what I trust you may be led to do today. I look back on my life, and while I have much to thank God for, much in which to see His Spirit's hand, yet when I feel my responsibilities and my shortcomings, my heart sinks within me. When I think of my transgressions, better known to myself than to anyone else, and remember, too, that they are not known even to me as they are to God, I feel all hope swept away and my soul left in utter despair, until I come anew to the cross and think of who it was who died there and why He died and what designs of infinite mercy are answered by His death.

It is so sweet to look up to the Crucified One again and say, "I have nothing but You, my Lord, no confidence but You. If you are not accepted as my substitute, I must perish; if God's appointed Savior is not enough I have no other. But I know You are the Father's well-beloved, and I am accepted in You. You are all I want and all I have.

CHARLES SPURGEON

# Hope for the Weak

*A bruised reed shall he not break,*
*and smoking flax shall he not quench.*
MATTHEW 12:20 KJV

Will Jesus accept such a heart as mine?—this erring, treacherous, traitorous heart? The past!—how many forgotten vows, broken covenants, prayerless days! How often have I made new resolutions, and as often has the reed succumbed to the first blast of temptation and the burning flax been well-near quenched by guilty omissions and guiltier commissions. Oh, my soul, you are low indeed—the things that remain seem "ready to die." But your Savior-God will not give you "over unto death." The reed is bruised; but He will not pluck it up by the roots. The flax is reduced to a smoking ember, but He will not fan the decaying flame. Why wound your loving Savior's heart by these repeated declensions? He will not—cannot—give you up! Go, mourn your weakness and unbelief. Cry unto the Strong for strength.

Weary and faint one! You have an Omnipotent arm to lean on. "He faints not, neither is weary!" Listen to His own gracious assurance, "Fear not, for I am with you. Do not be dismayed, for I am your God. I will strengthen you; yes, I will help you with the right hand of my righteousness!" Leaving all your false props and refuges, let this be your resolve—"I trust in the Lord for protection!"

JOHN MACDUFF

# More on Prayer

*Where can I flee from your presence?*
PSALM 139:7 NIV

Another report on Brother Lawrence's conversation with a reporter about practicing the presence of God in everyday life.

※

It is a great delusion to think that times of prayer ought to differ from other times in our day. According to him, prayer is recognizing the presence of God; it isn't different than any other time in your day. When your appointed times of prayer were past, he found no difference, because he still continued with God, praising and blessing Him with all his might, so that he passed his life in continual joy; yet he hoped that God would give him somewhat to suffer, when he should grow stronger.

That we ought, once for all, heartily to put our whole trust in God and make a total surrender of ourselves to Him, secure that He would not deceive us.

That we ought not to be weary of doing little things for the love of God, who regards not the greatness of the work, but the love with which it is performed. That we should not wonder if, in the beginning, we often failed in our endeavors, but that at last we should gain a habit, which will naturally produce its acts in us, without our care, and to our exceeding great delight.

BROTHER LAWRENCE

# The Omnipotent Prayer

*Father, I will that they also,*
*whom thou hast given me,*
*be with me where I am;*
*that they may behold my glory.*

JOHN 17:24 KJV

This is not the petition of a suppliant but the claim of a conqueror. There was only one request He ever made, or ever can make, that was refused. It was the prayer wrung forth by the presence and power of superhuman anguish, "Father if it is possible, let this cup pass from me." Had that prayer been answered, never could one consolatory word of Jesus have been ours. "If it be possible"—but for that gracious parenthetical phrase, we would have been lost forever.

In His unmurmuring submission, the bitter cup was drained; all the dread penalties of the law were borne, the atonement completed, an all-perfect righteousness wrought out; and now, as the stipulated reward of His obedience and sufferings, the Divine Victor claims His trophies.

What are those trophies? Those that were given Him by the Father—the countless multitudes redeemed by His blood. These He wills to be with Him where He is. They are the spectators of His glory and partakers of His crown. Wondrous word and will of a dying testator. His last prayer on earth is an importunate pleading for their glorification. His parting wish is to meet them in heaven—as if these earthly jewels were needed to make His crown complete—their happiness and joy the needful complement of His own.

JOHN MACDUFF

# Hope to Defeat the Enemy

*Be of sober spirit, be on the alert.*
*Your adversary, the devil,*
*prowls about like a roaring lion,*
*seeing someone to devour.*
*But resist him, firm in your faith.*

1 PETER 5:8–9 NASB

We have a subtle adversary of great power and malignity. It has become unpopular to say much about the devil; people have become so incredulous respecting his existence. This state of things is doubtless the result of his infernal agency, since, if men doubt his existence, they will more readily become his prey.

The Bible requires people to pass the time of the sojourning here with fear. It represents him as possessing great subtlety and being ready to take a thousand advantages, even turning himself into an angel of light to delude and destroy souls. And what man is able to resist him—to detect all the villainies and sophistries of a mind as old and malevolent as his? I have often felt that the devil would just as certainly have my soul, in spite of all my endeavors against him, if Christ did not save me, as I existed. As well expect to escape a devouring lion, whose strong power had already encompassed you about. Who can protect us? Our Christian journey lies all the way through an enemy's country, and throngs of devils are prowling about on all sides—and if the Lord does not deliver us, the devil will have the whole of us.

CHARLES G. FINNEY

# The Gentleness of God

*Your gentleness has made me great.*
PSALM 18:35 NLT

We wonder sometimes when God is so great, so terrible in majesty, that He uses so little violence with us, who are so small. But it is not His way. His way is to be gentle. He seldom drives, but draws. He seldom compels, but leads. He remembers we are dust. We think it might be quicker work if God threatened and compelled us to do right. But God does not want quick work, but good work. God does not want slave work, but free work. So, God is gentle with us all—molding us and winning us many a times with no more than a silent look. Course treatment never wins souls. So God did not drive the chariot of His omnipotence up to Peter and command him to repent. God did not threaten him with thunderbolts of punishment. God did not even speak to him. That one look laid a spell upon his soul which was more than voice or language through all his afterlife.

God may be dealing with us in some quiet way just now and we do not know it. So mysteriously has all our life been shaped, and so unobtrusive the fingers which mold our will, that we scarce believe it has been the hand of God at all. But it is God's gentleness. And the reason why God made Peter's heart sensitive, and yours and mine, was to meet His gentleness.

HENRY DRUMMOND

# Full Dependence on God

*He only is my rock and my salvation:*
*he is my defense;*
*I shall not be moved.*
PSALM 62:6 KJV

No soul can be really at rest until it has given up all dependence on everything else and has been forced to depend on the Lord alone. Feelings may change, and will change, with our changing circumstances; prayers may seem to lose their fervency; promises may seem to fail; everything that we have believed in or depended upon may seem to be swept away, and only God is left, just God, the bare God, if I may be allowed that expression; simply and only God.

Promises may be misunderstood or misplaced or misapplied, and, at the moment when we are leaning all our weight upon them, they may seem utterly to fail us. But the Promiser, who stands behind His promises and is infinitely more than His promises, can never fail nor change. The little child does not need to have promises from his mother to make him content; it has its mother himself, and she is enough. Mother is better than a thousand promises. In our highest ideal of love or friendship, promises do not enter. The personality of lover or friend is better than all their promises. If every promise should be wiped out of the Bible, we would still have God left, and God would be enough. Again I repeat it, only God, He himself, just as He is, without addition of anything on our part, whether it be disposition or feelings or experiences or good works or sound doctrine or any other thing either outward or inward.

HANNAH WHITALL SMITH

# Comforts

*For whatsoever things were written*
*aforetime were written for our learning,*
*that we through patience and comfort*
*of the scriptures might have hope.*
ROMANS 15:4 KJV

How much important matter do we find condensed in this single verse! What a light and glory does it throw on the Word of God! It has been well noted that we have here *its authority;* as it is a written word; *its antiquity,* as it was written aforetime; *its utility,* as it is written for our learning. We may also infer from what immediately follows, *its divine origin;* for, if by means of the holy scriptures, and the power of the Holy Spirit (Isaiah 59:21), God imparts to our soul patience and comfort and hope, because He is the God of patience and comfort and hope. He is the fountain of these gifts and graces, which by the channel of His inspired Word, flow into our hearts and lives, to strengthen us for service.

There is hope connected with the scriptures. The Word is intended to work in us a good hope. People with a hope will purify themselves and will rise to a high and noble character. By this hope of the scriptures we understand it to mean:

(1) The hope of salvation (1 Thessalonians 5:8); (2) the blessed hope, and the appearing of our Lord (Titus 2:13); (3) the hope of the resurrection of the dead (Acts 23:6); (4) the hope of glory (Colossians 1:27).

This is a good hope, a lively hope; it is the hope set before us in the gospel.

S. D. GORDON

# New Birth Hope

*Blessed be the God and Father of our Lord Jesus Christ,*
*which according to his abundant mercy*
*hath begotten us again unto a lively hope.*

1 PETER 1:3 KJV

Preacher and social reformer John Wesley experienced the presence of hope in his life. The great revivals of eighteenth-century England were the results of this man's expectation of the Holy Spirit's work.

A scriptural mark of those who are born of God is hope. Thus Peter delivers our text, speaking to all the children of God who were then scattered abroad. Notice, "a lively hope." There is also a dead hope. As well as a dead faith, a hope which is not from God, but from the enemy of God and man. Every man with living hope can say, "Beloved, now are we the sons of God, and we shall see Him as He is."

New birth hope implies first the testimony of our own spirit or conscience that we walk "in simplicity and godly sincerity." Secondly, the testimony of the Spirit of God, "bearing witness with," or to "our spirit, that we are the children of God."

As we and you have one Lord, so we have one Spirit: As we have one faith, so we have one hope also. We are sealed with one "Spirit of promise," the earnest of our inheritance: the same Spirit bearing witness with our spirit "that we are the children of God" (Romans 8:14–16).

JOHN WESLEY

# Hope That Burns

*Did not our heart burn within us,*
*while he talked with us by the way,*
*and while he opened to us the scriptures?*
LUKE 24:32 KJV

Look back to the road that leads to Emmaus, and to two men, one named Cleopas, the other a nameless disciple. Listen to them, on this day after the Crucifixion, speaking among themselves. They had lost their hope, and they had lost their confidence in Jesus' ability to do what they thought He was going to do. Their attitude toward Jesus was the attitude of men who should say, "Oh, we believe in Him, we love Him. He meant well, but He has not succeeded. We had *hoped* that it was He who should redeem Israel." Their hope was gone. The hope which had been burning like a beacon before them in the days when He was still among them had died out into gray ashes.

This is the picture of these men as they set their faces toward Emmaus. [Until a Stranger joins them on the road and engages them in conversations concerning the events in Jerusalem. When at last the Stranger sits with the men for a meal, they recognize Him as Jesus.]

How did Christ deal with these hopeless men? I freely confess I am surprised at the wonder of His coming to these men. Why does He come? He comes because He is seeking love. It was there in those doubt-shadowed hearts, and He knew it. What were the things He said to them? Nothing new. He opened the scriptures to them. When they were quiet, they heard Him speak to them. Then their hearts burned with hope.

G. CAMPBELL MORGAN

# Object of Christian Hope

*Paul, an apostle of Christ Jesus*
*by the command of God our Savior*
*and of Christ Jesus our hope.*

1 TIMOTHY 1:1 NIV

For hope to be genuine hope and not foolishness or presumption, it must be grounded in the Holy Word.

The stated object of Christian hope: (1) It is the future hope of the resurrection of the dead (Acts 23:6); (2) the promises given to Israel (Acts 26:6–7); (3) the redemption of the body and the whole creation (Romans 8:23–25); (4) eternal glory (Colossians 1:27); (5) eternal life and the inheritance of the saints (Titus 3:5–7); (6) the return of Christ (Titus 2:11–14); (7) transformation into the likeness of Christ (1 John 3:2–3); (8) the salvation of God (1 Timothy 4:10); (9) or simply Christ (1 Timothy 1:1).

Hope is basic to the Christian view of life. Along with faith and love, hope is an enduring virtue of the Christian life (1 Corinthians 4–5). In fact, faith and love spring from hope. Faith and hope produce holiness in the lives of Christians. While faith, hope, and love work together to mold believers into disciples (1 Thessalonians 1:3).

BASED ON ANONYMOUS SOURCES

# Day Is Breaking

*There shall be no night there.*
REVELATION 21:25 KJV

Is it night wherever you are? Are you wearied with these mid-night tossings on life's tumultuous sea? Take hope! The day is breaking. Soon your Lord will be appearing. That glorious appearing shall disperse every cloud and usher in an eternal noontide that knows no twilight. "The sun will never set; the moon will not go down. For the Lord will be your everlasting light—the everlasting light of the Three-in-One. Your days of mourning will come to an end."

Everlasting light! Wondrous secret of a nightless world—the glories of an ever-present God. My soul waits for the Lord more than those who wait for the morning.

Strange realities! A world without night—a heaven without a sun; and a greater wonder still, yourself in this world; a joyful citizen of this nightless, sinless, sorrowless, tearless heaven! And you will be singing, "Holy, holy, holy is the Lord God Almighty—the one who always was, who is, and who is to come."

God Himself shall be with you and shall be your God. You shall see His face. And who will see Him? Who will stand in His presence and look upon His face? It is the pure in heart who will see Him.

JOHN MACDUFF

# Claim Your Crown

*And when the head Shepherd comes,*
*your reward will be a never-ending share*
*in His glory and honor.*

1 PETER 5:4 NLT

What! Is the beggar to be "raised from the ash-heap, set among Princes, and made to inherit a throne of glory?" Is dust and ashes, a puny rebel, a guilty traitor—to be pitied, pardoned, loved, exalted from the depths of despair, raised to the heights of heaven; gifted with kingly honor—royally fed—royally clothed—royally attended—and, at last royally crowned?

Oh, my soul, forward with joyous emotion to that day of wonders, when He whose head shall be crowned with many crowns shall be the royal dispenser of royal diadems to His people. "Unto him that loved us, and washed us from our sins in his own blood, and hath made us kings. . .to him be glory and dominion forever and ever. Amen" (Revelation 1:5).

It is the hope of every man and woman to be among the number. Will you be among them? While the princes and monarchs of the earth wade through seas of blood for a corruptible crown or barter it for some perishable nothings of earth, oh that you would awake to your high destiny and live up to your privileges as a citizen of a kingly commonwealth, a member of the royal family of heaven.

JOHN MACDUFF

# Hope to Be Dead to Sin

*Know ye not, that so many of us
as were baptized into Jesus Christ
were baptized into his death?
Therefore we are buried with him
by baptism into death.*

ROMANS 6:3–4 KJV

John Chrysostom (345–407) was one of the finest preachers in the early church. He studied law but then turned his attention to the Christian faith and was baptized in 368.

❧

Believe that Christ was raised from the dead, and believe the same of yourself. Just as His death is yours, so also is His resurrection; if you have shared in the one, you shall share in the other. As of now the sin is done away with.

Paul sets before us a demand: to bring about a newness of life by a changing of habits. For when a fornicator becomes chaste, when the covetous man becomes merciful, he who is harsh becomes quiet, a resurrection has taken place, foreshadowing of the final resurrection that is to come.

The apostle goes on to say, "As Christ was raised up from the dead by the glory of the Father, even so we also should walk in newness of life" (Romans 6:4). Here Paul tells of the importance of the resurrection.

How is it a resurrection? It is a resurrection because sin has been mortified and righteousness has risen in its place; the old life has passed away, and new, angelic life is now being lived.

JOHN CHRYSOSTOM

# A Father's Hope Realized

*I will set out and go back to my father.*
LUKE 15:18 NIV

Like the prodigal son (John 15:11–32), the sinful end up in the mire of the pig's slop, reduced to the greatest wretchedness, and are in a worse state than any disordered person. But when the prodigal was willing, he became suddenly young by his decision. As soon as he said, "I will return to my father," the one phrase conveyed to him all the blessings; or rather, not the phrase alone, but the deed that he added to the phrase. He did not say, "I will return," and then stay where he was.

Thus, let us also do this, no matter where we are on our journey. Let us go back to our Father's house, not lingering over the length of the journey. For we shall find, if we be willing, that the way back again is very easy and very speedy.

And how am I to go back again? Start by avoiding vice, going no farther into it, and you have come home. When a person who is sick does not get any worse it is a sign that he is getting better, and so is the case with vice. Go no further and your deeds of wickedness will have an end.

Let us leave this strange land of sin where we have been drawn away from the Father. For our Father has a natural yearning toward us and will honor us if we are changed. He finds great pleasure in receiving back his children.

JOHN CHRYSOSTOM

# Great and Wonderful Things

*Now those who were scattered*
*went from place to place,*
*proclaiming the word.*

ACTS 8:4 NRSV

It was during the turmoil of seventeenth-century Puritan England that George Fox was born and grew up. He became the founder and leader of the Quakers. Fox's *Journal* helped introduce a genre of spiritual writing.

❧

After I was set at liberty from Nottingham Jail, where I had been kept prisoner a pretty long time, I traveled as before, with hope and in the work of the Lord.

Coming to Mansfield-Woodhouse, I found there a distracted woman under a doctor's hand with her hair loose around her ears. He was about to let her blood, she being first bound and many people around her, holding her by violence, but he could get no blood from her.

I desired them to unbind her and let her alone, for they could not touch the spirit in her body by which she was tormented. So they did unbind her; and I was moved to speak to her and in the name of the Lord to bid her to be quiet, and she was so. The Lord's power settled her mind, and she mended. Afterwards she received the truth and continued in it to her death; and the Lord's name was honored.

Many great and wonderful things were wrought by the heavenly power in these days; for the Lord made bare His omnipotent arm and manifested His power, to the astonishment of many, by the healing virtue whereby many have been delivered from great infirmities. And the devils were made subject through His name.

GEORGE FOX

# A Living Hope

*Phillip began to speak,
and starting with this scripture,
he proclaimed to [the eunuch]
the good news about Jesus.*

ACTS 8:35 NRSV

One morning, as I was sitting by the fire, a great cloud came over me, and a temptation beset me; but I sat still. And it was said, "All things come by nature"; and the elements and stars came over me so that I was in a manner quite clouded with it. But inasmuch as I sat, still and silent, the people of the house perceived nothing. And as I sat still under it and let it alone, a living hope arose in me, and a true voice, which said, "There's a living God who made all things." And immediately the cloud and temptation vanished away, and life rose over it all, and my heart was glad, and I praised the living God.

On a certain time, as I was walking in the fields, the Lord said unto me, "Thy name is written in the Lamb's book of life, which was before the foundation of the world"; and as the Lord spoke it I believed and saw it in the new birth.

Then, some time after, the Lord commanded me to go abroad into the world, which was like a briery, thorny wilderness, and when I came in the Lord's mighty power with the word of life into the world, the world swelled and made a noise like the great raging waves of the sea. Priests and professors, magistrates and people, were all like a sea when I came to proclaim the day of the Lord and preach repentance.

GEORGE FOX

# A Mystery of Hope

*For what is your life?*
*It is even a vapor that appears for a little time*
*and then vanishes away.*
JAMES 4:14 NKJV

Your life is a transitory thing. It is a thing of change. There is no endurance in it, no settling down in it, no real home for it here. Therefore God calls life a *pilgrimage*—a passing on to a something that is to be. It means there is no real substance in it. It is a going and coming for a moment, then a passing away forever. Life is a mysterious thing. We do not understand life—why it should begin, why it should end. There is some meaning in it somewhere that has baffled every search; some meaning beyond, some more real state than itself. So the Bible calls life a *sleep*, a *dream*, the *wind*. No book but the Bible could have called our life a sleep. The great book of the Greeks has called death a sleep: "Death's twin brother, sleep."

But the Bible has the profounder thought—life is the sleep. Death is but the waking. And the great poets and philosophers of the world since have found no deeper thought of life than this; and the greatest of them all has used the very word—our little life is rounded with a sleep. It seems to have been a soothing thought to them, and it may be a sanctifying thought to us, that this life is not the end; and therefore it is a wise thing to turn round sometimes in our sleep and think how there is more beyond than dreams.

HENRY DRUMMOND

# In God's Hand

*Thou hast also given me the shield of thy salvation:*
*and thy right hand hath holden me up,*
*and thy gentleness hath made me great.*

PSALM 18:35 KJV

What we should be most diligent about, I think, is this. First, we must continually ask God in our prayers to keep us in His hand, and bear constantly in mind that, if He leaves us, we shall at once be down in the depths, as indeed we shall be. So we must never have any confidence in ourselves—that would simply be folly.

But most of us must walk with that special care and attention, and watch what progress we make in the virtues, and discover if, in any way, we are either improving or going back. This is especially in our love for each other, and in our desire to be thought least of, and in ordinary things. If we look to this and beg the Lord to give us light, we shall at once discern whether we have gained or lost. Do not suppose, then, that when God brings a soul to such a point He lets it go so quickly out of His hand that the devil can recapture it without much labor. His majesty is so anxious for it not to be lost that He gives it a thousand interior warnings of mankind, and thus it cannot fail to perceive danger.

TERESA OF AVILA

# Hopeful Love

*Charity. . .*
*beareth all things, believeth all things,*
*hopeth all things, endureth all things.*
1 CORINTHIANS 13:4, 7 KJV

Indeed charity [love] does by no means destroy prudence, and, out of mere simplicity and silliness, believe every word. Wisdom may dwell with love, and charity be cautious, but it is apt to believe well of all, to entertain a good opinion of them when there is no appearance to the contrary; nay, to believe well when there may be some dark appearances, if the evidence of ill be not clear.

All charity is full of candor, apt to make the best of everything and put on it the best face and appearance for the support of a kind opinion; but it will go into a bad with the utmost reluctance, and fence against it as much as it fairly and honestly can. And when, in spite of inclination, it cannot believe well of others, it will yet hope well, and continue to hope as long as there is any ground for it. It will not presently conclude a case desperate, but wishes the amendment of the worst of men and is very apt to hope for what it wishes.

How well-natured and amiable a thing is Christian charity! How lovely a thing would Christianity appear to the world, if those who profess it were more actuated and animated by this divine principle.

MATTHEW HENRY

# Take Courage

*Be of good courage.*
NUMBERS 13:20 NKJV

If we were well accustomed to the exercise of the presence of God, all bodily diseases would be much alleviated. God often permits that we should suffer a little, to purify our souls and oblige us to continue with Him.

Take courage; offer Him your pains incessantly. Pray to Him for strength to endure them. Above all, get a habit of entertaining yourself often with God, and forget Him the least you can. Adore Him in your infirmities, offer yourself to Him from time to time, and, in the height of your suffering, beseech Him humbly and affectionately (as a child his father) to make you comfortable to His holy will.

God has many ways of drawing us to Himself. He sometimes hides Himself from us, but faith alone ought to be our support and the foundation of our confidence, which must be all in God.

I would willingly ask of God a part of your sufferings. But I know my weakness, which is so great that if He left me one moment to myself, I should be the most wretched man alive. And yet I know not how He can leave me alone, because faith gives me as strong a conviction as sense can do—and I know that He will never forsake me. Let us fear to leave Him. Let us be always be with Him. Let us live and die in His presence.

BROTHER LAWRENCE

# Hope in Christ's Power

*"I am the way and the truth and the life.*
*No one comes to the Father except through me."*
JOHN 14:6 NIV

Christ is the power of God for salvation—the counter fact to the power of sin for destruction. Christ is the Way—He is also the Truth and the Life. This power, this life, is within our reach each moment of our life; as near, as free, as abundant as the air we breathe.

A breath of prayer in the morning, and the morning life is sure. A breath of prayer in the evening, and the evening blessing comes. So our life is redeemed from destruction. Breath by breath our life comes into us. Inch by inch it is redeemed. So much prayer today—so many inches redeemed today. So much water in life today—so many turns of the great wheel of life today.

Therefore, if we want to be saved—whatsoever will, let him take of the water of life freely. If you want to be saved, breathe the breath of life. And if you cannot breathe, let the groans which cannot be uttered go up to God, and the power of life will come. To all of us alike, if we but ask we shall receive. For God makes surpassing allowances, and He will do the least of us exceedingly abundantly above all that we ask or thing.

HENRY DRUMMOND

# A Condition in Chastisement

*Wherein ye greatly rejoice, though now for a season,
if need be, ye are in heaviness through manifold temptations.*

1 PETER 1:6 KJV

Three gracious words, "If need be." Not one of all my tears has been shed for nothing! Not one stroke of the rod has been unneeded, or that might have been spared.

Your heavenly Father loves you too much, and too tenderly, to bestow harsher correction than your case requires. Is it loss of health or loss of wealth or loss of beloved friends? Be still, there was a "need be." We are no judges of what that "need be" is; often though, in spite of aching hearts we are forced to exclaim, "Your judgments are greatly deep."

God here pledges Himself, that there will not be one unnecessary thorn in the believer's crown of suffering. No burden too heavy will be laid on him; and no sacrifice too great exacted from him. He will "temper the wind to the shorn lamb." Whenever the "need be" has accomplished its end, then the rod is removed—the chastisement suspended—the furnace quenched.

"If need be"! Oh, what a pillow on which to rest your aching head—that there is not a drop in all your bitter cup but what a God of love saw to be absolutely necessary. Will you not trust His heart, even though you cannot trace the mystery of His dealings? Not too curiously prying into the "Why it is?" or "How it is?" but satisfied that "So it is," and therefore, that all must be well.

Although you cannot see Him, yet judgment is before Him; therefore trust in Him.

JOHN MACDUFF

# *Our Refuge*

*The LORD is my rock, and my fortress,*
*and my deliverer;*
*the God of my rock; in him will I trust;*
*he is my shield, and the horn of my salvation,*
*my high tower, and my refuge, my savior;*
*thou savest me from violence.*

2 SAMUEL 22:2–3 KJV

We see that our dwelling place is also our fortress and our high tower and our rock and our refuge. We all know what a fortress is. It is a place of safety, where everything that is weak and helpless can be hidden from the enemy and kept in security. And when we are told that God, who is our dwelling place, is also our fortress, it can only mean one thing, and that is, if we will but live in our dwelling place, we shall be perfectly safe and secure from every assault of every possible enemy that can attack. "For in the time of trouble he shall hide me in his pavilion: in the secret of his tabernacle shall he hide me; he shall set me up upon a rock" (Psalm 27:5). "He that dwelleth in the secret place of the most High shall abide under the shadow of the Almighty" (Psalm 91:1). He shall hide us in the secret of His presence from the pride of man; He shall keep us secretly in a pavilion from the strife of tongues.

Trials may come in abundance, but they cannot penetrate into the sanctuary of the soul, and we may dwell in perfect peace even in the midst of life's fiercest storms.

HANNAH WHITALL SMITH

# The Hope of God's Work Within

*It is God who works in you
both to will and to do for His good pleasure.*

PHILIPPIANS 2:13 NKJV

It is simply by faith that we receive the Spirit of Christ to work in us to will and to do according to His good pleasure. He sheds abroad His own love in our hearts, and thereby kindles ours. Every victory over sin is by faith in Christ; and whenever the mind is diverted from Christ, by resolving and fighting against sin, whether we are aware of it or not, we are acting in our own strength, rejecting the help of Christ, and are under a specious delusion. Nothing but the life and energy of the Spirit of Christ within us can save us from sin, and hope is the uniform and universal condition of the working of this saving energy within us.

When we open the door by implicit trust, He enters and takes up His abode with us and in us. By shedding abroad His love, He enlivens our whole soul into sympathy with Himself, and in this way, and in this way alone, He purifies our hearts through faith. He sustains our wills in the attitude of devotion. He enlivens and regulates our affections, desires, appetites, and passions, and becomes our sanctification.

No one can ask for any greater experience than this: the set-apart life in Christ.

CHARLES G. FINNEY

# Hope in God Alone

*I called upon the LORD in distress:*
*the LORD answered me,*
*and set me in a large place.*
*It is better to trust in the LORD*
*than to put confidence in man.*
*It is better to trust in the LORD*
*than to put confidence in princes.*

PSALM 118:5, 8–9 KJV

You must despair of finding help anywhere else. While a person runs to any and everybody and puts more confidence in men than in God, he may go to the best man on earth, to an apostle or an angel, and it will avail him nothing. He might as well go to a child, as far as efficient help is concerned. I have told sinners sometimes, "I won't pray for you, nor have anything to do with you, if you are going to depend on me and put me in the place of the Savior. Go to Christ if you want help."

It is a species of trusting in an arm of flesh that God abhors. Many will flee to books, to anything, and sometimes even to the Bible and put it in the place of God and cleave to such vain help, until God compels them to look to Him alone. My advice: Look to Jesus Christ and prove God herewith, and you shall find that God "will open the windows of heaven, and pour you out a blessing that there shall not be room enough to receive it" (Malachi 3:10).

CHARLES G. FINNEY

# Remaining in Christ

*I follow after,*
*if that I may apprehend that for which also*
*I am apprehended of Christ Jesus.*
PHILIPPIANS 3:12 KJV

Paul's expression, and its application to the Christian life, can be best understood if we think of a father helping his child mount the side of some steep precipice. The father stands above and has taken the son by the hand to help him. He points him to the spot on which he will help him plant his feet, as he leaps upward. The leap would be too high and dangerous for the child alone, but, the father's hand is his trust, and he leaps to get hold of the point for which his father has taken hold of him. It is the father's strength that secures him and lifts him up and so urges him to use his utmost strength.

Such is the relation between Christ and you, oh weak and trembling believer. Fix first your eyes on the purpose for which He has apprehended you. It is nothing less than a life-abiding, unbroken fellowship with himself to which He is seeking to lift you up. All that you have already received—pardon and peace, the Spirit and His grace—are but preliminary to this. And all that you see promised to you in the future holiness and fruitfulness and glory everlasting are but its natural outcome. Union with Himself, and so with the Father, is His highest object. Fix your eye on this and gaze until it stands out before you clear and unmistakable: Christ's aim is to have me abiding in Him.

ANDREW MURRAY

# There Is Hope in Humility

*Be clothed with humility,*
*for "God resists the proud,*
*but gives grace to the humble."*

1 PETER 5:5 NKJV

Is there such humility to be found, that men shall indeed still count themselves "less than the least of all saints," the servants of all? There is. "Love vaunteth not itself, is not puffed up, seeketh not its own" (1 Corinthians 13:4–5).

Where the spirit of love is shed abroad in the heart, where the divine nature comes to a full birth, where Jesus the meek and lowly Lamb of God is truly formed within, there is given the power a perfect love that forgets itself and finds its blessedness in blessing others, in bearing with them and honoring them, however feeble they be. Where this love enters, God enters. And where God has entered in His power and reveals Himself as all, there the creature becomes nothing before God; it cannot be anything but humble toward the fellow creature.

The presence of God becomes not a thing of times and seasons, but the covering under which the soul ever dwells, and its deep abasement before God becomes the holy place of His presence whence all its words and works proceed.

ANDREW MURRAY

# Strength and Power

*God is my strength and power:*
*and he maketh my way perfect.*
2 SAMUEL 22:33 KJV

Man was dependent on the power of God in his first estate, but he is more dependent on His power now; he needs God's power to do more things for him and depends on a more wonderful exercise of His power.

It was an effect of the power to make man holy at the first; but more remarkably so now, because there is a great deal of opposition and difficulty in the way. It is a more glorious effect of power to make that holy that was so depraved and under the dominion of sin, than to confer holiness on that which beforehand had nothing of the contrary. It is a more glorious work of power to rescue a soul out of the hands of the devil and from the powers of darkness and to bring it into a state of salvation, than to confer holiness where there was no prepossession or opposition.

So it is a more glorious work of power to uphold a soul in a state of grace and holiness and to carry it on till it is brought to glory, when there is so much sin remaining in the heart resisting, and Satan with all his might opposing, than it would have been to have kept man from falling in the first place, when Satan had nothing in man.

Thus, the redeemed are dependent on God for all their good, as they have all of Him.

JONATHAN EDWARDS

# The Master's Touch

*I will do whatever you ask in my name.*
JOHN 14:13 NIV

Probably we have heard the sermon illustration about the wearied and discouraged young artist who put his head down on the table and slept beside the oil painting he had struggled over for weeks. No one could accuse him of not giving the work his best try. He had poured all the talent that he had into the picture.

While the artist slept, his painting master quietly entered the room and went to the sleeping boy, picked up a brush, and with his skilled hands began painting. With just a few touches, the beauty that had eluded the young artist began to appear. In just a few minutes the canvas became all that the young artist wanted it to be.

While that kind of teaching may be questionable, many of us need to be reminded that when we are tired and spent and lay down whatever our toiling might be, our own great Master will make perfect our endeavors for Him. From our service He will remove every stain, every blemish, and every failure. To our service He will give the brightest luster and highest honor. Shall we not bring ourselves to the One who can make us better?

WILLIAM "BILLY" SUNDAY

# The Subject Is the Tongue

*If anyone considers himself religious
and yet does not keep a tight rein on his tongue,
he deceives himself and his religion is worthless.*

JAMES 1:26 NIV

Most of us often forget this, but it's true: Noise, anger, explosive tones, superlatives, and exaggerations of passions add nothing to the force of what we say. Instead, they rob our words of the power that belongs to them. But utterances that show a spirit subdued by truth and mastered by wisdom is the utterance that sweeps away opposition, that persuades and overcomes.

Go into a heated political convention, and you will find that it is not the speakers who get angry and storm and swear who carry the day. But it's the participants who never lose their tempers and never raise their voices, who keep talking quietly and placidly as if they are discussing the weather, who win.

This is a truth that all of us who seek to influence our fellow beings in the family, in the church, in the school, in society, in politics, anywhere, must take to heart. Parents who shout at their children have raucous sons and daughters who scream at everyone and anyone.

The soft tongue breaks the bone. The tamed tongue subdues the adversary.

WASHINGTON GLADDEN

# The Hope of Love

*The greatest of these is love.*
1 CORINTHIANS 13:13 NIV

Love is the medicine of all moral evil. By it the world is to be cured of sin. Love is the wine of existence. When you have taken that, you have taken the most precious drop that there is in the cluster.

Love is the seraph, and faith and hope are the wings by which it flies. The nature of the highest love is to be exquisitely sensitive to the act of forcing itself unbidden and unwelcomed upon another. The finer, the stronger, the higher love is, the more it is conditioned upon reciprocation. No man can afford to invest his being in anything lower than faith, hope, and love, these three, the greatest of which is love.

Finish then Thy new creation; pure and spotless let us be. Let us see Thy great salvation, perfectly restored in Thee: Changed from glory into glory, till in heaven we take our place, till we cast our crowns before Thee, lost in wonder, love, and praise [Charles Wesley].

HENRY WARD BEECHER

# Legacy at Death

*Peace I leave with you,*
*My peace I give to you;*
*not as the world gives.*
JOHN 14:27 NKJV

How we treasure the last sayings of a dying parent. How specially cherished and memorable are his last looks and last words. This text is the last words—the parting legacy—of a dying Savior. It is a legacy of peace.

How different from the false and counterfeit peace in which so many are content to live and content to die. The world's peace is all well, so long as prosperity lasts, so long as the stream runs smoothly and the sky is clear; but when the flood is at hand or the storm is gathering, where is the world's peace? It is gone! There is no calculating on its permanency. Often when the cup is fullest, there is the trembling apprehension that in one brief moment it may be dashed to the ground. The soul may be saying to itself, "Peace, peace," but like the drawing in the sand, it may be obliterated by the first wave of adversity.

But, "not as the world gives" the peace of the believer is deep, calm, lasting, everlasting. The world, with all its blandishments, cannot give it. The world, with all its vicissitudes and fluctuations, cannot take it away. It is the brightest in the hour of trial; it lights up the final valley-like gloom.

JOHN MACDUFF

# Heavenly Illumination

*What I do thou knowest not now;*
*but thou shalt know hereafter.*
JOHN 13:7 KJV

As the natural sun sometimes sinks in clouds, so occasionally, the Christian who has a bright rising, and a brighter meridian, sets in gloom. It is not always "light" at his evening time; but this we know, when the day of immortality breaks, the last vestige of earth's shadows will forever flee away. To the closing hour of time, Providence may be to him a baffling enigma; but before the first hour has struck on heaven's chronometer, all will be clear. My soul, "in God's light you shall see the light." The book of His decrees is a sealed book now—"A greet deep" is all the explanation you can often give to His judgments; the why and the wherefore He seems to keep from us, to test our faith, to discipline us in trustful submission. To make us able to say, "Your will be done."

But rejoice, in that hereafter—light awaits you! "Now we see through a glass, darkly; but then face to face" (1 Corinthians 13:12). In the great mirror of eternity, all of the events of this present checkered scene will be reflected; the darkest of them will be seen to be bright with mercy—the severest dispensations, only the severe aspects of His love.

Pry not, then, too curiously; pronounce not to censoriously on God's dealings with you. Wait with patience until the grand day of disclosures; one confession shall then burst from every tongue, "Righteous are You, O Lord!"

JOHN MACDUFF

# Handbook for Hope

*I rejoice at Your word.*
PSALM 119:162 NKJV

The Bible has made an ineffaceable impression upon all human life. Upon it poets have fed their genius. Its thoughts lie like threads of gold upon the rich pages of each Browning or Wordsworth. Orators have quoted from it so largely that we may say that, in proportion as men are cultured, have they been students of the Bible.

Today its moral principles form the very substance and body of modern law and jurisprudence. For centuries it has been the book for patriots and reformers: It has been the slave's book; it has been the book for common people struggling upward; it has been a book of hope for all prodigals; it has been a medicine book for the brokenhearted, while its ideas furnish goals for society's future progress.

For the individual, the Bible—the Book of Life—teaches the art of individual growth, and it is a guide to conduct and character. For the state it is a handbook of universal civilization. For those who mourn, it is a loving bosom to flee to; for the young man and woman, it is the rule for godly attitudes and behavior; for the tempted, it shows how to live victoriously. For everyone, the Bible is a roadmap for salvation.

NEWELL DWIGHT HILLIS

# They Who Love

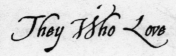

*Dear friends, let us love one another.*
1 JOHN 4:7 NIV

Nothing is sweeter than love, nothing more courageous, nothing higher, nothing wider, nothing more pleasant, nothing fuller nor better in heaven and earth, because love is born of God, and cannot rest but in God, above all created things.

Love feels no burden, thinks nothing of trouble, attempts what is above its strength, pleads no excuse of impossibility. It is therefore able to undertake all things, and it completes many things and warrants them to take effect, where he who does not love would faint and lie down. Love is watchful and sleeping, slumbering not. Though weary, it is not tired; though pressed, it is not straitened; though pressed, it is not confounded; but, as a lively flame and burning torch, it forces its way upward and securely passes all.

Three men are my friends—he that loves me, he that hates me, he that is indifferent to me. Who loves me teaches me tenderness; who hates me teaches me caution; who is indifferent to me teaches me self-reliance.

So long as we love, we serve. So long as we are loved by others, I would almost say we are indispensable, and no man is useless while he has a friend.

THOMAS À KEMPIS

# Hope for the Future

> My sheep hear my voice,
> and I know them, and they follow me:
> And I give unto them eternal life;
> and they shall never perish,
> neither shall any man pluck them out of my hand.
> My Father, which gave them me,
> is greater than all;
> and no man is able to pluck them out of my Father's hand.
>
> JOHN 10:27–29 KJV

It is true that, looking forward, there may be long avenues of tribulation, but the glory is at the end of them; battles may be foreseen, and woe to the person who does not expect them, but the eye of faith perceives the crown of victory. Deep waters are mapped upon our journey, but faith can see Jehovah fording these rivers with us, and she anticipates the day when we shall ascend the banks of the shore and enter into Jehovah's rest.

When we have received these priceless truths into our souls, we are satisfied with favor and full of the goodness of the Lord. I value the gospel not only for what it has done for me in the past, but for the guarantees which it affords me of eternal salvation. "I give unto them eternal life; and they shall never perish, neither shall any man pluck them out of my hand."

CHARLES SPURGEON

# His Everlasting Love

*I have loved you with an everlasting love;*
*therefore I have continued my faithfulness to you.*
JEREMIAH 31:3 NRSV

Reflect upon the everlasting love God has had for you. Before our Lord Jesus Christ as man suffered on the Cross for you, His Divine Majesty by His sovereign goodness already foresaw your existence and loved and favored you. When did His love for you begin? It began even when He began to be God. When did He begin to be God? Never, for He has been forever, without beginning and without end. So also He has always loved you from all eternity and for this reason He has prepared for you all these graces and favors.

Hence He speaks to you as well as to others when He speaks through the prophet [Jeremiah 31:3]. Among other things, He has thought of enabling you to make your resolution to serve Him.

O God, what resolutions are these which you have thought of and meditated upon and projected from all eternity! How dear and precious should they be to us! What should we not suffer rather than forget the least of them! Rather let the whole world perish! For all the world together is not worth one single soul and a soul is worth nothing without these resolutions.

Learn to despise exterior things and to give yourself to the interior, and you shall have hope that the kingdom of God will come to you [Thomas à Kempis].

FRANCIS DE SALES

# Finding Hope Within, Part 1

*Seek the LORD while he may be found,*
*call upon him while he is near.*
ISAIAH 55:6 NRSV

North of the village and over a hill lay a piece of woods, in which I was in the almost daily habit of walking when it was pleasant weather. It was now October, and the time was past for my frequent walks there. Nevertheless, instead of going to my [law] office, I turned and bent my course toward the woods, feeling that I must be alone and away from all human eyes and ears, so that I could pour my prayer to God.

I penetrated into the woods a quarter of a mile, went over the other side of the hill, and found a place where some large trees had fallen across each other, leaving an open space between. There I saw I could make kind of a closet. I crept into this place and knelt down for prayer. As I turned to go up into the woods, I recollect to have said, "I will give my heart to God, or I will never come down from there." I recollect repeating this as I went up—"I will give my heart to God before I ever come down again."

When I came to try, I found I could not give my heart to God. My inward soul hung back, and there was no going out of my heart to God. I began to feel deeply that it was too late; that it must be that I was given up of God and was past hope.

CHARLES G. FINNEY

# Finding Hope Within, Part 2

*"You will seek me and find me
when you seek me with all your heart."*
JEREMIAH 29:13 NIV

I said to myself, "I cannot pray. My heart is dead to God and will not pray."

Just at this moment I thought I heard someone approach me, and I opened my eyes. Right then the revelation of my pride of heart, as the great difficulty that stood in the way, was shown to me. An overwhelming sense of my wickedness in being ashamed to have a human being see me on my knees before God, took such powerful possession of me, that I cried at the top of my voice and exclaimed that I would not leave that place if all the men on earth and all the devils in hell surrounded me.

Just at that point this passage of scripture seemed to drop into my mind with a flood of light: "Then shall ye go and pray unto me, and I will hear unto you. Then shall ye seek me and find me, when ye shall search for me with all your heart." I instantly seized hold of this with my heart.

I knew that that was a passage of scripture. I knew it was God's Word, and it was God's voice that spoke to me. I cried to Him, "Lord, I take Thee at Thy word. Now thou knowest that I do search for Thee with all my heart, and that I have come here to pray to Thee, and Thou hast promised to hear me."

CHARLES G. FINNEY

# Finding Hope Within, Part 3

*You are all sons of God through faith in Christ Jesus.*
GALATIANS 3:26 NIV

The question was settled. I could that day perform my vow. The Spirit seemed to lay stress upon the idea in the text, "When you search for me with all your heart." I told the Lord that I would take Him at His Word; that He could not lie; and therefore I was sure that He heard my prayer, and that He would be found of me.

He gave me many other promises, both from the Old Testament and the New Testament, especially some of the most precious promises respecting our Lord Jesus Christ. I never can, in words, make any human being understand how precious and true those promises appeared to me.

I took the promises God gave me one after the other as infallible truth, the assertions of a loving God who could not lie. They did not seem so much to fall into my intellect as into my heart, to be put within the grasp of the voluntary powers of my mind; and I seized hold of them, appropriated them, and fastened upon them with the grasp of a drowning man.

*The future was bright. Lawyer Charles Finney anticipated the tomorrows of his life. "[His] hope was built on nothing less, than Jesus' blood and righteousness."*

CHARLES G. FINNEY

# The Glorified One

*Your life is now hidden with Christ in God.*
*When Christ, who is your life, appears,*
*then you also will appear with him in glory.*
COLOSSIANS 3:3–4 NIV

This life of hope abides close to the Glorified One. In Him we find our reason for existence; it's to fellowship with Him.

❧

This life in Christ is a life of full fellowship with the Father's love and holiness. Jesus often gave prominence to this thought with His disciples. His death was a going to the Father. He prayed: "Glorify me, O Father, with Thyself, with the glory which I had with Thee" (John 17:5).

As the believer, abiding in Christ the Glorified One, seeks to realize and experience what His union with Jesus on the throne implies. The believer apprehends how the unclouded light of the Father's presence is His highest glory and blessedness. In Him is the believer's portion.

The believer learns the sacred art of "always"—always in fellowship with his exalted head; always dwelling in the secret of the Father's presence. Further, when Jesus was on earth, temptation could still reach Him: In glory, everything is holy and in perfect harmony with the will of God.

So the believer who abides in him experiences that; in this high fellowship his spirit is sanctified into growing harmony with the Father's will. The heavenly life of Jesus is the power that casts out sin.

ANDREW MURRAY

# Until I Reach the Shore

*Love your enemies,*
*do good to those who hate you.*
LUKE 6:27 NIV

Dwight L. Moody occasionally ended his sermon with this prayer from an anonymous Romanian Christian who had suffered much for his faith.

🌿

I have not yet reached the shore where there is no hatred. The clouds of unjust struggles have not yet passed. The scars of wounds endured have not yet closed. Warm trust in men lies totally dead. From the springs of forgetting, I have not drunk wisdom.

Weary memories still poison me. From the glades of forgiveness I am still absent. From the sanctuary of refuge I am a great way separated.

Lord, will you give me back my hope and bring me to the clear dawn of other days? May all painful shadows depart from me. Let me look with tender emotion on the scars of my wounds and with meek goodness upon the faces of my enemies. Bring me to the dawn whilst the way is so long, but Lord do not hinder my striving until I reach the shore. Amen.

A ROMANIAN CHRISTIAN

# Written from Bedford Gaol

*As a prisoner for the Lord, then,*
*I urge you to live a life worthy of*
*the calling you have received.*
EPHESIANS 4:1 NIV

If John Bunyan were alive today, he would tearfully tell us of the dark days and spiritual doubting he experienced for several years after serving in the British army. But when he answered God's call to preach, he was "filled with overriding hope that could not be denied." Imprisoned for twelve years for his to-the-point preaching, Bunyan wrote and published his spiritual biography—*Grace Abounding*.

My hope is found in this: [Jesus Christ] wrestled with justice, that I might have rest; He wept and mourned, that I might laugh and rejoice; He was betrayed, that I might go free; He was apprehended, that I might escape; He was condemned, that I might be justified, and was killed, that I might live; He wore a crown of thorns, that I might wear a crown of glory; and He was nailed to the cross with his arms wide open, to show with what freshness all His merits shall be bestowed on those who come to Him. He will receive them into His bosom.

Hope has a thick skin and will endure many a blow; it will put on patience as a vestment, it will wade through a sea of blood, it will endure all things if it be of the right kind, for the joy that is set before it. It is hope that makes the soul exercise patience, until the time comes to enjoy the crown.

JOHN BUNYAN

## *Peace in Hope*

*Peace I leave with you; my peace I give you.*
*I do not give to you as the world gives.*

JOHN 14:27 NIV

"You will keep him in perfect peace, whose mind is stayed on You" (Isaiah 26:3 NKJV). "Perfect peace"—what a blessed attainment. Dear reader, is it yours? Do you have the sense of hope that peace brings about?

If you have all that the world calls enviable and happy, unless you have peace in God and with God, all else is unworthy of the name. Perfect peace! What is it? It is the peace of forgiveness. It is the peace arising out of a sense of God reconciled through the blood of the everlasting covenant—resting on the bosom and work of Jesus.

My soul, stay yourself on God, so that this blessed peace may be yours. You have tried the world. It has deceived you. Prop after prop of earthly scaffolding has yielded and tottered and fallen. Has our God ever done that? False and counterfeit world peace may do well for the world's work and worldly prosperity. But test it in the hour of sorrow—what can it do for you when it is most needed?

On the other hand, even if you have no other blessing on the earth to call your own, you are rich indeed if you can look up to heaven and say with a smile, "I am at peace with God."

JOHN MACDUFF

# Words of Hope

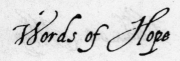

*We also rejoice in our sufferings,*
*because we know that suffering produces perseverance;*
*perseverance, character; and character, hope.*
*And hope does not disappoint us.*

ROMANS 5:3–4 NIV

Christianity is not a voice in the wilderness, but a life in the world. It is not an idea in the air, but has feet on the ground—going God's way. It is not an exotic to be kept under glass, but a hardy plant to bear twelve months of fruits in all kinds of weather.

Fidelity to duty is its root and branch. Nothing we can say to the Lord, no calling Him by great or dear names, can take the place of the plain doing of His will. We may cry out about the beauty of eating bread with Him in His kingdom, but it is wasted breath and a rootless hope, unless we plow and plant in His kingdom here and now.

To remember Him at His table and to forget Him at ours is to have invested in bad securities. True hope is found in absolute truth—there is no substitute for plain everyday goodness.

The tests of life are to make, not break us. The blow at the outward man may be the greatest blessing to the inner man. If God puts or permits anything hard in our lives, be sure that the real peril, the real trouble, is that we shall lose if we flinch or rebel.

M. D. BABCOCK

# The Cross Holds out Hope

*Let us fix our eyes on Jesus,*
*the author and perfector of our faith,*
*who for the joy set before him endured the cross,*
*scorning its shame,*
*and sat down at the right hand of the throne of God.*

HEBREWS 12:2 NIV

In the cross of Christ we glory, because we regard it as a matchless exhibition of the attributes of God. We see there the love of God, desiring a way by which He might save mankind, aided by His wisdom, so that a plan is perfected by which the deed can be done without violation of truth and justice.

In the cross we see a strange conjunction of what once appeared to be two opposite qualities—justice and mercy. We see how God is supremely just; as just as if He had no mercy, and yet infinitely merciful in the gift of His Son.

Mercy and justice, in fact, become counsel upon the same side and irresistibly plead for the acquittal of the believing sinner. We can never tell which of the attributes of God shines most glorious in the sacrifice of Christ; they each one find a glorious high throne in the person and work of the Lamb of God, that taketh away the sin of the world. Since it has become the disc which reflects the character and perfections of God, it is meet that we should glory in the cross of Christ, and none shall stay us of our boasting.

CHARLES H. SPURGEON

*The LORD watches over the way of the righteous.*

PSALM 1:6 NIV

A parable on hope that reflects "trees planted by streams, which yield their fruit in its season."

Did you ever see a man sitting in his own orchard with the trees (which he planted with his own hand) pouring down their ripened fruit upon him, and he and his children and his grandchildren rejoicing in its beauty?

That is the picture of a man who took hope and planted it, and now he is sitting under the boughs that overarch him. His trees of hope were watered by faith in God's word, enriched with his love to God, and cultivated by faith in His promises. The man was faithful in attending to every phase of the orchard's growth. The glory of hope cannot be overestimated. It brings its positive influence wherever it is planted, nurtured, and allowed to bloom.

This orchard of hope becomes a bountiful gift to the man's antecedents and descendents. It is a vision of what is ahead, as well as what the man has pledged in other days. The result of the hope? His days are happy, and his life is full of joy and usefulness. Hope affects the man's life, as well as his future in the kingdom of God.

THOMAS BROOKS

# Anticipation and Joy

*You ought to live holy and godly lives*
*as you forward to the day of God and speed its coming.*
2 PETER 3:11–12 NIV

If you would keep young and happy, cultivate hope, live a high moral life, practice the principles of the brotherhood of man, send out good thoughts and prayers to all, and think evil of no man. . .

This is in obedience to God's great natural law; to live otherwise is to break this Divine law. Other things being equal, it is the cleanest, purest minds that live long and are happy. The man who is growing in his soul and developing intellectually does not grow old like the man who has stopped advancing; but when ambition, aspiration, and hope halt, old age sets in.

There is nothing like God-given hope to keep your mind fresh, provide you with a quicker step, offer you restful sleep at night, brighten your eyes, and put a smile on your face.

A Christian will part with anything rather than his hope; he knows that hope will keep the heart both from aching and breaking, from fainting and sinking. The Christian knows that hope is a beam of God, a spark of glory that nothing can extinguish till the soul is filled with glory.

THOMAS BROOKS

# The Fire of Hope

*Fan into flame the gift of God.*
2 TIMOTHY 1:6 NIV

Look at a coal covered with ashes; there is nothing else in the hearth, only the dead ashes. There is neither light, nor smoke, nor heat; and yet when these embers are stirred to the bottom, there are found some living gleams which do not contain fire, yet these gleaming embers are apt to propagate fire.

Many a Christian breast is like this hearth; no life of grace has appeared there for a long time. There is no vision or anticipation for tomorrows. All seems cold and dead; yet still there is a secret coal in his bosom, which upon gracious motion of the Almighty, will stir up the Divine fire to a perfect flame of hope.

Let no man, therefore, deject himself or censure others, for the utter extinction of that spirit which hides in the soul can be fanned into flame.

HERBERT SPENCER

## *A Quiet Hope*

*Be still, and know that I am God.*
PSALM 46:10 KJV

It is not easy to be still in this rough and restless world. Yet God says, "Be still"; and He also says, "In returning and rest shall ye be saved; in quietness and in confidence shall be your strength" (Isaiah 30:15).

Be still, and know that I can put all enemies to shame. The Lord shall hold them in derision. Who shall contend with Him who made the heavens and the earth? Remember, I am God.

Be still, and know that I can uphold My own truth in a day of error. Is not My truth precious to me? And My book of truth, is it not above all books in My eyes? Remember, I am God.

Be still, and you shall know that I can say to the nations, "Peace, be still." The waves rise, but I am mightier than all. Remember, these tumults do not touch My throne. Take no alarm; I am still God.

Be still, and you shall see the glorious issue of all these confusions. Know that this world is My world, and you shall see it to be so. Remember, this earth shall yet be the abode of the righteous, because I am God.

HORATIUS BONAR

# Practicing His Presence, Part 1

*Am I now seeking human approval,*
*or God's approval?*
*Or am I trying to please people?*
GALATIANS 1:10 NRSV

Brother Lawrence discourses with me very frequently, and with great openness of heart, concerning his manner of going to God. He tells me that all consists in one hearty renunciation of everything to which we are sensitive does not leave to God, that we might accustom ourselves to a continual conversation with Him, with freedom and in simplicity. That we need only to recognize God intimately present with us, to address ourselves to Him every moment, that we may beg for His assistance for knowing His will in things doubtful, and for rightly performing those we plainly see He requires of us, offering them to Him before we do them, and giving Him thanks when we have done.

In this hope-filled conversation with God, we are also employed in praising, adoring, and loving Him incessantly for His infinite goodness and perfection.

BROTHER LAWRENCE AND HIS INTERVIEWER

# Practicing His Presence, Part 2

*If I were still pleasing people,*
*I would not be a servant of Christ.*

GALATIANS 1:10 NRSV

As Brother Lawrence has found such an advantage in walking in the presence of God, it is natural for him to recommend it earnestly to others—to those who have lost all hope for personal devotion—but his example is a stronger inducement than any arguments he could propose.

His very countenance is edifying; such a sweet and calm devotion appearing in it, as could not but affect the beholders. And it is observed, that in the greatest hurry of business in the kitchen, he still preserves his heavenly-mindedness. He is never hasty nor loitering, but he does each thing in its season, with an even uninterrupted composure and tranquility of spirit; he says, "To me the time of business does not differ the time of prayer; and in the noise and clutter of my kitchen while at the same time several brothers are at the same time calling for my attention, I possess God in as great tranquility as if I were upon my knees at the Sacrament.

"The most excellent method I have of going to God is in doing my common business without any view of pleasing men. My hope of glory is found in performing purely for the love of God."

BROTHER LAWRENCE AND HIS INTERVIEWER

# God Wills Our Good

*He no longer should live*
*the rest of his time in the flesh. . .*
*but to the will of God.*
1 PETER 4:2 KJV

Perfection is founded entirely on the love of God, and the perfect love of God means the complete union of our will with God's: It follows then, that the more one unites his will with the divine will, the greater will be his love of God.

The greatest glory we can give to God is to do His will in everything. Our Redeemer came on earth to glorify His heavenly Father and to teach us by His example and how we can do the same. Our Lord frequently declared that He had come on earth not to do His own will, but solely that of His Father. He spoke in the same strain in the garden when He went to meet His enemies who had come to seize Him and to lead Him to death: Furthermore, He said He would recognize as His brother him who would do His will.

If we would completely rejoice the heart of God, let us strive in all things to conform ourselves to whatever dispositions God makes of us. Conformity signifies that we join our wills to the will of God. Uniformity means more—it means that we make one will of God's will and ours, so that we will only what God wills; that God's will alone is our will. This is the summit of perfection and to it we should always aspire; this should be the goal of all our works, desires, meditations, and prayers.

ALPHONSUS DE LIGOURI

# No More Sin or Sorrow

*He will wipe every tear from their eyes.*
*There will be no more death or mourning or crying or pain,*
*for the old order of things has passed away.*
REVELATION 21:4 NIV

The most glorious of all will be the change that will take place on the poor, sinful, miserable children of men. These had fallen in many respects, as from a greater height, so into a lower depth, than any other part of the creation. But they shall "hear a great voice out of heaven saying, Behold, the tabernacle of God is with men, and he will dwell with them, and they shall be his people, and God himself shall be. . .their God" (Revelation 21:3).

Thus will arise an unmixed state of holiness and happiness far superior to that which Adam enjoyed in Paradise. In how beautiful a manner is this described by the apostle: "God shall wipe away all tears from their eyes; and there shall be no more death, neither sorrow, nor crying, neither shall there be any more pain; for the former things are done away!" As there will be no more death and no more pain or sickness, as there will be no more grieving for or parting from friends, so there will be no more sorrow or crying. But there will be an even greater deliverance than all this, for there will be no more sin. And to crown all, there will be a deep and intimate uninterrupted union with God, a constant communion with the Father and His Son Jesus Christ through the Spirit, a continual enjoyment of the Three-in-One God, and of all the creatures in Him!

JOHN WESLEY

# Atonement for Sin

*If when we were enemies we were reconciled to*
*God through the death of His Son, much more,*
*having been reconciled, we shall be saved by His life.*
ROMANS 5:10 NKJV

Sin is power in our life; let us fairly understand that it can only be met by another power. The fact of sin works all through our life. The death of Christ, which is the atonement, reconciles us to God, makes our religion possible, puts us in the way of the power which is to come against our sin and deliver our life from destruction. But the water of life, which flows from the life of Christ, is the power itself.

He redeemeth my life, by His life, from destruction. This is the power, Paul says, which redeemed his life from destruction. Christ's life, not His death, living in his life, absorbing it, impregnating it, transforming it: "Christ," as he confessed, "in me."

Paul meant no disrespect to the atonement when he said, "We shall be saved by his life." He was bringing out in relief one of the great facts of salvation. If God gives atoning power with one hand and power to save the life from destruction with the other, there is no jealousy between. Both are from God. Atonement is from God. Power to resist sin is from God. Christ is all in all, the beginning and the end.

HENRY DRUMMOND

# Great Is Your Reward

*Rejoice, and be exceeding glad:*
*for great is your reward in heaven.*

MATTHEW 5:12 KJV

The text speaks to you who are patiently suffering for truth's sake. For to you it is given not only to believe, but also to suffer, and perhaps remarkably, too, for the sake of Jesus! This is a mark of your discipleship, an evidence that you do live godly in Christ Jesus. Fear not, therefore, neither be dismayed. Be not weary and faint in your minds. Jesus, your Lord, your life, comes, and His reward is with Him.

Though all men forsake you, He will not: No, the Spirit of Christ and of glory shall rest upon you. Think it not strange concerning the fiery trial by which you are or may be tried. The Devil rages, knowing that he has but a short time to reign. He or his emissaries have no more power than what is given them from above: God sets their bounds, which they cannot pass; and the very hairs of your head are all numbered. Fear not; no one shall set upon you to hurt you without your heavenly Father's knowledge. The Lord shall reveal Himself to you, as to the man who was born blind. Jesus Christ shall take you up. Fear not; the God whom you serve is able to deliver you: or, if He should suffer the flames to devour your bodies, they would only serve, as so many fiery chariots, to carry your souls to God.

Dare, dare to live godly in Christ Jesus, though you suffer all manner of persecution.

GEORGE WHITEFIELD

# *Hope of Victory*

*Thanks be to God!*
*He gives us the victory through our Lord Jesus Christ.*
*Therefore, my dear brothers, stand firm.*
*Let nothing move you.*
*Always give yourselves fully to the work of the Lord,*
*because you know that your labor in the Lord is not in vain.*

1 CORINTHIANS 15:57–58 NIV

O Christian, only believe that there is a victorious life! Christ the victor is your Lord. He will undertake for you in everything and will enable you to do all that the Father expects from you. Be of good courage. Will you not trust Him to do this great work for you who has given His life for you and has forgiven your sins?

Dare, in His power, to surrender yourself to the life of those who are kept from sin by the power of God. Along with the deepest conviction that there is no good in you, confess that you see in the Lord Jesus all the goodness of which you have need, for the life of a child of God. Begin to literally to live "by the faith of the Son of God, who loved me, and gave himself for me" (Galatians 2:20).

Thank God, a life of victory is sure for those who have a knowledge of their inward ruin and are hopeless in themselves. But, who, in "the confidence of despair" have looked to Jesus, and, in faith in His power to make the act of surrender possible for them, they have done it, in His might, and now rely on Him alone every day and every hour.

ANDREW MURRAY

# Christian Blamelessness

*"Walk before me, and be blameless."*

GENESIS 17:1 NRSV

The presence of God calms the soul and gives it quiet and repose even during the day and in the midst of busyness. But we must be given up to God without reserve. When we have once found God, we have nothing to seek among men; we must make the sacrifice of our dearest friendships. The best of friends has entered into our hearts, that jealous Bridegroom who requires the whole of it for Himself.

It takes no great time to love God, to be refreshed by His presence, to elevate our hearts to Him, or to worship Him in the depths of our souls, to offer Him all we do and all we suffer. This is the true kingdom of God within us, which cannot be disturbed. When the distractions of the senses and the vivacity of the imagination hinder the soul from a sweet and peaceful state of recollection, we should at least be calm as to the state of the will. In that case, the will to be recollected is a sufficient state of recollection for the time being. We must return toward God and do everything that He would have us do with a right intention.

Let us separate ourselves from all that does not come from God. Let us suppress our superfluous thoughts and reveries. Let us utter no useless word. Let us seek God within us, and we shall find Him without fail. With Him, joy and peace.

FRANÇOIS FENELON

# *Hope for Maturity*

*Go on toward maturity.*

HEBREWS 6:1 NIV

Maturity [perfection] consists in doing the will of God, not in understanding His designs. The designs of God, the good pleasure of God, the will of God, the operation of God, and gift of His grace are all one and the same thing in the spiritual life. It is God working in the soul to make it like himself. Maturity is neither more nor less than the faithful cooperation of the soul with the work of God, and is begun, grows, and is consummated in the soul unperceived and in secret. The designs of God and His divine will accepted by a faithful soul with simplicity produces this divine state in it without its knowledge, just as a medicine taken obediently will produce health, although the sick person neither knows nor wishes to know anything about medicine. As fire gives out heat, so the designs of God and His holy will work in the soul for its sanctification, not speculations of curiosity as to this principle and this state.

When one is thirsty, one quenches one's thirst by drinks, not by reading books that discuss this condition. The desire to know increases this thirst. Therefore, when one thirsts after sanctity, the desire to know about it only drives it further away. Speculation must be laid aside, and everything arranged by God as regards actions and sufferings must be accepted with simplicity, for those things that happen at each moment by the divine command or permission are always the most holy, the best and the most divine for us.

JEAN-PIERRE DE CAUSSADE

# God's Word to Us

*Let the word of Christ dwell in you richly*
*as you teach and admonish one another with all wisdom,*
*and as you sing psalms, hymns, and spiritual songs*
*with gratitude in your hearts to God.*

COLOSSIANS 3:16 NIV

That which is sent us at the present moments is the most useful because it is intended especially for us. We can only be well instructed by the words that God utters expressly for us. No one becomes learned in the science of God either by the reading of books or by the inquisitive investigation of history. That which instructs us in what happens from one moment to another producing in us that experimental science which Jesus Christ himself willed to acquire before instructing others. It is impossible to perfectly understand anything that experience has not taught us, by suffering or by action.

We must listen to God from moment to moment to become learned in the theology of virtue that is entirely practical and experimental. Do not attend therefore to what is said to others, but listen to that which is said to you and for us; there will be enough to exercise your faith because this interior language of God exercises, purifies, and increases it by its very obscurity.

JEAN-PIERRE DE CAUSSADE

# Hope in God's Patience

*I will have mercy on whom I have mercy,*
*and I will have compassion on whom I have compassion.*
*It does not, therefore, depend on man's desire or effort,*
*but on God's mercy.*

ROMANS 9:15 NIV

Because He [God] would confer eternal life upon man, He patiently endures the filthy righteousness of this life wherein we must dwell until the last day, for the sake of His chosen people and until the number is complete. For so long as the final day is deferred, not all to have eternal life are yet born. When the time shall be fulfilled, the number completed, God will suddenly bring to an end the world with its governments, its jurists and authorities, its conditions of life; in short, He will utterly abolish earthly righteousness, destroying physical appetites and all else together.

Every form of human holiness is condemned to destruction; yet for the sake of Christians, to whom eternal life is appointed, and for their sake only, all these must be perpetuated until the last saint is born and has attained life everlasting. Were there but one saint yet to be born, for the sake of that one the world must remain. For God regards not the world nor has He need for it, except for the sake of His Christians.

MARTIN LUTHER

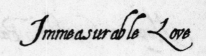

*"I have loved you with an everlasting love."*
JEREMIAH 31:3 NIV

Sometimes the Lord Jesus tells His church His love thoughts. The Holy Spirit is often pleased, in a most gracious manner, to witness with our spirits of the love of Jesus. No voice is heard from the clouds, and no vision is seen in the night, but we have a testimony more sure than either of these. If an angel should fly from heaven and inform the saint personally of the Savior's love to him or her, the evidence would not be one bit more satisfactory than that which is borne in the heart by the Holy Spirit.

Ask those of the Lord's people who have lived the nearest to the gates of heaven, and they will tell you that they have had some seasons when the love of Christ toward them has been a fact so clear and sure that they could no more doubt it than they could question their own existence.

You and I have had times of refreshing from the presence of the Lord, and then our faith and hope have mounted to the topmost heights of assurance. We have had confidence to lean our heads upon our Lord's bosom, and we have had no more questions about our Master's affection for us than John did when in that blessed posture; no, nor so much: For the dark question, "Lord, is it I who will betray you?" has been put far from us. He has kissed us with the kisses of His mouth and killed our doubts by the closeness of His embrace. His love has been sweeter than wine to our souls.

CHARLES SPURGEON

# Hope in Submission

*Submit yourselves, then, to God.*
JAMES 4:7 NIV

At the beginning of each day, declare to God that you desire to belong to Him entirely, and that you will devote yourself wholly to acquiring the spirit of prayer and of the interior life.

Make it your chief study to conform yourself to the will of God even in the smallest things, saying in the midst of the most annoying contradictions and with the most alarming prospects for the future: "My God, I desire with all my heart to do Your holy will; I submit in all things and absolutely to Your good pleasure for time and eternity, I wish to do this, O God, for two reasons: First, because You are my Sovereign Lord and it is but just that Your will should be accomplished; second, because I am convinced by faith and by experience that Your will is in all things as good and beneficent as it is just and adorable, while my own desire is corrupt, because I nearly always long for what would do me harm. Therefore, from this time forward, I renounce my own will to follow Your will in all things; dispose of me, O God, according to Your good will and pleasure."

This continual practice of submission will preserve that interior peace as the foundation of the spiritual life.

JEAN-PIERRE DE CAUSSADE

# More Than Conquerors

*In all these things we are more than conquerors through him that loved us.*

ROMANS 8:37 KJV

A joyous man, such as I have now in my mind's eye, is for all intents and purposes a strong man. He is strong in a calm, restful manner. Whatever happens he is not ruffled or disturbed. He is not afraid of evil tidings; his heart is fixed, trusting in the Lord. The ruffled person is ever weak. He is in a hurry and does things poorly. The man full of joy within is quiet. He bides his time and crouches in the fullness of his strength. Such a man, though he is humble, is firm and steadfast; he is not carried away with every wind or bowed by every breeze; he knows what he knows and holds what he holds. The golden anchor of his hope enters within the veil and holds him fast.

His strength is not pretentious but real. The happiness arising from communion with God breeds in him no boastfulness; he does not talk of what he can do, but he does it! He does not say what he could bear, but he bears all that comes his way. He does not always know what he could do; his weakness is the more apparent to himself because of the strength which the Holy Spirit puts upon him. When the time comes, his weakness only illustrates the divine might, while the man goes calmly on, conquering.

CHARLES H. SPURGEON

# Hope in a Changed Life

*For to me to live is Christ,*
*and to die is gain.*
PHILIPPIANS 1:21 KJV

What went on between Paul's heart and God we do not know. We do not know how deep repentance ran, nor where nor how the justifying grace came down from heaven to his soul. Whether just then he went through our conversion formula—the process which we like to describe in technical words—we do not know. But we know this—there came a difference into his life. His life was changed. It was changed at its most radical part. He had changed centers. During the process, whatever that was, this great transfer was effected. Paul deliberately removed the old center from his life and put a new one in its place. Instead of "to me to live is Saul," it was now, "to me to live is Christ."

Of course, when the center of Paul's life was changed, he had to take his whole life to pieces and build it up again on a totally different plan. This change, therefore, is not a mere incident in a man's life. It is a revolution; a revolution of the most sweeping sort. There never was a life so filled up with anti-Christian thoughts and impulses that was brought to such a complete halt. There never was such a total eclipse of the most brilliant worldly prospects nor such an abrupt transition from a career of dazzling greatness to humble and obscure ignominy.

HENRY DRUMMOND

# The Wisdom of Christ

> *My purpose is that they. . .*
> *may have the full riches of complete understanding,*
> *in order that they may know the mystery of God,*
> *namely, Christ, in whom are hidden all the treasures of*
> *wisdom and knowledge.*
>
> COLOSSIANS 2:2–3 NIV

Expect from Him most confidently whatever teaching you may need for a life to the glory of the Father. In all that concerns your spiritual life, abide in Jesus as your wisdom. The life you have in Christ is a thing of infinite sacredness. It is far too holy and high for you to know how to act it out. It is He alone who can guide you to know what is becoming your dignity as a child of God. He will help you understand what will hinder your inner life, and especially your abiding in Him.

Do not think of it as a mystery or a difficulty you have to solve, whatever questions come up regarding the possibility of abiding perfectly and uninterruptedly in Him, and of really obtaining all the blessings that come from it. Always remember that He knows everything; it is all perfectly clear to Him. He is my wisdom. Just as much as you need to and are capable of understanding, He will communicate to you. But you must trust Him! Never think that Jesus has hidden away the riches of wisdom and knowledge, as in a treasure chest without a key or of your way as a path without a light. Jesus, who is your wisdom, is guiding you, even when you can't see it.

ANDREW MURRAY

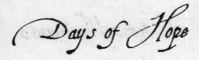

*"The righteous will live by faith."*
ROMANS 1:17 NIV

October 31, 1517, Martin Luther posted his ninety-five theses on the door of the church in Wittenberg. In 1546 the Wittenberg pastor delivered "A Christian sermon over the body and at the funeral of the venerable Dr. Martin Luther."

When Martin Luther noticed that his hour had come, the following is what he prayed.

O my heavenly Father, one God and Father of our Lord Jesus Christ, God of all comfort, I thank you that you have revealed to me your dear Son, Jesus Christ, in whom I believe, whom I have preached and confessed, whom I have loved and praised. I implore you, my Lord Jesus Christ, let my little soul be commended to you.

O heavenly Father, although I must leave this body and be snatched away from this life, I am, nevertheless, certain that I will remain with you eternally and that no one will tear me out of Your hands.

*And then he said three times:* Into your hands I commend my spirit. You have redeemed me, my faithful God. My hope for eternal life is found in this: "For God so loved the world that he gave his only begotten Son so that all who believe in him will not be lost but have eternal life."

*And then he folded his hands and gave up his spirit to Christ in grand silence.*

MARTIN LUTHER

# For All Saints

*We are surrounded by such a great cloud of witnesses.*

HEBREWS 12:1 NIV

For all the saints, who from their labors rest,
Who Thee by faith before the world confessed,
Thy Name, O Jesus, be forever blessed.
Alleluia, alleluia!

Thou wast their Rock, their Fortress, and their Might:
Thou Lord, their Captain in the well-fought fight;
Thou, in the darkness drear, their one true Light.
Alleluia, alleluia!

O may Thy soldiers, faithful, true, and bold,
Fight as the saints who nobly fought of old,
And win with them the victor's crown of gold.
Alleluia, alleluia!

And when the strife is fierce, the warfare long,
Steals on the ear the distant triumph song,
And hearts are brave again and arms are strong.
Alleluia, alleluia!

But lo! There breaks a yet more glorious day;
The saints triumphant rise in bright array;
The King of Glory passes on His way.
Alleluia, alleluia!

From earth's wide bounds, from oceans farthest coast,
Through gates of pearl stream in the countless host,
Singing to Father, Son, and Holy Ghost.
Alleluia, alleluia!

WILLIAM WALSHAM HOW

# *Needs Supplied*

*My God shall supply all your need according to*
*His riches in glory by Christ Jesus.*
PHILIPPIANS 4:19 NKJV

If it is a throne of grace, then all the wants of those who come to it will be supplied. The King from off such a throne will not say, "You must bring Me gifts; you must offer Me sacrifices." It is not a throne for receiving tribute; it is a throne for dispensing gifts.

Come then, you who are poor as poverty itself; come you who have no merits and are destitute of virtues; come you who are reduced to a beggarly bankruptcy by Adam's fall and by your own transgressions.

This is not the throne of majesty which supports itself by the taxation of its subjects, but a throne that glorifies itself by streaming forth like a fountain with floods of good things. Come you, now, and receive the wine and milk, which are freely given. Yes, come, buy wine and milk without money and without price. All the petitioner's wants shall be supplied, because it is a throne of grace.

And the one upon this throne is your salvation. When sinners approach His throne, He holds out a welcoming hand and says, "Come to me." And the Apostle Paul? He reminds you who are here tonight, "My God shall supply all your needs."

CHARLES H. SPURGEON

# Good-bye, Brother Lawrence

*The LORD is good.*
*When trouble comes,*
*he is a strong refuge.*

NAHUM 1:7

This is a portion of the final teaching letter from Brother Lawrence, the lay brother who practiced the presence of God.

❧

1691. God knows best what is needful for us, and all that He does is for our good. If we knew how much He loves us, we should be always ready to receive equally and with indifference from His hand the sweet and the bitter; all that comes from Him would please. All of our sufferings will lose their bitterness and become even matter of consolation.

Let us not amuse ourselves to seek or to love God for any sensual or sentimental reasons. Such reasons cannot bring us as near to God as does faith in one simple act. Let us seek Him often by faith. He is within us; do not seek Him elsewhere. We are rude and deserve blame if we leave Him alone in order to busy ourselves about trifles, which do not please Him and probably offend Him. We should fear these trifles; one day they will cost us dear.

Let us begin to be devoted to Him earnestly. Let us cast everything except what is eternal out of our hearts. He wants to possess them alone. Beg this favor of Him. If we do what we can on our part, we shall soon see the changes that we want.

I hope from His mercy to see Him in a few days. Let us pray for one another.

*Lawrence took to his bed two days after and died within the week.*

BROTHER LAWRENCE

# Good and False Hope

*This is eternal life:*
*that they may know you,*
*the only true God, and Jesus Christ,*
*whom you have sent.*

JOHN 17:3 NIV

A good hope naturally secures its object. For example, a young man hopes to become a good minister. What will be the effect of this hope? First, he will get before his mind the true ideal of a good minister. He cannot intelligently hope for such a result without this ideal. The very ideal is a first and necessary step toward the attainment of the end. Then, his hope will set him upon efforts. It will make him ever wakeful and ever earnest in the attainment of his object. His hope becomes both condition and stimulus of attainment.

A false hope must and will reveal itself in many ways. It will reveal itself by its obviously mistaken end. Suppose it to be the common hope of being a Christian. A man has a hope, he says; you ask him what he hopes for, and he tells you he hopes he is a Christian. This man perhaps does not at all conceive what constitutes eternal life. He has never thought of it as being an eternal likeness to Jesus Christ and an eternal sympathy with Him. On the contrary, he thinks of it only, or at least chiefly, as an escape from hell. Now by natural consequence, this hope will reveal itself as we often see it—no energizing after holiness—no laboring to be prepared to live forever with Christ; but anything else, rather than this. Yet who does not see that the result of the Christian hope must be a most earnest preparation for the employments of heaven?

CHARLES G. FINNEY

# The New Nature

*Therefore, if anyone is in Christ,*
*he is a new creation;*
*the old has gone, the new has come!*
2 CORINTHIANS 5:17 NIV

Christ has been pleased to make us new people. His saints are the "new creatures in Christ Jesus." They have a new nature. God has breathed into them a new life. The Holy Spirit, though the old nature is still there, has been pleased to put within them a new nature. There is now a contending force within them—the old carnal nature inclining to evil and the new God-given nature panting after perfection. They are new men and women, "begotten again unto a lively hope by the resurrection of Jesus Christ."

This new nature is moved by principles. The old nature needed to be awed with threatenings or bribed with rewards; the new nature feels the impulse of love. Gratitude is its mainspring: "We love Him because He first loved us."

This new nature is conscious of new emotions. It loves what once it hated; it hates what once it loved. It finds blight where once it sought for bliss, and finds bliss where once it found nothing but bitterness. It leaps at the sound that was once dull to its ears—the name of Jesus. It rejoices in hopes that once seemed idle as dreams. It is filled with a divine enthusiasm that it once rejected as fanatical. It is conscious now of living in a new element, breathing a fresh air, partaking of new food, drinking out of new wells not dug by men or filled from the earth. The new person is absolutely new—new in principles and new in emotions.

CHARLES H. SPURGEON

# The Cab Horse Charter

*While we were still sinners,*
*Christ died for us.*
ROMANS 5:8 NIV

William Booth, founder of the Salvation Army, was convinced that it was mandatory to make an attempt to provide some physical stability to London's homeless and destitute—before the hope of eternal life could be appreciated and accepted. Reader, how does this apply to you?

❧

When in the streets of London a cab horse, weary or careless or stupid, trips and falls and has stretched out in the midst of traffic, there is no question of debating how he came to stumble before we try to get him on his legs again. The cab horse is a very real illustration of poor, broken-down humanity—he usually falls down because of overwork and underfeeding. If you put him on his feet without altering his conditions, it would only be to give him another dose of agony; but first of all you'll have to pick him up again.

These are the two points of the Cab Horse Charter. When he is down he is helped up, and while he lives he has food, shelter, and work. That, although a humble standard, is at present absolutely unattainable by many of our fellowmen and women in this country.

Can the Cab Horse Charter be gained for human beings? I answer yes! If you can get your fallen fellow on his feet again, you hold out to him the promise of hope.

We know by our experience that life is very different when we have found the hope and peace of God.

WILLIAM BOOTH

# *Hope Found in Abiding*

> *"If you [abide] in me,*
> *and my words [abide] in you,*
> *ask whatever you wish,*
> *and it will be given you."*
>
> JOHN 15:7 NIV

The child of God replenishes his hope in the reality of God's promises by abiding in close proximity to his Creator—the Giver and Sustainer of his life. A rereading of this familiar parable cannot help but cause hope and anticipation to bloom even more keenly. Note: Andrew Murray and the King James Version use the word "abide," where "remain" is the word used in contemporary translations.

❧

The reason the vine and its branches are such a true parable of the Christian life is because all nature has one source and breathes one spirit. The plant world was created to be for man an object lesson teaching him that his entire dependence is upon God, and his security in that dependence.

He who clothes the lilies will much more clothe us; He who gives the trees and vines their beauty and their fruit, making each what He meant it to be, will much more certainly make us what He would have us be.

The only difference is that what God works in the trees is by a power of which they are not conscious. He wants to work in us with our consent. This is the nobility of man, that he has a will that can cooperate with God in understanding and approving and accepting what He offers to do.

ANDREW MURRAY

# Abiding and Asking

*"If you [abide] in me
and my words [abide] in you,
ask whatever you wish."*

JOHN 15:7 NIV

It's the hope and desire of every person who has ever lived to get what he or she asks for, but for the child of God, it's the abiding—that's where the hope is found.

❧

If we are to live a true prayer life, with the love and the power and the hope of prayer marking it, there must be no question about the abiding. And if we abide, there is no question about the liberty we have in asking what we will and the certainty of its being done.

Jesus presents us with one condition, though: "If you abide in me." There must be no hesitation about the possibility and the certainty of it. We must gaze at that little branch and its wonderful power to bear such beautiful fruit until we understand the full meaning of abiding in Christ.

And what is the secret of that little branch? It is to be wholly occupied with Jesus. Sink the roots of your being in faith and love and hope and obedience deep down into Him. Come away out of every other place to abide here in the Vine. Give up everything for the privilege of being a branch here on earth—a branch of the Son of God. Let Christ be first. Let Christ be all. Do not be occupied with the abiding—be occupied with Christ! He will hold you; He will keep you abiding in Him. He will abide in you.

ANDREW MURRAY

# Abiding in His Love

*"As the Father has loved me,
so have I loved you."*
JOHN 15:9 NIV

So, if Christ loves us with such an intense and infinite love, what is it that hinders it from triumphing over every obstacle and getting full possession of us? The answer is simple; even as the love of the Father is to Christ, so His love to us is a divine mystery. That is, too high for us to comprehend or attain by any effort of our own. It is only the Holy Spirit who can shed that love abroad and reveal it in its all-conquering power.

It is the vine itself that must give the branch its growth and fruit. It is Christ Himself, who by His Holy Spirit must dwell in the heart; then shall we know and have in us the love that passes all knowledge.

Shall we not draw near to the personal living Christ and trust Him? Shall we not yield all of ourselves to Him, that He may love this kind of love into us? Just as He knew and rejoiced every hour in the knowledge that "The Father loves Me!"—we too may live in the unceasing consciousness—as the Father loved Him, so He loves me.

Dear Lord, I am only beginning to apprehend how important the life of the vine is to the branch. You are the Vine, because the Father loved You and poured His love through You. And so You love me, and my life as a branch is to be like You, a receiver and a giver of heavenly love.

ANDREW MURRAY

# Whose Slave Are You?

*We should no longer be slaves.*

ROMANS 6:6 NIV

John Newton was born in 1725. His life as a seafaring slave-ship captain is well known.

❧

My conversion took place on March 10, 1748. On that day the Lord came from on high and delivered me out of deep waters. The storm was terrific: When the ship went plunging down into the trough of the sea, few on board expected her to come up again. I said to the captain, "The Lord have mercy upon us!" Then I thought, "What mercy can there be for me?" This was the first desire I had breathed for mercy in many years. About six in the evening the hold was free from water, and then came a gleam of hope. I thought I saw the hand of God displayed in my favor. I began to pray. I could not utter the prayer of faith. I could not draw near to a reconciled God and call Him Father.

My prayer for mercy was like the cry of ravens, which yet the Lord does not disdain to hear. In the gospel I saw at least a possibility of hope; on every side I was surrounded with black, unfathomable despair. But I staked everything on the possibility of hope. I sought mercy—and found it!

*Depth of mercy! Can there be*
*Mercy still reserved for me?*

JOHN NEWTON

## *Hope in Restoration*

*Restore to me the joy of your salvation
and grant me a willing spirit.*

PSALM 51:12 NIV

You must not rest while there is any unrepented, unconfessed sin between your soul and Jesus Christ. You must keep a clear channel open. I will explain what I mean.

You have seen two friends who have been a long time agreed and have taken sweet counsel together. But by and by a little difference creeps in between them—a little mist begins to obscure the channel. Now when they meet, you will begin to see it in their eyes and countenances. There is a little disturbance in their manner; and unless it be immediately removed, it will increase, until, finally, they turn their backs upon each other.

So with a husband and a wife—how carefully they should be to keep a clear channel of communication open between them. Suppose a husband has grieved his wife. Now, if he is a man of sensibility, he cannot be at ease; he goes to pray, and he remembers the wound which he has inflicted. He discovers he can pray no further; he rises from his knees and goes and confesses to his wife the injury he has done to her. The cloud is now removed from the channel, and both the husband and wife are happy. So with the Christian. If he has grieved Christ and injured His tender feelings, he can have no further communion with Him until he has repented and confessed his faults, allowing the tender breathings of mutual love to be restored.

CHARLES G. FINNEY

# The Hope of Love

*God is love.*
1 JOHN 4:8 KJV

What a mystery love is! We cannot define it. We can only indicate it by describing the occasion on which it arises in the soul. If human love is inexplicable, divine love is an ocean too deep for the plummet of man or archangel, too broad to be bounded by the thought of the loftiest intelligence in the universe.

Love is not a product of the reason. It is the free play of the spiritual sensibilities in the possession of its object. God is not only love, but He is love revealed. The perfect love of God toward mankind is designed to call forth perfect love toward God in man's bosom. Though the mirror on which that is reflected is broken into uneven planes and reflects a distorted image, though the human soul at its best earthly estate under grace is shattered by infirmities and incurable imperfections, yet the love which man cherishes toward God may flow with all the united force of his being.

The history of God's involvement with men is the chronicle of His love. We can contemplate no more sublime and ennobling theme. The brightness of the material universe pales before the splendors of the Divine character—that central fire which kindles the souls of seraphs in heaven and melts the hearts of sinners on earth. Thus is the science of the divine Heart infinitely above the science of the almighty hand.

DANIEL STEELE

# Earthly Needs, Heavenly Blessings

*Hallowed be thy name. Thy kingdom come.*
*They will be done in earth, as it is in heaven.*
*Give us this day our daily bread.*
*And forgive us our debts, as we forgive our debtors.*

MATTHEW 6:9–12 KJV

When we say, "Hallowed be thy name. Thy kingdom come. Thy will be done on earth as it is in heaven," this last is at times wrongly interpreted by some as meaning "in body and spirit"— these blessings will be retained forever. They begin in this life, of course; they are increased in us as we make progress, but in their perfection—which is to be hoped for in the other life— they will be possessed forever. But when we say, "Give us this day our daily bread. And forgive us our debts, as we forgive our debtors. And lead us not into temptation, but deliver us from evil," who does not see that all these pertain to our needs in the present life? In that life eternal—where we all hope to be—the hallowing of God's name, His kingdom, and His will in our spirit and body will abide perfectly and immortally. But in this life we ask for "daily bread" because it is necessary, in the measure required by soul and body, whether we take the term in a spiritual or bodily sense, or both. And here, too, it is that we petition for forgiveness, where the sins are committed; here, too, are the temptations that allure and drive us to sinning; here, finally, the evil from which we wish to be freed. But in that other world none of these things will be found.

AUGUSTINE

# Hope in Times of Despair

*We are troubled on every side, yet not distressed;*
*we are perplexed, but not in despair.*
2 CORINTHIANS 4:8 KJV

What if the rain is falling and the wind blowing; what if we stand alone, or, more painful still, have some dear one beside us, sharing our despair. What even if the window be not shining, because the curtains of good inscrutability are drawn across it; let us think to ourselves, or say to our friend, "God is; Jesus is not dead; nothing can be going wrong, however it may look so to hearts unfinished in childness."

Let us say to the Lord, "Jesus, are You loving the Father in there?" Then we out here will do His will, patiently waiting until He opens the door. We shall not mind the wind or the rain much. Perhaps you are saying to the Father, "Your little ones need some wind and rain: their buds are hard; the flowers do not come out. I cannot get them blessed without a little more winter weather." Then perhaps the Father will say, "Comfort them, My Son Jesus, with the memory of Your patience when you were missing Me. Comfort them that You were sure of Me when everything about You seemed so unlike Me, so unlike the place You had left."

Let us be at peace, because peace is at the heart of things— peace and utter satisfaction between the Father and the Son—in which peace they call us to share; in which peace they promise that at length, when they have their good way with us, we shall share.

GEORGE MACDONALD

# The Great Heart of God

*For as high as the heavens are above the earth,*
*so great is his love for those who fear him;*
*as far as the east is from the west,*
*so far has he removed our trangressions from us.*
*As a father has compassion on his children,*
*so the LORD has compassion on those who fear him.*

PSALM 103:11–13 NIV

Does it not make a person glad to know that though once his sins had provoked the Lord, they are now all blotted out, and not one of them remains? Though once he was estranged from God through wicked works, and far away from Him, yet he is brought near by the blood of Christ.

The Lord is no longer an angry judge pursuing us with a drawn sword, but He is a loving Father into whose bosom we pour our sorrows and find ease for every pang of the heart. Oh, to know that God actually loves us! I cannot preach upon that theme, for it is a subject to muse upon in silence, a matter to sit by the hour together and meditate upon.

The Infinite to love an insignificant creature, a shadow that declines, is this not a marvel? For God to pity me I can understand, for God to condescend to have mercy upon me I can comprehend; but for Him to love me, for the pure to love a sinner, for the infinitely great to love a worm, is matchless, a miracle of miracles! Such thoughts must comfort the soul.

CHARLES H. SPURGEON

# Resurrection and Life

*I am the resurrection,*
*and the life:*
*he that believeth in me,*
*though he were dead,*
*yet shall he live.*
JOHN 11:25 KJV

The power of Christ, His sovereign power: "I am the resurrection and the life," the fountain of life, and the head and author of the resurrection. Martha believed that at His prayer, God would give anything, but He would have her know that by His word He could work anything.

Martha believed in a resurrection at the last day; Christ tells her that He has the power lodged in His own hand, that if the dead were to hear His voice, whence it was easy to infer, He could raise a world of men who had been dead many ages; doubtless He could raise one man [her brother Lazarus] who had been dead but four days.

Note, this is an unspeakable comfort to all Christians—that Jesus Christ is the resurrection and the life, and will be so to them. Resurrection is a return to life; Christ is the author of that return, and of that life to which it is a return. We look for the resurrection of the dead and the life of the world to come, and Christ is both.

He who lives and believes is he who by faith is born again into a heavenly and divine life, to whom to live is Christ—that makes Jesus Christ the life of his soul.

MATTHEW HENRY

# Trust His Guidance

*The LORD will guide you continually.*
ISAIAH 58:11 NKJV

The docile soul will not seek to learn by what road God is conducting him. When God makes Himself the guide of a soul, He exacts from it an absolute confidence in Him and a freedom from any sort of disquietude as to the way in which He conducts it. This soul, therefore, is urged on without perceiving the path traced out before him. He does not imitate either what he has seen, or what he has read, but proceeds by his own action and cannot do otherwise without grave risk.

The divine action is ever fresh; it never retraces its steps, but always marks out new ways. Souls that are conducted by it never know where they are going; their ways are neither to be found in books, nor in their own minds. The divine action carries them step by step, and they progress only according to its movement.

When you are led by a guide through the unknown country, at night across fields where there are no tracks, by his own skill, without asking advice from anyone or giving you any inkling of his plans, how can you choose to abandon yourself? Of what use is it attempting to find out where you are, ask a passerby, or consult maps? The plans of a guide who insists on being trusted would not allow this. He would take pleasure in overcoming the anxiety and distrust of the soul and would insist on an entire surrender to his guidance. If one is convinced that he is a good guide, one must have faith in him and abandon oneself to his care.

JEAN-PIERRE DE CAUSSADE

# Evening Light

*At evening time it shall be light.*
ZECHARIAH 14:7 KJV

How inspiring the thought of our coming glory! How would we rise above our sins and sorrows and sufferings, if we didn't live under the power of a world to come? Were faith always able to take its giant leap beyond a soul-trammeling earth and remember its brighter destiny. If we could stand on its highest mount and look above and beyond the mists and vapors of this land and its shadows, and rest on the better country. But, alas, in spite of ourselves, the wings often refuse to soar—the spirit droops—guilty fears depress—sin dims and darkens—God's providences seem to frown—God's ways are misinterpreted—the Christian belies his name and his destiny.

But, "at evening time it shall be light." The material sun, which wades through clouds and a troubled sky, sets often in a couch of lustrous gold. So, when the sun of life is setting, many rays of sunlight will shoot across memory's darkened sky and many mysterious dealings of the wilderness will then elicit an "All is well!"

How frequently is the presence and upholding grace of Jesus especially felt and acknowledged at that hour, and griefs and misgivings hushed with His own gentle accents, "Fear not! It is I: do not be afraid" (Matthew 28:10). A triumphant deathbed! It is no unmeaning word; the eye is lit with holy luster, the tongue with holy rapture, as if the harps of heaven were accompanying it. My soul! May such a life's evening time be yours.

JOHN MACDUFF

# The Spiritual Adoption

*You did not receive a spirit that
makes you a slave again to fear,
but you received the Spirit of sonship.
And by him we cry, "Abba, Father."
The Spirit himself testifies with our spirit
that we are God's children."*

ROMANS 8:15–16 NIV

He cannot be an unhappy man and still cry, "Abba, Father." The spirit of adoption is always attended by love, joy, and peace, which are the fruits of the spirit (Galatians 5:22). We have not received the spirit of bondage again to fear, but we have received the spirit of liberty and joy in Christ Jesus: "My God, my Father." How sweet the sound. But all children of God do not enjoy this, you say. Sadly, that is true, but it is their own fault.

It is the right and portion of every believer to live in the assurance that he is reconciled to God, that God loves him, and that he is God's child. If he does not live in that manner, he has himself only to blame. If there be any starving at God's table, it is because the guest stints himself, for the feast is superabundant.

If, however, a man comes to live habitually under a sense of pardon through the sprinkling of the precious blood and in a delightful sense of perfect reconciliation with the great God, he is the possessor of a joy unspeakable that is full of glory.

CHARLES H. SPURGEON

# Moody's Words of Hope

*A word fitly spoken is like*
*apples of gold in a setting of silver.*
PROVERBS 25:11 NRSV

When we find a person meditating on the words of God, my friends, that person is full of boldness and is successful.

The Lord didn't tell Joshua how to use his sword, but He told him how he should meditate on the Lord day and night, and then he would have good success.

One thing I have noticed in studying the Word of God is that when a man is filled with the Spirit, he deals largely with the Word of God, whereas the man who is filled with his own ideas refers rarely to the Word of God. He gets along without it, and you hear it mentioned in his discourses.

Now I am no prophet, nor the son of a prophet, but one thing I can predict: Every one of you new converts that goes to studying his Bible, and loves this book above every other book, is sure to hold out. The world will have no charm for him; he will get the world under his feet.

I find a great many people who want some evidence that they have accepted the Son of God. My friends, if you want any evidence, take God's Word for it. You can't find better evidence than that.

When a man is filled with the Word of God, you cannot keep him still. If a man has got the Word, he must speak or die.

DWIGHT L. MOODY

# David's Plea

*In thee, O LORD, do I put my trust:*
*let me never be put to confusion.*
*Deliver me in thy righteousness, and cause me to escape:*
*incline thine ear unto me, and save me.*
*Be thou my strong habitation*
*whereunto I may continually resort:*
*thou hast given commandment to save me;*
*for thou art my rock and my fortress.*
*Deliver me, O my God, out of the hand of the wicked,*
*out of the hand of the unrighteous and cruel man.*

PSALM 71:1–4 KJV

David professes his confidence in God and repeats the profession of his confidence. We praise God by telling Him (if it be indeed true) what an entire confidence we have in Him. "In Thee, O Lord! And in Thee only, do I put my trust. Whatever others do, I choose the God of Jacob for my help. Thou art my rock and my fortress. Thou art my hope and my trust. That is, I fly to Thee and am sure to be safe in Thee, and under Thy protection. If Thou secure me, none can hurt me. Thou art my hope and my trust. Thou has proposed Thyself to me in Thy Word as the proper object of my hope and trust. I have hoped in Thee and never found it in vain to do so."

David's confidence in his God is supported and encouraged by his experiences. "I have reason to hope that Thou wilt protect me. Thou that hast held me up hitherto wilt not let me fall now."

MATTHEW HENRY

# We Gather Together

*May God be gracious to us and bless us.*

PSALM 67:1 NIV

We gather together to ask the Lord's blessing.
He chastens and hastens His will to make known.
The wicked oppressing now cease from distressing.
Sing praises to His name; He forgets not His own.

Beside us to guide us, our God with us joining,
Ordaining, maintaining His kingdom divine;
So from the beginning the fight we are winning.
Thou, Lord, wast at our side—all glory be Thine!

We all do extol Thee, Thou leader triumphant,
And pray that Thou still our Defender wilt be.
Let Thy congregation escape tribulation:
Thy name be ever praised; O Lord, make us free!

NETHERLANDS FOLK HYMN,
TRANSLATED BY THEODORE BAKER

# Hope in Difficult Times

*Weeping may linger for the night,*
*but joy comes with the morning.*

PSALM 30:5 NRSV

The sanctified are sometimes in heaviness through manifold temptations. Now don't infer, if you see them so, that they are not holy. Christ had His sorrows and knew what it was to resist even unto blood, striving against temptation to sin; and the servant need not expect to fare better than his Lord.

The truth is, these trials are useful—they are but for a moment, but they prepare us for a far more exceeding and eternal weight of glory. Under the pressure of temptations the soul is in agony and cries out, "Help, oh Lord, help," and He comes forth and scatters the insulting foe, and the soul bounds up like a rocket, giving glory to God.

The warfare of the true Christian greatly strengthens his virtue. When he is greatly tried and obligated to gather up all his energy to maintain his integrity, when he wrestles with some fiery trial until he is all in a perspiration, as it is sometimes necessary for him to do, it must be that when he comes out from such a scene as this, his virtue is greatly strengthened and improved.

CHARLES G. FINNEY

# The Throne of Grace

*"Hear from heaven their prayer and their plea,*
*and uphold their cause."*
1 KINGS 8:45 NIV

If in prayer I come before a throne of grace, then the faults of my prayer will be overlooked. The groanings of your spirit are such that you think there is nothing in them. What a blotted, blurred, smeared prayer it is. Never mind; you are not come to the throne of justice, otherwise when God perceives the fault in the prayer He would spurn it—your gaspings and stammerings are before a throne of grace.

When any of us has presented his best prayer before God, if he saw it as God sees it, he would lament over it. For there is enough sin in the best prayer that was ever prayed to secure its being cast away from God. But our King does not maintain a stately etiquette in His court like that which has been observed by princes, where a little mistake or a flaw would secure the petitioner's being dismissed with disgrace. No, the faulty cries of His children are not criticized. Our Lord Jesus Christ takes care to alter and amend every prayer before He presents it, and He makes the prayer perfect and prevalent with His own merits. God looks upon the prayer as presented through Christ and forgives all its own inherent faultiness.

How this ought to encourage any of us who feel ourselves to be feeble, wandering, and unskillful in prayer. If you feel as if somehow or other you have grown rusty in the act of supplication, never give up, but come still, come more often, for it is a throne of grace to which you come.

CHARLES H. SPURGEON

# Our Glorified Bodies

*But now, O LORD, thou art our father;*
*we are the clay, and thou our potter;*
*and we all are the work of thy hand.*

ISAIAH 64:8 KJV

The Protestant reformer once told his children, "Simple speech is the best and truest eloquence." His own writing, though pointed and outspoken, reflects this.

❧

Think of the honor and the glory Christ's righteousness brings even to our bodies! How can this poor, sinful, miserable, filthy, polluted body become like unto that of the Son of God, the Lord of Glory? What are you—your powers and abilities, or those of all men—to effect this glorious thing? But Paul says human righteousness, merit, glory, and power have nothing to do with it. They are mere filth and pollution and condemned as well. Another force intervenes, the power of Christ the Lord, who is able to bring all things unto Himself at will, He is also able to glorify the pollution and filth of this wretched body, even when it has become worms and dust. In His hands it is as clay in the hands of the potter, and from the polluted lump of clay He can make a vessel that shall be a beautiful, new, pure, glorious body, surpassing the sun in its brilliance and beauty.

MARTIN LUTHER

# Abiding in Christ

*Abide in me, and I in you.*
JOHN 15:4 KJV

Abide in me: These words are no law of Moses, demanding from the sinful what they cannot perform. They are the command of love, which is ever only a promise in a different shape. Think of this until all feeling of burden and fear and despair pass away, and the first thought that comes as you hear of abiding in Jesus be one of bright and joyous hope—it is for me, I know I shall enjoy it.

You are not under law, with its inexorable "Do!" but under grace, with its blessed, "Believe what Christ will do for you." And if the question be asked, "But surely there is something for us to do?" the answer is, "Our doing and working are but the fruit of Christ's work in us."

It is when the soul becomes utterly passive, looking and resting on what Christ is to do, that its energies are stirred to their highest activity, and that we work most effectively because we know that He works in us. It is as we see in those words "in me" the mighty energies of love reaching out after us to hold us, that all the strength of our will is roused to abide in Him.

ANDREW MURRAY

# Hope in His Power

> *"I am going to send you what my Father has promised;*
> *but stay in the city until you have been clothed*
> *with power from on high."*
>
> LUKE 24:49 NIV

There is a great difference between the peace and the power of the Holy Spirit in the soul and the way the disciples were before Pentecost. The disciples were Christians before that glorious day and, as such, had a measure of the Holy Spirit. They must have had the peace of sins forgiven and of a justified state, yet they had not the provision of power necessary to the accomplishment of the work assigned to them. They had the peace that Christ had given them, but not the power that He had promised.

This may be true of all Christians, and right here is, I think, the great mistake of the church and of ministry. They rest in conversion and do not seek until they obtain this provision of power from on high. Hence so many of those who profess have no power with either God or man. They prevail with neither. They cling to a hope in Christ, overlooking the admonition to wait until they are endued with power from on high. Let all converts lay all upon the altar and prove God herewith, and he shall find that God "will open the windows of heaven, and pour him out a blessing that there shall not be room enough to receive it."

CHARLES G. FINNEY

# There Is Joy in Faithfulness

*A faithful man shall abound with blessings.*
PROVERBS 28:20 KJV

All that we have, all that we are, all that we enjoy are only so many talents from God: If we use them to the ends of a pious and holy life, our five talents will become ten, and our labors will carry us into the joy of our Lord. If we abuse them to the gratification of our own passions, sacrificing the gifts of God to our own pride and vanity, we shall live here in vain labors and foolish anxieties, shunning religion as a melancholy thing, accusing our Lord as a hard master, and then fall into everlasting misery.

We may for a while amuse ourselves with names and sounds and shadows of happiness. We may talk of this or that greatness and dignity, but if we desire real happiness, we have no other possible way to it but by improving our talents, by piously using the powers and faculties of men in this present state, that we may be happy and glorious in the powers and faculties of angels in the world to come.

How ignorant, therefore, are they of the nature of religion, of the nature of man, and the nature of God, who think a life of strict piety and devotion to God to be a dull, uncomfortable state, when it is so plain and certain that there is neither comfort or joy to be found in anything else.

WILLIAM LAW

# Comfort and Hope

*A voice was heard in Ramah, lamentation, and bitter weeping;*
*[Rachel] weeping for her children refused*
*to be comforted for her children,*
*because they were not. Thus saith the LORD;*
*Refrain thy voice from weeping, and thine eyes from tears;*
*for thy work shall be rewarded, saith the LORD;*
*and they shall come again from the land of the enemy.*
*And there is hope in thine end, saith the LORD,*
*that thy children shall come again to their own border.*

JEREMIAH 31:15–17 KJV

When President Theodore Roosevelt lost his wife two days after childbirth, he is said to have sobbed, "The light has gone out of my life." Later, his daughter reported, "Daddy said the Lord is his light and salvation."

❧

The verses from Jeremiah only underscore the fact that though we mourn, we must not murmur. In order to repress inordinate grief, we must consider that there is hope in our end, hope that the trouble will not last, that it will be a happy end, and that that end will be peace. This is not hope-so, but it is Christian hope.

Though one generation falls in the wilderness, the next shall enter Canaan. Thy suffering work shall be rewarded. God makes His people glad according to the days wherein He has afflicted them, and so there is a proportion between the joys and the sorrows. Let them not tremble and lose their spirits; let them not trifle and lose their time, but with a firm resolution and a close application address themselves to their journey. Though they are laid waste and in ruins, they are your cities which your God gave you, and therefore turn again to them.

MATTHEW HENRY

# Do Something

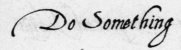

*Whatsoever thy hand findeth to do,*
*do it with thy might.*
ECCLESIASTES 9:10 KJV

Observe what Paul did at Athens. He did something. He was not the man to stand still and "confer with flesh and blood" in the face of a city full of idols. He might have reasoned with himself that he stood alone; that he was a Jew by birth; that he was a stranger in a strange land; that he had to oppose the rooted prejudices and old associations of learned men; that to attack the old religion of a whole city was to beard a lion in his den; that the doctrines of the gospel were little likely to be effective on minds steeped in Greek philosophy; that there was no reason to ruffle some feather.

But none of these thoughts seem to have crossed Paul's mind. He saw souls perishing: He felt that life was short and time was passing away: He had confidence in the power of his Master's message to meet every man's soul: He had received mercy himself and knew not how to hold his peace.

He acted at once, and what his hand found to do, he did with all his might. Oh, that we had more men of action these days!

JOHN CHARLES RYLE

# Come, Thou Long-Expected Jesus

*When the time had fully come,*
*God sent his Son. . .to redeem.*

GALATIANS 4:4 NIV

Come, thou long-expected Jesus,
Born to set Thy people free;
From our fears and sins release us,
Let us find our rest in Thee.

Israel's strength and consolation,
Hope of all the earth Thou art;
Dear desire of ev'ry nation,
Joy of ev'ry longing heart.

Born Thy people to deliver,
Born a child, and yet a King,
Born to reign in us forever,
Now Thy gracious Kingdom bring.

By Thine own eternal Spirit
Rule in all our hearts alone;
By Thine all-sufficient merit
Raise us to Thy glorious throne.

CHARLES WESLEY

# Publish Glad Tidings

*"Do not be afraid.*
*I bring you good news."*
LUKE 2:10 NIV

There is a tradition that Johann Gutenberg perfected his invention, the movable-type printing press, during the Advent season. Perhaps no one else, save the Son of God, has provided the world with more expectation and hope: "Tidings of great joy" in the languages of all people.

❧

God suffers in the multitude of souls that His holy Word cannot reach. Religious truth is imprisoned in a small number of manuscript books, which confine instead of spreading the public treasure.

Yes, it is a press, certainly, but a press from which shall soon flow, in inexhaustible streams, the most abundant and most marvelous refreshment that has ever flowed to relieve the thirst of men. Through it, God will spread His Word. A spring of pure truth shall flow from it; like a new star of hope it shall scatter the darkness of ignorance and cause a light heretofore unknown to shine amongst men.

JOHANN GUTENBERG

# Hope in Jesus the Christ

*I have set the Lord always before me. . .*
*Therefore my heart is glad.*
PSALM 16:8–9 NIV

Bernard, the twelfth-century saint from Clairvaux, gave the Christian world this hymn that is so appropriate for Advent and for any season.

Jesus, the very thought of Thee with sweetness fills my breast.
But sweeter far Thy face to see, and in Thy presence rest.

No voice can sing, no heart can frame, nor can the
memory find
A sweeter sound than Thy blest name, O Savior of mankind!

O Hope of ev'ry contrite heart, O Joy of all the meek,
To those who fall, how kind Thou art! How good to those
who seek!

But what to those who find? Ah, this nor tongue nor
pen can show.
The love of Jesus, what it is—None but His loved ones know.

Jesus, our only joy be Thou, as Thou our prize wilt be.
Jesus, be our glory now and through eternity.

ATTRIBUTED TO BERNARD OF CLAIRVAUX

# Days and Hours

*"You also must be ready,*
*because the Son of Man will come*
*at an hour when you do not expect him."*
LUKE 12:40 NIV

If *hope* and *anticipation* are synonyms, this excerpt from *The Imitation of Christ* should provide for some prayer introspection.

❧

Each morning remember that you may not live until evening, and in the evening do not presume to promise yourself another day.

Happy and wise is he who endeavors to be during his life as he wishes to be found at time of death. For this will afford us sure hope of a happy death, perfect contempt of the world, fervent desire to grow in holiness, love of discipline, the patience of penance, ready obedience, self-denial, the bearing of every trial for the love of Christ. While you enjoy health, you can do much good; but when sickness comes, little can be done. Few are made better by sickness, and those who make frequent pilgrimages seldom acquire holiness by doing so.

Do not rely on friends and neighbors, and do not delay the salvation of your soul to some future date, for men will forget you sooner than you think. It is better to make timely provision and to acquire merit in this life than to depend upon the help of others. And if you have no care for your own soul, who will have care for you in time to come? The present time is most precious; now is the accepted time, now is the day of salvation. It is said that you do not employ your time better, when you may win eternal life hereafter. The time will come when you will long for one day or one hour in which to amend; and who knows whether it will be granted?

THOMAS À KEMPIS

## Anticipation

*When you see all these things,*
*you know that it is near.*

MATTHEW 24:33 NIV

Anticipation and hope seem to walk hand in hand. While not a theological classic, these lines of verse remind that there are moments when the small things in life pique our anticipation and provide us with hope, perhaps small on God's great screen but so important to mortals like us.

I love preliminary things:
The tuning-up of flutes and strings;
The little scales musicians play
In varying keys to feel their way;
The hum—the hush in which it dies;
But most to see the curtain rise.

I love preliminary things:
The little box the postman brings
To cut the twine, to break the seals,
And to wonder what the lid reveals;
To lift the folds in which it lies
And watch the gift materialize.

The snowdrop and the daffodil,
The cattails standing straight and still,
The blossom on the orchard trees—
Do you know greater joys than these?
Each represents the hope that springs
In all preliminary things.

J. R. J.

# Prayer and Promise

*"I will give them an undivided heart
and put a new spirit in them."*
EZEKIEL 11:19 NIV

The great promises find their fulfillment along the lines of prayer. They inspire prayer, and through prayer the promises flow out to their full realization and bear their ripest fruit. In anticipation of what was to come, the prophet Ezekiel speaks a promise that finds its full, ripe, and richest fruit in the New Testament. What hope it gave those who walked in darkness:

"I will sprinkle clean water upon you, and ye shall be clean; from all your filthiness. . .a new heart I will give you, and a new spirit I will put within you."

God had promised through His prophets that the coming Messiah should have a forerunner. How many homes and wombs in Israel has longed for the coming of this great honor? How much hope was heaped on this event? Perchance Zacharias and Elizabeth were the only ones who were trying to realize by prayer this great dignity and blessing. At least we know that the angel said to Zacharias, as he announced to the old man the coming Messiah: "Your prayer is heard."

It was then that the word of the Lord, as spoken by the prophets and the prayers of an old priest and his wife, brought John the Baptist into the withered womb and into the childless home of Zacharias and Elizabeth.

God has never has put His Spirit into a human heart that hasn't ardently prayed for it.

E. M. BOUNDS

# Is There Not a Shorter Way?

*Be always ready to give an answer to every man*
*that asketh you a reason of the hope that is*
*in you with meekness and fear.*

1 PETER 3:15 KJV

Born in New York City into a devout home, Phoebe Palmer was one of the first women of the nineteenth century to become a celebrated public figure and speaker. She was involved in evangelism and social action.

❧

"I have thought," said one of the children of Zion to the other, as in love they journeyed onward in the way cast up for the ransomed of the Lord to walk in; "I have thought," said he, "whether there is not a shorter way of getting into this way of holiness than some of our brethren apprehend?"

"Yes," said the sister addressed, "yes, brother, there is a shorter way! Oh, I am sure this long waiting and struggling with the powers of darkness is not necessary. There is a shorter way." And then, with a solemn feeling of responsibility and with a realizing conviction of the truth uttered, she added, "But, brother, there is but one way."

How many, whom infinite love would long since have brought into this state, instead of seeking to be brought into the possession of the blessing at once, are seeking a preparation for the reception of it? They feel that their convictions are not deep enough to warrant an approach to the throne of grace with the confident expectation of receiving the blessing now. Just at this point some may have been lingering months and years. . . . "Plunge in today and be complete," as the old song advises.

PHOEBE PALMER

# Imitate Jesus Christ

*Be imitators of God, therefore,*
 *as dearly loved children and live a life of love,*
*just as Christ loved us and gave himself up*
*for us as a fragrant offering and sacrifice to God.*
EPHESIANS 5:1–2 NIV

Persons attempting to imitate others must give them close attention. This is essential to the success of a dramatic actor or any other artist.

The apostle commands us to put on Christ—to imitate Him—to give intense thought to get at the true idea of His character, and to commit the mind fully to the same end, to which He was devoted.

To enjoy a piece of poetry, you must put yourself into the same state of mind in which the author was in when he wrote the poem. Then as you read it, your tone of voice and manner of gestures will naturally represent him.

This is the difficulty with so many in reading hymns. They read as though they did not apprehend the sentiment, and without emotion. The reason is, either they have not the spirit of devotion or they have not at all given attention to the sentiment of the hymn.

To represent Christ we must catch His spirit and make His grand end and aim become ours. "Your attitude should be the same as that of Christ Jesus" (Philippians 2:5 NIV). Then we shall act as He would under like circumstances.

CHARLES G. FINNEY

## Hope in Love

*What shall I render unto the LORD*
*for all his benefits toward me?*

PSALM 116:12 KJV

Before the Word was made flesh, died on the Cross, came forth from the grave, and returned to His Father, the commandment had been uttered, "Thou shalt love the Lord thy God with all thine heart, and with all thy soul, and with all thy might." And it was not unjust for God to claim this from His own work and gifts. Why should not the creature love the Creator, who gave him the power to love? Why should not he love Him with all his being, since it is by His gift alone that he can do anything that is good?

I owe all that I am to Him who made me: but how can I pay my debt to Him who redeemed me? What reward shall I give to my Lord for all the benefits that He has given me? In the first creation He gave me myself; but in His new creation, He gave me Himself, and by that gift, restored to me the self that I had lost.

Created first and then restored, I owe Him myself twice over in return for myself. But what have I to offer Him for the gift of Himself? If I could multiply myself a thousandfold and then give Him all, what would that be in comparison with God?

BERNARD OF CLAIRVAUX

# God's Workmanship

*He who began a good work in you*
*will perfect it until the day of Christ Jesus.*

PHILIPPIANS 1:6 NASB

In the creation of the old world God first gave light, and afterward He created life—the life that crept, the life that walked, the life that dived, the life that flew in the midst of heaven. So has He fashioned in our hearts; He has given us the life that creeps upon the ground in humiliation for sin; the life that walks in service, the life that swims in sacred waters of repentance, the life that flies on the wings of faith in the midst of heaven.

As God separated the light from the darkness and the dry land from the sea, so in the new creature He has separated the old depravity from the new life. He has given to us a holy and incorruptible life that is forever separated from, and opposed to, the old natural death.

Then at last, when the old creation was all but finished, God brought forth man in His own image as the top stone. A similar work He will do in us as His new creatures. Having given us light and life and order, He will renew in us the image of God. Yes, that image is in every man who is in Christ Jesus. Though it is not yet complete, the outlines, as it were, are there. The great Sculptor has begun to chisel out the image of Himself in this rough block of human marble. You cannot see all the features, the lineaments divine are not yet apparent. Still, because it is in His design, the Master sees what we see not. He sees in our unhewn nature His own perfect likeness as it is to be revealed in the day of the revealing of our Lord and Savior Jesus Christ.

CHARLES H. SPURGEON

# *My God, My Strength*

*"I will strengthen you."*
ISAIAH 41:10 NKJV

God is able to do all things. Believer, until you can drain dry the ocean of omnipotence, until you can break into pieces the towering mountains of almighty strength, you never need to fear. Think not that the strength of man shall ever be able to overcome the power of God. The same God who directs the earth in its orbit, who feeds the burning furnace of the sun and trims the lamps of heaven, has promised to supply you with daily strength. While He is able to uphold the universe, think not that He will prove unable to fulfill His own promises.

Remember what He did in the days of old, in the former generations. Remember how He spoke and it was done; how He commanded, and it stood fast. Shall He who created the world grow weary? He hangs the world upon nothing; shall He who does this be unable to support His children? Shall He be unfaithful to His Word? How can He fail us? When He put such a faithful promise as this on record, will you think for a moment that He has outpromised Himself and gone beyond His power to fulfill? No! Doubt no longer.

You who are my God and my strength, I can believe that this promise shall be fulfilled. The boundless reservoir of Your grace can never be exhausted, and the overflowing storehouse of Your strength can never be emptied.

CHARLES H. SPURGEON

# Blessed Hope

*Looking for that blessed hope,*
*and the glorious appearing of*
*the great God and our Savior Jesus Christ. . .*
TITUS 2:13 KJV

The gospel teaches us not only how to believe and hope well, but also to live well, as becomes that faith and hope in this present world and as expectant of another and better.

There is the world that now is and that which is to come; the present is the time and place of our trial. The gospel teaches us to live well here, not, however, as our final state but with an eye chiefly to a future. It teaches us all to look for the glories of another world, to which a sober, righteous, and godly life in this world is preparative.

Hope, by a metonymy, is put for the thing hoped for, namely, heaven and the felicities thereof, called emphatically *that hope*, because it is the great thing we look and long and wait for; and a *blessed hope*, because when we attain, we shall be completely happy forever.

"And the glorious appearing of the great God and our Savior Jesus Christ." This denotes both the time of the accomplishing of our hope and the sureness and greatness of it. It will be at the second appearing of Christ, when He shall come in His own glory, and in His Father's and the holy angels'.

MATTHEW HENRY

## *Overcoming*

*Jesus. . .was in all points*
*tempted like as we are,*
*yet without sin.*
HEBREWS 4:14–15 KJV

Temptation, in some form, will exist forever. Satan and his angels and our first parents were actually tempted in their holy state. We know that Jesus Christ was tempted and had a mighty warfare; to such a degree as to have no appetite for food and to seek the wilderness in His distress, just as you and I have done under similar circumstances. We have gone into the woods or some other seclusion to be alone.

What Christian has not often felt so disposed? They are so weighed down and struggling inwardly that they can have no peace day or night and often seek a place where they can give vent to their prayers or groans alone.

Thus was Christ tempted, and thus, in His warfare, did He fly from the face of man and seek the solitude of the wilderness, where He might contest the point even unto death. He seems to have been assaulted in all the weakest points of human nature. When, finally, in His agony from fasting until He was famished, He was besieged through His appetite for food and in every other way the devil could invent, until he saw it was all in vain and left Him.

However sharp the conflict, if the soul prevails there is no sin. What trials had Jesus Christ? But He prevailed. So, if temptation should rush like a tornado upon any of you, if you will only hold on and fight it out, you have not sinned. The sharper the conflict, the greater the virtue of resistance.

CHARLES G. FINNEY

# The Glory of the Lord

*"And the glory of the LORD will be revealed,
and all mankind together will see it."*
ISAIAH 40:5 NIV

We anticipate the happy day when the whole world shall be converted to Christ, when kings shall bow down before the Prince of Peace and all nations shall call their Redeemer blessed. We know that the world and all that is in it one day will be burnt up, and afterwards we look for new heavens and for a new earth.

We are not discouraged by the length of His delays; we are not disheartened by the long period which He allots to the church in which to struggle with little success and much defeat. We believe that God will never suffer this world, which has once seen Christ's blood shed upon it, to be always the devil's stronghold.

Christ came to deliver this world from the detested sway of the powers of darkness. What a shout shall that be when men and angels shall unite to cry, "Hallelujah, hallelujah, for the Lord God Omnipotent reigneth!" What a satisfaction will it be in that day to have had a share in the fight, to have helped to break the arrows of the bow, and to have aided in winning the victory for our Lord! Happy are they who trust themselves with this conquering Lord, and who fight side by side with Him, doing their little in His name and by His strength!

CHARLES H. SPURGEON

# Truth Speaking

*Speaking the truth in love,*
*we will in all things grow up in him who is the Head,*
*that is, Christ.*
*From him the whole body,*
*joined and held together by every supporting ligament,*
*grows and builds itself up in love,*
*as each part does its work.*

EPHESIANS 4:15 NIV

We grow in the knowledge of Christ through the heart and not through the head. We do not know Jesus until we love Him, and the more we love, the more intimate our knowledge of Him. The more we familiarize ourselves with the perfect character of Jesus, the more we shall admire Him, just as by studying the works of Josephus we come to admire him as a historian much more.

But admiration is not love. It kindles no furnace-glow in the affections; it impels the soul onward through no losses and labors, self-denials and persecutions, to the martyr's stake. As the character of Christ folds its splendors beneath the long and earnest gaze of the student, he may be growing esthetically by familiarity with so many moral beauties, and he may become more perfectly grounded in his theological beliefs respecting the divinity of the Man of Nazareth, and yet he may, in his own heart, be refusing to receive and enthrone Him as his rightful King.

DANIEL STEELE

# The World Conquered

*In the world ye shall have tribulation:*
*but be of good cheer;*
*I have overcome the world.*

JOHN 16:33 KJV

Shall I be afraid of the world, which is already conquered? The Almighty Victor, within view of His crown, turns round to His faint and weary soldiers and bids them to take courage. They are not fighting their way through the untried enemies. The God-Man Mediator "knows their sorrows." "He was in all points tempted." "Both He (that is, Christ) who sanctifies, and they (His people) who are sanctified are all of one (nature)."

As the great Predecessor, He heads the pilgrim band, saying, "I will show you the path of life." The way to heaven is consecrated by His footprints. Every thorn that wounds them has wounded Him before. Every cross they can bear, He has borne before. Every tear they shed, He has shed before. There is one respect, indeed, in which the identity fails—He was "yet without sin." This recoil of His holy nature from moral evil gives Him a deeper and more intense sensibility toward those who still have corruption within responding to temptation without.

Reader, are you ready to faint under your tribulations? Is the world seducing you? Have you a wandering, wayward heart? Consider Him who endured. Listen to your wonderful redeemer, stooping from His throne, and saying, "I have overcome—so can you."

JOHN MACDUFF

# The Light of Hope

*God is light,*
*and in him is no darkness at all.*

1 JOHN 1:5 KJV

Come to God with all your desires and instincts, all your lofty ideals, all your longing for purity and unselfishness, all your yearning to love and be true, all your aspirations after self-forgetfulness and childlikeness; come to Him with all your weaknesses, all your shames, all your futilities; with all your helplessness over your own thoughts; with all your failure, all your doubts, fears, dishonesties, meannesses, paltinesses, misjudgments, wearinesses, disappointments, and stalenesses. Be sure of this, He will take you and all your misery into His care, for liberty in His limitless heart. He is light, and in Him there is no darkness at all. If he were a king, a governor, if the name that described Him were the Almighty, you may well doubt whether there could be light enough in Him for you and your darkness. But, He is your Father, and more your Father than the word can mean in any lips but His who said, "My father and your father, my God and your God."

Such a Father is light, an infinite, perfect light. If He were any less or any other than He is, and you could continue growing, you must at length come to the point where you wouldn't be dissatisfied with Him; but He is light, and in Him is no darkness at all.

GEORGE MACDONALD

# The Supreme Investiture

*All power is given unto me*
*in heaven and earth.*
MATTHEW 28:18 KJV

What an empire is this! Heaven and earth—the church militant—the church triumphant—angels and archangels—saints and seraphs. At His mandate the billows were hushed—demons crouched in terror—the grave yielded its prey! Upon His head are many crowns. He is made head over all things to His church. Yes! Over all things, from the minutest to the mightiest. He holds the stars in His right hand—He walks in the midst of the seven golden candlesticks, feeding every candlestick with the oil of His grace, and preserving every star in its own spiritual orbit.

The Prince of Darkness has a power, but, God be praised, it is not an all-power, potent but not omnipotent. Christ holds the Prince of Darkness on a chain. He has set bounds that he may not pass over. "Satan," we read in the book of Job, "went out [with permission] from the presence of the Lord." He was not allowed to enter the herd of swine until Christ permitted it. He only desired to have Peter that he might "sift him." There was a mightier Countervailing Agency at hand: He said, "I have prayed for you, that your faith fail not."

"Heaven and earth shall pass away, but my words shall not pass away" (Matthew 24:35).

JOHN MACDUFF

# A Mother's Hope

*For God so loved the world
that he gave his one and only Son,
that whoever believes in him
shall not perish but have eternal life.*

JOHN 3:16 NIV

The glorious truth is, that when our hope is based in the Heavenly Father, it is promised to have a happy ending. There are times, though, when our hope depends upon the response of a fellow human being. In that case, a guaranteed happy ending cannot be taken for granted.

In a remote district of Wales a baby boy lay dangerously ill. The widowed mother walked five miles through the night in drenching rain to get the village doctor.

When confronted by the mother, the doctor hesitated about making the unpleasant trip. He questioned himself, "Would it pay?" He knew he that he would receive little money for his services, and besides, if the child recovered, he would have no future; he would probably be little more than a poor laborer.

But love for humanity and a sense of professional responsibility conquered, and the little boy's life was saved.

Years later, when this same child became first Chancellor of the Exchequer and later Prime Minister of England, the old doctor confessed, "I never dreamed that in saving that child on the farm hearth, I was saving the life of a national leader. But there was something about the hope I saw in that mother's tears." God is constantly justified in the responsibilities He has placed upon our hearts.

AUTHOR UNKNOWN

# The Star

*We have seen his star.*
MATTHEW 2:2 KJV

Christ is our star of Hope. I want my deathbed to be under that star. All other light will fail. The light that falls from the scroll of fortune, the light that flashes from the gem in the beautiful apparel and materialism, the light that flashes from the lamps of a theatre or a banquet—but this light of hope burns on and on.

Paul kept his eye on that star until he could say, "I have finished my course."

The dullard and the intellectual can both follow the star of hope. Rich and poor alike have access to the star. Magi were brought to Messiah by the star, so we find the star of hope when we come to Jesus Christ.

The renowned preacher Edward Payson kept his eye on that star until he lay on his death bed and could say, "The breezes of heaven fan my brow."

Intellectual John Tennant kept his eye on that star until his eyes began to close and he could say, "Welcome, Lord Jesus; welcome, eternity."

No other star ever pointed a man into so safe a harbor. No other star ever brought so much good out of a man, thanks to the Bright and Morning Star.

THOMAS DEWITT TALMAGE

# I Am What I Am

*By the grace of God I am what I am.*
1 CORINTHIANS 15:10 KJV

Two or three years before the death of the eminent servant of Christ, John Milton [writer of *Paradise Lost*] of London, formerly of Olney, when his sight was become so dim that he was no longer able to read, I called on my longtime contemporary friend and fellow minister to breakfast.

Family prayer followed, and the portion of scripture for the day was read to him. In it occurred the verse, "By the grace of God I am what I am." It was the pious man's custom on these occasions to make a short familiar exposition on the passage read. After the reading of this text, he paused for some moments and then uttered this affecting soliloquy, "I am not what I ought to be—ah, how imperfect and deficient! I am not what I wish to be—I abhor what is evil, and I would cleave to what is good! I am not what I hope to be—soon, soon shall I put off mortality, and with mortality all sin and imperfection.

"Yet though I am not what I ought to be, nor what I wish to be, nor what I hope to be, I can truly say, I am not what I once was—a slave to sin and Satan—and I can heartily join with the apostle and acknowledge, 'By the grace of God I am what I am.' "

A FRIEND OF JOHN NEWTON

# Real Hope of the World

*Every tongue confess that Jesus Christ is Lord,*
*to the glory of God the Father.*

PHILIPPIANS 2:11 NIV

There are those who say that Julius Caesar was the greatest man who ever lived. Professor Ridpath says that he was head and shoulders above the age in which he lived.

*But,* did angels announce the birth of Julius Caesar? Did the sun refuse to witness his assassination in the senate chamber? Did Julius Caesar have the power to lay down his life, then take it up again? Was it at the name the name of Julius Caesar that apostles proclaimed and martyrs died? Caesar and his kingdom are things of the past, and were it not for recorded history, they would have been forgotten.

*But,* today the name of Jesus is lauded more than ever before. You may go to the most remote isles of the sea and you will find His name there. You may visit every land and clime and His name is there. Go to the highest point on earth and down to the lowest, and the name of Jesus will be known and loved. His name spans eternity past and eternity to come. There have been great names that have held out kinds of hope, but only one is the genuine Hope of the world.

A. B. SIMPSON

# The Hope of Christmas

*"You are to give him the name Jesus,*
*because he will save his people from their sins."*
MATTHEW 1:21 NIV

Imagine, if you can, a preacher named Isaiah standing before sin-infected Israelites declaring, "For a child has been born to us, a son given to us. . .and he will be named Wonderful Counselor, Mighty God, Everlasting Father, Prince of Peace" (Isaiah 9:6).

Now we look at ourselves, when day after day we struggle and it appears that we will never be released from the overwhelming power of sin and we hope against hope because we know that a loving God can do it. Then we consider that year after year we struggle with the same annoying sinful habits and practices, and realize that God has promised to make things right.

But then year after year goes by without the return of Jesus Christ; the world becomes darker and sin abounds more and more. We can lose hope and believe that God has forgotten us, that God has not remembered His promise. The world is anything but saved!

And then we light a Christmas candle, and we remember that God has kept his promise. It is I who has forgotten God. Christmas tells us that no matter what things look like in the world, we have the hope of the Old Testament prophets who foretold His mission and an angel who announced to a virgin in Nazareth, "He will save his people from their sins." We have hope because of the promise of God.

RODNEY "GIPSY" SMITH

# A Great Mystery

*The shepherds said one to another,*
*Let us now go even unto Bethlehem,*
*and see this thing which is come to pass.*

LUKE 2:15 KJV

The mystery of Christmas Eve was compounded to the shepherds by angels and the baby who was promised to bring them hope.

Let us go with the shepherds to contemplate that miracle to which the angel directed them, the Nativity of Christ. Luke says of the blessed virgin, "She brought forth her firstborn Son, and wrapped Him in swaddling clothes, and laid Him in a manger."

The God of heaven and earth, the Divine Word, who had been in glory with the Eternal Father from the beginning, lay in His mother's arms, to all appearances helpless and powerless, and was wrapped by Mary in an infant's bands and laid to sleep in a manger. The Son of God, who created the worlds, became flesh.

He became flesh as truly as if He had ceased to be what He was and had actually been changed into flesh. He submitted to be the offspring of Mary, to be taken up in the hands of a mortal, to have a mother's eye fixed upon Him, and to be cherished at a mother's bosom. What an emptying of His glory to become a man and to inherit all the infirmities and imperfections of our nature which were possible to a sinless soul.

What were His thoughts? What mystery is there from first to last in the Son of God becoming man! Yet in proportion to the mystery is the grace and mercy of it, and as is the grace, so is the greatness of the fruit of it.

JOHN HENRY NEWMAN

# A Christmas Carol

*The time came for the baby to be born. . .and she gave birth. . . .
She. . .placed him in a manger,
because there was no room for them in the inn.*

LUKE 2:6–7 NIV

Our God, Heaven cannot hold him,
Nor earth sustain;
Heaven and earth shall flee away
When he comes to reign:
In the bleak midwinter
A stable-place sufficed
The Lord Almighty
Jesus Christ.

Angels and archangels
May have gathered there;
Cherubim and seraphim
Thronged the air,
But only his mother
In her maiden bliss
Worshipped the Beloved
With a kiss.

What can I give him
Poor as I am?
If I were a shepherd
I would bring him a lamb;
If I were a wise man
I would do my part—
Yet what I can I give him,
Give my heart.

CHRISTINA ROSSETTI

# The Reality of Hope

*After Jesus was born in Bethlehem in Judea, during the time of King Herod, Magi from the east came to Jerusalem and asked, "Where is the one who has been born king of the Jews? We saw his star in the east and have come to worship him."*

MATTHEW 2:1–2 NIV

No man has given such joy to the world as Jesus Christ has given. Have you seen Christ's star in the east? That is a sight which we may never behold: But we may see a greater sight than that. We may see Him!

It will be a happy day when we are more eager to see Christ than we are to see any symbol of Him that could be found, either in the heavens or on the earth. I do not want you as fellow students of the Word, to care about baptism and the Lord's Supper and the Sabbath day and the church built with hands—except as these may lead you further into the inner sanctuary where is enthroned Christ Himself.

If I found men now earnestly searching the heavens with the most scientifically constructed telescopes, hoping to find a star resembling what the Persian sages saw, that they, too, might be following its guiding light to some distant Bethlehem, I would say to them, "Christ is not here nor there; He is not to be found in sign or symbol; He is to be found in our consciousness; He is to be the answer to our sin; He is to be the satisfaction of our hunger; He is to be the light of our firmament; He is to be the glory of our spiritual hope."

JOSEPH PARKER

# The Source: Christ in Me

*I pray that out of his glorious riches he may. . .
dwell in your hearts.*

EPHESIANS 3:16–17 NIV

Remember, "Christ can be within me" is what the apostle told us long ago; but in this age of the world, over and above his word, we have the experience of many centuries for our comfort. We have his own history to show us how Christ within us is stronger than the world around us and will prevail—the hope of every child of God.

We have the history of his fellow-sufferers, of all the Confessors and Martyrs of early times and since, to show us that Christ's arm "is not shortened, that it cannot save"; that faith and love have a real abiding-place on earth; that, come what will, His Grace is sufficient for His church, and His strength is made perfect in weakness.

His grace will carry and deliver His church through whatever the powers of evil give challenge. Meantime, while Satan only threatens, let us possess our hearts in patience; try to keep quiet; aim at obeying God in all things—little as well as great; do the duties of our calling which lie before us, day by day. And, "take no thought for the morrow, for sufficient unto the day is the evil thereof" (Matthew 6:34).

JOHN HENRY NEWMAN

# A New Heart

*I will give you a new heart
and put a new spirit in you.*
EZEKIEL 36:26 NIV

"Behold," says Christ, "I make all things new." What a wonder it is that a man should ever have a new heart! You know if a lobster loses its claw in a fight it can get a new claw, and that is thought to be marvelous. It would be exceedingly wonderful if a person should be able to grow new arms and new legs, but whoever heard of a creature that grew a new heart? You may have seen a tree bough lopped off, and you may have thought that, perhaps, the tree will sprout again, and there will be a new limb, but whoever heard of old trees getting new sap and a new core? But my Lord and Master, the crucified and exalted Savior, has given new hearts and new cores; He has put the vital substance into man afresh and made them into new creatures. I am glad to notice the tear in your eye when you think of past years, but wipe that tear away and look up to the cross and say—

> Just as I am, without one plea,
> But that Thy blood was shed for me,
> And that Thou bid'st me come to Thee,
> O Lamb of God, I come.

"Make me a new creature!" If you have said that from your heart, you are a new creature, dear brothers and sisters, and we will rejoice together in this regenerating Savior.

CHARLES H. SPURGEON

# *Hope for Today*

> *"But while [the foolish virgins] were*
> *on their way to buy the oil,*
> *the bridegroom arrived. . .*
> *And the door was shut."*
>
> MATTHEW 25:10 NIV

The foolish virgins of Christ's parables faced the fact that there is a point in life at which no excuses will avail.

The door was shut. There was absolutely nothing to be done about it. All action should have been taken beforehand. Now it was too late. But the important thing to remember is that the arrival at the inexorable point of hopelessness is always the culmination of what has gone before, and that this desperate plight is avoidable if we are continually ready.

Many of us believe we are going to become people of hope. We will break the sense of hopelessness—tomorrow! But tomorrow never comes. For the only day we have is today. And this corrupting habit of running behind schedule—even in small things—has for its inevitable result the bringing of us face-to-face with a shut door.

The demand that life makes on all of us is to be ready at all times, to live neither in the past nor in the future, but in the present. Until we learn that lesson, we cannot escape the certain consequence that we shall one day stand, sorrowful but too late, before the one door through which we desire to enter but cannot—because it is shut.

WILLIAM "BILLY" SUNDAY

# Hope for a Country Boy

*He too shared in their humanity so that*
*by his death he might destroy him who*
*holds the power of death—that is, the devil—*
*and free those who all their lives were*
*held in slavery by their fear of death.*

HEBREWS 2:14–15 NIV

In 1801, when I was in my sixteenth year, my father, my eldest half brother, and myself attended a wedding about five miles from home, where there was a great deal of drinking and dancing.

Some days after this, I retired to a cave on my father's farm to pray in secret. My soul was in an agony; I wept, I prayed, "Now, Lord, if there is any hope for me, let me find it," and it really seemed to me that I could almost lay hold of the Savior and realize a reconciled God. All of a sudden, such a fear of the devil fell upon me that it really appeared to me that he was surely present in the room, to seize and drag me down to hell.

Then months rolled away, and still I did not find the blessing of hope. In the spring a revival had broken out at Cane Ridge [Kentucky]. The people crowded to the meetings from far and near. On Saturday evening I was with weeping multitudes and bowed before the stand and earnestly prayed for mercy. In the midst of my solemn struggle of soul, an impression was made on my mind, as though a voice said to me, "Thy sins are all forgiven thee."

I rose to my feet, opened my eyes, and it really seemed as if I was in heaven. The Lord had forgiven my sins and gave me hope.

PETER CARTWRIGHT

# Imitating Christ

*"Man does not live by bread alone,
but on every word that comes from the mouth of God."*

MATTHEW 4:4 NIV

As an old year closes, have you become a hope-filled person over the past twelve months? Looking ahead, plan to take to heart these suggestions from John Wesley's abridgement of Thomas à Kempis's *Imitation of Christ*.

❧

Press toward the mark and do not despise this assistance offered you. The following advices are proposed, concerning the issue of reading.

First: Assign some stated time every day for this employment.

Secondly: Prepare yourself for reading, by purity of intention, aiming at the good of your soul.

Thirdly: Be sure to read, not cursorily or hastily, but with great attention, with proper pauses and intervals, and that you may allow time for enlightenings of the divine grace.

THOMAS À KEMPIS

# Scripture Index